The Political Culture
of Judaism

The Political Culture of Judaism

MARTIN SICKER

PRAEGER

Westport, Connecticut
London

Library of Congress Cataloging-in-Publication Data

Sicker, Martin.
    The political culture of Judaism / Martin Sicker.
      p. cm.
    Includes bibliographical references and index.
    ISBN 0–275–97257–7 (alk. paper)—0–275–97429–4 (pbk. : alk. paper)
    1. Judaism and politics.   2. Ethics, Jewish.   I. Title.
  BM645.P64S547   2001
  296.3′82—dc21   2001021646

British Library Cataloguing in Publication Data is available.

Library of Congress Catalog Card Number: 2001021646
ISBN: 0–275–97257–7
      0–275–97429–4 (pbk.)

First published in 2001

Praeger Publishers, 88 Post Road West, Westport, CT 06881
An imprint of Greenwood Publishing Group, Inc.
www.praeger.com

Printed in the United States of America

The paper used in this book complies with the
Permanent Paper Standard issued by the National
Information Standards Organization (Z39.48–1984).

10 9 8 7 6 5 4 3 2 1

Contents

Introduction

It is a curious fact that because the modern era has produced several major schools of religious thought and practice that constitute contemporary Judaism—Orthodox, Conservative, Reform, and Reconstructionist—it is very difficult if not impossible to offer a definition of Judaism that would be universally acceptable. It therefore becomes important for the purposes of this study to indicate at the outset just what we mean when we use the term "Judaism" and the adjective "Judaic."

To provide a baseline from which the exploration of the subject matter of this work may proceed, "Judaism" will be used here to describe the framework that encompasses the central religious beliefs and values that most of the Jewish people have considered normative from antiquity to modern times. We will refer to these beliefs and values generally as "traditional Judaism," to draw a distinction from the modern Orthodox and Conservative movements, both of which claim to represent historical Judaism. The qualifier "Judaic" will therefore be used here in preference to "Jewish," because the two terms are not necessarily synonymous, the former referring to a religious value system and the latter to a national or ethnic identity. Thus, while figures as diverse as Theodor Herzl, Sigmund Freud, and Albert Einstein might be characterized as Jewish thinkers, they should not be considered Judaic thinkers, because their views on nationalism, the mind, and the universe are not predicated on or derived from the sources of traditional Judaic thought.

Moreover—and it is important that this be clearly understood at the outset—the discussion that follows relates only peripherally to the present

State of Israel, which, although intended by its founders to be a Jewish state, is not in any significant sense a Judaic state. That is, although certain Judaic values and norms may inform legislation and policy as well as jurisprudence to one degree or another, and although many of its citizens are Judaic in personal orientation, the state itself is essentially secular, as are its basic law and its principal institutions. As a result, contemporary Israel cannot be considered an embodiment of the political culture of Judaism.

The burden of the present work is to identify and examine, from a Judaic perspective, the fundamental norms of civic conduct considered to be essential to the emergence and continuing moral viability of the "good society" envisioned in the source documents and traditions of Judaism. The principles underlying the indicated behavioral norms constitute the ethical underpinnings of the civilization adumbrated by Mosaic teaching; they set forth the parameters, or boundary conditions, for the public conduct of human relations in a political society infused with Judaic values.

In considering how these principles are conceived and articulated in Judaic thought, it is important to acknowledge that the basic norms of social behavior essential to the good society were never deemed by the classical Judaic thinkers to have originated in the revelation of the Torah. On the contrary, it was always considered a truism that every society must, if it is to be viable, have some set of norms in accordance with which its members are expected to conduct their affairs. The sages of the talmudic period referred to such societal norms of conduct as *derekh eretz*—literally, "the way of the land." In fact, the sage R. Samuel b. Nahman went so far as to assert, "*Derekh eretz* preceded the Torah by twenty-six generations."[1] This statement appears to be based on the biblical tradition that Moses, the lawgiver, lived in the twenty-sixth generation following the creation of man; what R. Samuel is suggesting is that such fundamental societal norms are as old as humanity itself. Moreover, he clearly implies that the Israelites, as was the case with all other ancient peoples, conducted their lives in conformity with some basic set of common normative behavioral expectations even prior to the revelation of the Torah.

There is, of course, nothing surprising in this. It seems self-evident that every group of people must evolve standards of acceptable conduct. All peoples are therefore held to live according to some ethic, although the specific behaviors and patterns of socially desirable or acceptable conduct may and often do vary significantly from one group to another. These norms are distinctive in that they reflect the peculiar culture of the particular society, although one may be able to detect in them certain principles that would appear to be universal in character. Exemplary teachers have posited such guiding principles in diverse societies, and theorists throughout history have risen to the intellectual challenge of defining and articulating the bases for sustained and stable social relations.

One may ask, however: if Judaism admits the prior existence of the basic norms essential to any ordered society, what value-adding component does it contribute to the mix? Is there something distinctive in Judaism's approach to the basic issues of politics and society that is not readily to be found in other political cultures? This book suggests that there are indeed distinguishing characteristics of Judaic political thought, parts of which have long served as the basic value components of Western democracies, that are *sui generis* and merit the attention of those seriously concerned about how to bring about the good society.

In the political culture of Judaism, the fundamental precepts of social conduct that have come to be considered normative may be seen to have resulted from the convergence of three distinct, though interrelated, intellectual currents. These are represented by the work of the three different types of religious and intellectual leaders—prophet, priest, and sage—who have been the standard bearers of Judaic values throughout the long history of the Jewish people. These teachers, serially and each in his own way, contributed significantly to what we now refer to as traditional or rabbinic Judaism.[2]

The prophets—beginning with Moses, who is considered by the biblical author to have been without peer in his vocation[3]— transmitted and articulated the standards of individual conduct and social behavior that were to be adopted and adhered to by the people of Israel. The distinctiveness of the Judaic way of life was given its stamp by Moses, who, as the paramount prophet of Judaism and principal mentor of the people of Israel, undertook to "show them the way wherein they must walk, and the work that they must do" (Exod. 18:20). This guidance is presented as Moses' authoritative legacy to his people in the five biblical books attributed to him, collectively known as the Torah, or Pentateuch, which set forth the fundamental norms for a Judaic society. The prophets who followed Moses served principally as the moral guides of the society, interpreting and urging, forcefully and publicly, conformity with those norms.

The priests, by contrast, were intended to be the disseminators of the teachings of the Torah in a more limited, technical sense. That is, in addition to their biblically prescribed sacerdotal functions, they were assigned the pedagogic role of expounding the precepts of the Torah to the public. "They shall teach Jacob Thine ordinances, and Israel Thy Law" (Deut. 33:10).[4] However, over time, the moral authority of the priesthood declined dramatically, especially during the Hellenistic period, inaugurated with the Macedonian conquest of the Middle East in the latter part of the fourth century b.c.e. As a result, the responsibility of the priesthood for the moral education of the public was taken over successively by scribes and sages, the intellectual elite of the post-biblical period.

The ancient sages, who were expected to be thoroughly familiar with the teachings of the priests, were imbued with a profound sense of the moral responsibility they had inherited from the prophets. Not only did they have to be proficient in knowledge of the fundamental precepts of the Torah, but they also bore the burden of recommending how the underlying principles were to be applied under the exigencies of a given time and place in the tortuous history of Israel.

The sages, and the rabbis, scholars, and teachers who followed in their footsteps, clearly recognized that the fundamental societal norms set forth in the Torah had been intended by their author to be universal in character and were therefore already to be found to some degree in all organized societies. This is suggested explicitly in the rabbinic teaching that the Torah had initially been made available to all peoples but had been formally accepted only by Israel.[5] What principally distinguished the fundamental and universal societal norms reflected in the precepts of the Torah from even comparable ethical teachings of other societies and cultures was the matter of compliance. That is, adherence by the Israelites and their descendants to these norms or precepts is considered obligatory under the terms of the biblical covenant between God and the people of Israel. In societies and cultures without a comparable covenant-imposed ethic, compliance with ethical and social norms is more likely to be voluntary or merely demanded by custom, even if coerced in some instances. This study explores the implications of adherence to these norms for the ethos of a Judaic society, one motivated and informed by the guidelines held to be provided in the Torah, as these have been understood and interpreted throughout the centuries by Judaic thinkers.

We begin with a consideration of the underpinnings of a Judaic civilization as conceived and articulated by Scripture and its traditional interpreters over the millennia. By the term "Judaic civilization" we refer to the instituted norms of civil conduct deemed necessary to bring about the just and good society. Accordingly, "civilization" is used here in its most fundamental meaning, as the process of ensuring appropriately civil relations between persons, individually and collectively.

Because the Torah clearly sets forth a political theology, it is often assumed that it advocates theocracy as the appropriate organizing principle for society.[6] However, as the ensuing discussion of the meaning of theocracy in Judaic thought makes clear, the Judaic concept of theocracy is radically different from the manner in which it is usually conceived in Western thought. We will next consider the tensions in Judaic thought regarding the concept of democracy as a paradigm for Judaic governance, including the theological and moral implications of democracy that cast doubt on its appropriateness as a political ideal or desideratum.

The role of popular consent as a legitimating factor in the Judaic polity, and the character of the resulting grassroots democracy as recognized and legitimized in Judaic thought, are then considered, as a prelude to a discussion of "nomocracy." The latter term, as used in this study, refers to the distinctively Judaic approach to the ordering of civil relations in society within the constitutional context of a regime based on *halakhah*, which may be understood for present purposes as Judaism's own dynamic system of canon law.

Having discussed and set forth the conceptual basis for the Judaic political society, we turn to a consideration of three fundamental societal issues. First, we explore the status of the individual within the society and the relationship of the citizen to the state. Included under this heading are discussions of the Judaic concept of, and applied concern for, human dignity and the ramifications for public policy, individual rights, and the right to property, as well as the always troubling question of the legitimacy of civil disobedience. Second, we take up the matter of the Judaic approach to realizing the biblical imperative of social justice, which includes consideration of the elemental requirements of justice in a nomocratic society and of the fundamental social welfare policies appropriate to such a society. Also included in this discussion are the notion of prescriptive equality and the important principle of equality before the law.

Last is a substantial discussion of the classical Judaic approach to dealing with the problems of ensuring national security. This discussion includes consideration of the basic authority of the government to undertake or initiate war, which is viewed in Judaism as equivalent to imposing a death sentence on an unspecified number of soldiers. Also examined is the classification of various types of war and their corollary legal implications, as well as the legitimacy of preventive war. We will also consider the character and implications of the biblical rules of mobilization and military conduct, the appropriateness of military assistance to third parties, and finally, the requirements of a Judaic national security policy and the parameters and conditions for negotiating peace with an enemy.

The general Judaic approach to dealing with these issues represents the essence of what may properly be considered the political culture of Judaism, a culture that reflects the values and ideas that would characterize a polity structured in consonance with the teachings of traditional Judaism.

NOTES

1. *Leviticus Rabbah* 9:3.

2. Hayyim Z. Reines, *Torah uMusar*, p. 5.

3. "And there hath not arisen a prophet since in Israel like unto Moses" (Deut. 34:10).

4. This role of the priest is also reflected in the text: "Now for a long time Israel was without the true God, and without a teaching priest, and without law" (2 Chron. 15:3).

5. "And it was for the following reason that the nations of the world were asked to accept the Torah: In order that they should have no excuse for saying: Had we been asked we would have accepted it. For behold, they were asked and they re-

fused to accept it, for it is said[,] . . . Why was the Torah not given in the land of Israel? In order that the nations of the world should not have the excuse for saying: Because it was given in Israel's land, therefore we have not accepted it. . . . To three things the Torah is likened: To the desert, to fire, and to water. This is to tell you that just as these three things are free to all who come into the world, so also are the words of the Torah free to all who come into the world" (*Mekilta de-Rabbi Ishmael*, vol. 2, pp. 234–237, on Exod. 20:2).

6. For an extensive discussion of the political theology of the Torah, see the author's *What Judaism Says about Politics: The Political Theology of the Torah*.

The Political Culture
of Judaism

Chapter 1

The Foundations of
Judaic Civilization

A contemporary scholar, Michael Fishbane, has described Judaism as "the religious expression of the Jewish people based upon a Torah believed given them by God and on the teachings of this Torah as elaborated by trained sages for the sake of sanctifying human behavior and guiding nearness to God."[1] This formulation, which might be considered a reasonable definition of what we intend by the phrase "traditional Judaism," is of particular interest because it makes the case that Judaism, as "the religious expression of the Jewish people," is rooted in a particular social and communal foundation. Put another way, traditional Judaism may be considered to constitute the national ideology of the Jewish people. This would clearly distinguish it from most, if not all, other major religions, notwithstanding its many teachings of universal scope and interest.

But, it may be asked, cannot one believe in and practice Judaism without being a member of the Jewish people? The answer to this question, from a Judaic standpoint, has always been somewhat ambivalent. Thus, the talmudic sage R. Johanan strenuously objected to non-Jews studying Torah, "for it is written, 'Moses commanded us a law for an inheritance' [Deut. 33:4]; it is *our* inheritance, not theirs." On the other hand, R. Meir is recorded as having taught that a non-Jew who studies and practices the Torah "is as a High Priest."[2] In his codification of the halakhah, Maimonides sets forth what appears to be a compromise position. On the one hand, he agrees with the negative position of R. Johanan with regard to such matters as study of the Torah and observance of the Sabbath. On the other hand, he asserts that "a non-Jew that wishes to perform any other precept of the Torah for the purpose of attaining merit, should not be hindered from performing it properly."[3]

The prophets and sages of Judaism were generally not favorably disposed to the idea of proselytizing outside the community of Israel. Nonetheless, the sages did in fact postulate a number of basic principles considered critical to the establishment of an ordered and just society, principles that they held to be universal in scope and application. These are designated in traditional Judaic thought as the "Noahide Laws"—that is, the laws held in rabbinic tradition to have been divinely ordained, the observance of which was commanded of the descendents of the biblical Noah. These laws are considered to reflect the minimum requisite norms for a viable civilization and are held to be applicable to all peoples and societies.[4] In this regard, the sages taught, "Seven precepts were the sons of Noah commanded: social laws; to refrain from blasphemy; idolatry; adultery; bloodshed; robbery; and eating flesh cut from a living animal."[5]

The category of "social laws" was also presumed to be the Torah-derived basis for legitimate governmental authority in the non-Judaic state, obligating all residents, including Jews, to honor the laws promulgated by it. Teaching in the third century, the sage Samuel propounded the principle that "the law of the kingdom is the law"[6] as a guideline for his coreligionists. However, just what Samuel meant by this is a continuing topic of scholarly controversy, even though the principle continues to be recognized as operative in determining the political obligations of Jews residing in non-Jewish societies. The thirteenth-century Jacob ben Abba Mari Anatoli argued that the principle had been widely misconstrued and that its scope had to be qualified: the laws promulgated had to be consistent with the teachings of the Torah in order to be deemed legitimate and morally authoritative.[7]

It should come as no surprise that these Noahide precepts, with the exception of those concerning idolatry and flesh cut from a living animal, are also to be found in the ancient codes of cuneiform law, the Hammurabi Code, the Assyrian Laws, and the Hittite Code. There can be little doubt that such precepts, particularly those concerned with the promulgation of "social laws" and the maintenance of civic order, are indeed essential to the viability and stability of any organized society. This was already clearly recognized in remote antiquity and further acknowledged at the outset of modern times. Indeed, since the existence of the ancient cuneiform codes was unknown in the seventeenth century, the renowned Dutch scholar Hugo Grotius often cited the Jewish traditional literature as a source for the Noahide Laws, which he considered one of the bases of international law.[8]

From the Judaic standpoint, all peoples are encouraged, indeed obligated, to abide by the Noahide Laws, which are fully incorporated within the more comprehensive Mosaic Law that constitutes the essence of Judaism.[9] The Mosaic Law itself, however, at least from the standpoint of many of its Judaic exponents, has always been considered the exclusive property of the Jewish people. With few exceptions, pertaining primarily to non-Jews living within a Judaic society, traditional Judaism has frowned upon the observance of its rituals and religious practices as such by non-Jews. The latter category includes all persons who were not born Jews and have not undergone the rite of conversion that formally makes them members of the Jewish people.[10]

The reason for this constraint is that the rabbis were particularly concerned about the misappropriation and modification or dilution of the religious teachings and precepts of the Torah by persons whose allegiance to it might be tenuous at best. As Maimonides put it, no one is permitted to introduce innovations into the religion or to devise new precepts or commandments. Accordingly, non-Jews have the choice between becoming true proselytes—accepting the precepts or commandments of the Torah, as understood in the tradition, in their entirety, neither adding nor subtracting anything from them—or continuing to adhere to their own religions.[11] Presumably, introducing such innovations into the religion would be immeasurably more difficult for someone on the inside, who at least until contemporary times would be subject to constraining communal pressures.

Many will find this obviously exclusionary perspective difficult to fathom. For one thing, it would seem to negate the notion of Judaism as a universal religion. If the Mosaic Law does indeed reflect the profound teachings so valued by its adherents, why should these not be available to everyone? The answer to this challenge can only be that Judaism is not and never was intended to be a universal religion. Indeed, it is not a religion at all, in the sense in which the term is usually employed. Judaism as a faith and creed is inextricably bound up with the people of Israel and can have no independent existence. The modern concept of religion as a matter of personal belief, and therefore of individual choice, is essentially unknown to traditional Judaism. The biblical terms for Jews—"people of Israel," the "children of Israel"—reflect national rather than individual religious identity. It is for this reason that the proponents of traditional Judaism tend to insist upon the exclusive application of the ritual and "religious" aspects of the Mosaic Law to members of the faith community of Israel. To universalize Judaism, in all its aspects and dimensions, would be to uproot it from its moorings in history and to transform it into a lifeless intellectual abstraction.

Judaism may therefore also be understood as the basis of a unique civilization that is predicated on a distinctive and all-encompassing religious culture.[12] As such, Judaism is vitally concerned not only with matters of the spirit but also with the sanctification of the prosaic. Its essential task becomes that of bringing every aspect of human existence within the embrace of the holy, including the ethical and political dimensions of the civilization that it inspires. Mordecai Kaplan wrote in this regard:

The main elements of a civilization are organically inter-related. It is this essential and organic inter-relation that differentiates a civilization from a religion, a religious philosophy, or a literary culture.... Language is a vehicle of the group memories and devotions, literature and other arts their storehouse. Law and mores are the social cement among contemporaries and generate the sense of continuity with preceding generations. The religious elements of a civilization constitute the sanctions of the ideals and purposes of the group. They heighten the values of the civilization and protect it against absorption or destruction. But though these elements are distinguishable, they are organically related to each other, and the organic character of Judaism is the crucial fact about it.[13]

There is, however, a dimension, or aspect, of Judaism not captured in the description cited above, and it is crucial to an understanding of its political culture. Greek-speaking Jews of the first century C.E. first coined the term "Judaism" (Ioudaismos) to describe the faith and religious culture of the people of Judaea.[14] Judaism should therefore also be understood to relate both to a place and to its principal inhabitants—the descendants of the ancient Israelite kingdom of Judah, the Judahites, or Jews. As a contemporary writer, André Chouraqui, puts it, "the ethos of Judaism is expressed in the union of a God—that of Sinai—a people—Israel—and a country—the Holy Land. The history of Judaism, therefore, is that of a trinity: we cannot separate the message from the people that receives it, and we can understand the people only in the context of its land."[15]

In light of these considerations, Judaism may be conceived of as the religiously oriented civilization of a national community that is intimately bound up with the land that it traditionally has believed to be its divinely awarded patrimony, in accordance with its founding covenant. Some will raise the obvious objection that the majority of Jews have not had the implied intimate connection with the land of Israel for millennia; how does such a characterization apply to them? I have dealt with this complex issue at length elsewhere, and to reprise the involved arguments here would require a significant digression from our present subject.[16] Suffice it to note that the idea and ideals of Judaic civilization can be fully realized only within a territorial context, where Jews are empowered to create their distinctive political, social, and religious structures.

Jews living in various parts of the world continue to practice the religious aspects of Judaism, but from a traditional Judaic perspective, this cannot properly be construed as participating fully in a Judaic civilization. This point, disconcerting to many, was driven home unequivocally by the great eighteenth-century rabbinic authority Elijah, the Gaon of Vilna, who rejected as mere illusion the notion of being able to live a completely Judaic life in the Diaspora. Speaking of the precepts of the Torah, he taught, "The essential fulfillment of the precepts is dependent on the Land, but everyone is obligated to study and become familiar with the performance of the precepts that will be required practice when they come to the Land."[17] In other words, the precepts of Judaism are designed to shape a unique civilization, and that civilization can only be realized completely in the Holy Land. Jews are obligated to fulfill as many as possible of the precepts in the course of their lives in the Diaspora, but because a great many are applicable only in the land of Israel, the effective value of such observance is primarily anticipatory and prospective. Indeed, even a casual reading of the biblical works will reveal that the context of all the divine commitments to the patriarchs and to Israel is their fulfillment in the land promised to them, where they were to build their unique Judaic civilization.

The central defining feature of that civilization is the covenantal basis that it claims. Every aspect of traditional Judaism—whether sacral, theological, ethical, social, or political—is predicated on the existence of an eternal, indefeasible covenant between God and the people of Israel. This covenantal relationship, which is grounded in the Exodus—the emancipation of the people of Israel from servitude in Egypt, which constitutes the paramount historical event in Jewish history—is the foundation upon which the entire edifice of Judaic civilization and culture rests. Needless to point out, both biblical scholars and historians of the ancient world have called the historicity of those events into serious question. But—and this point cannot be stressed too emphatically—the historical verifiability of the Exodus tradition is essentially irrelevant: what is at issue here is Israel's sacred history, not its political history. Israel's sacred history reflects Judaism's foundation myth, and the ultimate importance of the mythopoeic saga of the Exodus for the formation of a Judaic civilization can be neither bolstered through scientific corroboration, even if the latter were possible, nor weakened by its absence.

In the biblical view, the divine intervention in history that resulted in the liberation of the ancient Israelites from their bondage in Egypt was undertaken solely in order that they should have the freedom necessary to devote themselves as a people to the service of their redeemer. God intervened in history so that "they shall know that I the Lord am their God, that brought them out of the land of Egypt that I might abide among them" (Exod. 29:46). The primary concern of the biblical writers was therefore not with the notion of "freedom from" but "freedom to." That is, freedom from the oppression of the Egyptians was not an end in itself. Scripture is not concerned with the notion of absolute liberty as the basis for individual self-determination. Instead, it holds that the Exodus was the result of a divine intervention into history meant to give the Israelites the freedom from external constraint necessary to carry out God's will, as it would be revealed to them. In other words, the liberation of the Israelites took place not so they could lead their lives as they chose but so that they might be free to choose to lead their lives as they ought, in accordance with the divine purpose. Thus, the divine message delivered by Moses to Pharaoh is, "Let My people go, that they may serve Me" (Exod. 7:26). The purpose of the Exodus was to transfer the Israelites from servitude to Pharaoh to servitude to God.

Perhaps even more suggestive in this regard is the biblical passage that states, "But you hath the Lord taken and brought forth out of the iron furnace, out of Egypt, to be unto Him a people of inheritance, as ye are this day" (Deut. 4:20). This text sets forth, albeit implicitly, the theory that the subjugation and subsequent liberation of the Israelites took place for the sole purpose of conditioning them to serve the divine will. Their ordeal of servitude in Egypt is analogized to the purification process that ore undergoes in the heat of a smelter. They are presumed to have emerged from this ordeal essentially and collectively purged of all previous cultural predisposition and prepared to reconstitute themselves as a unique people, as a society committed, within the context of the divine purpose, to fulfilling its assigned role in history.

This extraordinary act of divine providence became the basis for the founding covenant with the children of Israel, revealed through Moses acting as interlocutor on their behalf, a covenant to which they, as well as their descendants throughout all subsequent history, were to become parties. "Neither with you only do I make this covenant and this oath; but with him that standeth here with us this day before the Lord our God, and also with him that is not here with us this day" (Deut. 29:13–14). That is, even those Israelites who were not present, such as future generations, are included within the covenant, as surely as those who actually witnessed its enactment at Mount Sinai. In other words, the covenant was made in perpetuity with the people of Israel as a collectivity, not merely with those Israelites who were inclined to accept it at the time.

But how could Moses unilaterally enter into a covenant with, and impose obligations on, persons who were not explicit parties to it? How could the covenant encompass and obligate all future generations of the children of Israel? What theory of politics, presumably accepted and advocated by Moses, permitted him to conclude such a covenant and accorded legitimacy to open-ended obligation of the unborn?

It would appear that Moses employed a concept of patriarchalism predicated on a presumed natural reciprocity between parents and children, leading to the principle that one is generally obligated to fulfill the commitments made by one's parents or their surrogates. That is, just as one receives life and nurture from one's parents, one incurs certain obligations, one of which is to fulfill the agreements to which one's parents and their ancestors subscribed. In other words, in the Mosaic worldview, it is the family rather than the individual that constitutes the basic building block of society and civilization. Since the covenant between Moses and the elders cannot, as such, be logically binding on future generations, it must be in effect renewed in each generation through the patriarchal relationship between parent and child, providing a continuous link throughout the generations.

This also accounts for the strong patriarchal and tribal bias to be found in the Torah.[18]

Scripture assures us that even though the provisions of the covenant were not subject to negotiation, the children of Israel collectively accepted them without reservation. "And Moses came and told the people all the words of the Lord, and all the ordinances; and all the people answered with one voice, and said: 'All the words which the Lord hath spoken will we do'" (Exod. 24:3). We thus have a bilateral covenant, the essential provisions of which, including the reciprocal obligations of both parties to the agreement, are set forth in the Torah, traditionally believed to be the textual embodiment of the divine word.

Israel's duties and obligations, which are elaborated upon in the traditional literature of Judaism, are defined in terms of general and specific precepts that are to inform and guide the lives of the people. These precepts are justified and made normative on the basis of the collective obligations undertaken by the people of Israel, either explicitly or implicitly, as a consequence of their redemption in the Exodus. They entail not only those religious obligations that Israel, both collectively and individually, is considered to have with respect to God but also the general behavioral norms that are expected to prevail in relationships between persons in a properly ordered Judaic society.

The biblical writings repeatedly and explicitly emphasize the linkage between the precepts and the Exodus. One example of this is the biblical demand concerning the observance of the Sabbath as one of Israel's collective obligations under the covenant. The Torah states: "And thou shalt remember that thou wast a servant in the land of Egypt, and the Lord thy God brought thee out thence by a mighty hand and by an outstretched arm; therefore the Lord thy God commanded thee to keep the Sabbath day" (Deut. 5:15). Let us put aside the modern notion of the perceived, if not self-evident, benefits of a regular day of rest from one's usual regimen of labor and work-related activity, a day that can be devoted to spiritual revitalization. The biblical institution of the weekly Sabbath clearly represents a unique and unprecedented intervention into the social and economic order, the only justification for which in antiquity was the imposition by the covenant of obligatory Sabbath observance.

It is true that the biblical writings also offer an alternative rationale, unrelated to the events of the Exodus—that the justification for observance of the Sabbath is rooted in the story of the creation of the universe. "For in six days the Lord made heaven and earth, the sea, and all that in them is, and rested on the seventh day; wherefore the Lord blessed the Sabbath day, and hallowed it" (Exod. 22:11). How can these disparate rationales for observance of the Sabbath be reconciled? It is particularly instructive to observe how the rabbis synthesized these two rather different ideas, by paying meticulous attention to the way in which the biblical writings present them. In the traditional prayer of sanctification, the *Kiddush*, recited before partaking of the Sabbath evening feast, we bless God, who "with love and favor gave us His holy Sabbath as a heritage, a remembrance of creation. For that day is a prologue to the holy convocations, a memorial of the Exodus from Egypt."[19] This text asserts, in effect, that the rationale for the remembrance of the Sabbath per se is the sanctification it received in the culmination of the divine process of creation. However, the rationale for the actual keeping or observance of the Sabbath is that it serves as "a memorial of the Exodus."

Concerning the obligations one has to one's fellow man as well as to society, the Torah demands, "Thou shalt not pervert the justice due to the stranger, or to the fatherless; nor take the widow's raiment to pledge. But thou shalt remember that thou wast a bondman in Egypt, and the Lord thy God redeemed thee thence; therefore I command thee to do this thing" (Deut. 24:17–18). Here the Torah insists on compassion for the disadvantaged, something that is rare even in modern societies, where the law is often applied inappropriately as a surrogate for justice, regardless of its practical consequences. Such an ethical demand can be given moral force either by a commanding humanitarian impulse or by its being viewed as a divinely imposed obligation. Acutely sensitive to the foibles of men, the Torah prefers to base it on the latter. However, once again, the obligation to refrain from the proscribed acts is directly predicated on the Exodus-based covenant.

Similarly, the Torah demands," Just balances, just weights . . . shall ye have: I am the Lord your God, who brought you out of the land of Egypt" (Lev. 19:36). That is, as quid pro quo for their liberation in the Exodus, the children of Israel are obligated to practice honesty and integrity in their commercial activities. In this instance, the covenantal imperative might appear to be superfluous, since honest weights and measures are surely demanded in every ordered society. Nonetheless, and reflecting a profound insight into human nature, the Torah is wary of man's capacity to rationalize and justify his behavior, no matter how egregious; it therefore demands strict conformity with the precept as a matter of covenantal obligation. This implicitly reflects the view that in a properly constituted and motivated Judaic society, the people may be less prepared to violate the divine covenant than laws enacted by other mere mortals.

As a consequence of its covenantal foundations, the often-asserted criticism that Judaism is, or appears to be, overly "legalistic" completely misses the point, as do the equally misguided apologetics sometimes offered in rebuttal of such criticism. Judaism's fundamental concern is with the articulation and elaboration of the precepts that constitute the operative clauses of the covenant, tasks that represent the principal preoccupation of the traditional literature and teachings of Israel. Consequently, its legalistic character is in fact one of its primary virtues, not a failing. Covenants by their very nature imply the formalization of bilateral or multilateral obligations between contracting parties. To the extent that such obligations remain ill defined or amorphous, they tend to become both ineffectual and ultimately inconsequential, or to be interpreted so broadly as to become overly oner-ous, often to the point of precluding voluntary compliance. Normative Ju-daic thought is therefore vitally concerned with the systematic attempt to ascertain, clarify, delimit, and establish the dimensions and substantive content of such covenantal obligations within the bounds of reason, includ-ing their application in practice under changing historical circumstances and conditions. This aspect of Judaism has been characterized as a "limit culture," within which "every aspect of life is held to be equally divine, and the task of human behavior is to find one's way through the maze of pre-scriptions and proscriptions that constitute reality."[20]

The task of defining behavioral limits and constraints that impact di-rectly on the lives of people, individually and collectively, within the con-text of dynamic interpersonal, social, and political environments is inherently and necessarily highly legalistic in character. If one of Judaism's concerns is the establishment of an ordered society in which men need have no fear of their neighbors, it becomes essential to clearly define the free-doms and limits of each with respect to the other, and these may not at all be self-evident.

It seems clear that any ordered society must proscribe theft, but as Saadia Gaon observed more than a millennium ago, "Although reason con-siders stealing objectionable, there is nothing in it to inform us how a per-son comes to acquire property so that it becomes his possession. [It does not state, for instance,] whether this comes about as a result of labor, or is ef-fected by means of barter, or by way of inheritance, or is derived from what is free to all, like what is hunted on land and sea."[21] Accordingly, if one facet of the ordering of society is the prohibition of stealing or the misappropria-tion of property, a clear understanding becomes essential of what consti-tutes "property" and of how "private property" may be distinguished from that in the public domain. In Anglo-American societies this is achieved through the medium of the common law, which defines and characterizes property on the basis of traditional, customary practices. In other societies, enacted law must define property and all that pertains to it. Judaism essen-tially provides a synthesis of both approaches.

Similarly, if another facet of the covenant involves an obligation of the in-dividual toward God, one must know how and when such obligation is to be discharged. If one is required to abstain from food and drink on the Day of Atonement, one must first know precisely when the day begins and ends, and how much ingested matter would constitute an infraction of the rule. Moreover, one must know whether or not the rule remains operative when one is ill, when compliance might cause substantial harm to one's health through the self-denial of needed nourishment. In other words, an ordered existence, spiritual as well as physical, requires the demarcation of boundaries and limits. Judaism strives to establish those societal and per-

sonal norms that, if adhered to, will help man order his individual and collective life in consonance with the divine will, as the expositors of Judaism
profess it to be revealed in the Torah. These norms of conduct constitute the
halakhah (which will be discussed at length later in this work).

This is not to suggest that Judaism's sole concern is the definition and observance of limits and bounds, however essential these are to it. There are
circumstances in which what is licit may not be just, where what is acceptable is not desirable. Judaism therefore encourages and assigns great moral
and religious merit to those who are prepared, of their own volition, to go
beyond the legal requirements of the specified precept or law to ensure justice and to show compassion, thereby benefiting their fellow men. To facilitate such conduct, the sages of the talmudic period elaborated the ethical
principle of *lifnim mishurat hadin* (literally, "within the line of the law") as a
social and moral desideratum. This principle is believed by some to derive
from the biblical teaching, "And thou shalt do that which is right and good
in the sight of the Lord" (Deut. 6:18).[22] The principle was held in such high
regard by some ancient homilists that they suggested that if it were con-
ceivable that God prayed, His prayer would be to that effect. "What does
He pray? R. Zutra b. Tobiah said in the name of Rab: 'May it be My will that
My mercy may suppress My anger, and that My mercy may prevail over
My [other] attributes, so that I may deal with My children in the attribute of
mercy and, on their behalf, stop short of the limit of strict justice [*lifnim
meshurat hadin*]."[23]

Great virtue is attributed to those who go beyond the strict requirements
of the law by acting *as if* the virtuous actions they freely elect to take are actually "within the line of the law"—that is, as though they were legally required of them. In other words, it is considered meritorious in some
instances, in the interests of social justice and communal harmony, not to
insist upon what may legally be due to oneself. Some of the sages went so
far as to assert that Jerusalem had been destroyed by the Romans because
the communal authorities rendered their judgments strictly in accordance
with the letter of the law, not "within the line of the law."[24] That is, they suggested that a society in which strict adherence to the letter of the law is always construed unequivocally as justice may not merit preservation.

Nonetheless, realism demands acknowledgment that not all people are,
or are likely to become or to behave like, saints. Consequently, and as a
practical matter, a requirement to conform one's conduct to this higher
principle cannot be mandated. It must be voluntary. For this reason, normative Judaism places its greatest emphasis on defining and articulating the
basic parameters of the religious and social life that may reasonably be expected of the average person, while leaving the door open for, and encouraging, the righteous to exceed those basic expectations.

THE NATURE OF THE COVENANT

It hardly need be stressed that each of the parties to a covenant or contract must be able to fulfill the agreed-upon conditions. In the biblical covenant between God and Israel, the assurance that if Israel fulfills its obligations it will receive its due reward, in tangible forms of compensation, is predicated on the fundamental concept of divine sovereignty over the universe. That is, God can unquestionably fulfill his part of the bargain, because the ultimate disposition of the universe, its peoples, lands, and resources is under divine jurisdiction and control.

This concept of divine sovereignty is exemplified in traditional rabbinical thought, in which every aspect of Scripture—including, according to some, the order and sequence of the texts—is assumed to be purposive and significant. R. Isaac, one of the sages of the talmudic era, raised the rhetorical question of why Scripture begins with the story of the creation of the universe instead of the story of the Exodus, since it is the latter that lays the foundation for the national covenant with God. After all, the primary purpose of Scripture, from the rabbinic standpoint, is to transmit the constitution by which Israel is to live and thrive in accordance with the divine promise. R. Isaac's response was that the Torah began with the story of creation in order to make clear to all the extent of God's ultimate power over the universe and all that is contained within it. God is the sovereign of all that exists and is therefore free to do with it whatever He pleases. Accordingly, if it pleased God to award a particular portion of it to Israel in fulfillment of the covenant, His will was not to be contraverted. "He hath declared to His people the power of His works, in giving them the heritage of the nations" (Ps. 111:6).[25]

The great medieval commentator Rashi, who proved to be a remarkably prescient interpreter of R. Isaac's assertion, later elaborated upon that view. He suggested that R. Isaac's teaching was intended to provide a response to the challenge that would be levied by Israel's enemies against the legitimacy of its claim to the Land of Israel, a charge that continues to be made by Israel's enemies to this very day.[26] R. Isaac evidently anticipated the assertion that Israel had originally usurped the land from its previous owners. He therefore insisted that Scripture makes it unmistakably plain that the entire universe is under the sovereignty of its Maker and that it was He who gave the land to Israel after revoking the tenancy of the nations that had occupied it, thereby validating their ultimate dispossession. Viewed from this perspective, Israel's claim to the land is not vulnerable to legitimate challenge.

It is noteworthy that the Torah itself took a somewhat different approach to the issue, although arriving at the same conclusion. It asserts, in effect, that the so-called original owners of the land at the time of the Mosaic covenant were themselves but temporary occupants, who had conquered and absorbed or displaced the people they found there, who in turn had earlier displaced others. This represents an essentially accurate assessment of the demographic history of the territory in ancient times. It also suggests implicitly that the Mosaic covenant itself should be considered the culmination of a covenant formation process that began centuries earlier with God's initial covenant with the patriarch Abraham. According to this approach, the earlier covenant had long before established the basis for Israel's ultimate claim to the land—a claim that could not be asserted at the time of Abraham because, as the biblical text put it, "the iniquity of the Amorite is not yet full" (Gen. 15:16).

In exchange for Israel's compliance with the precepts set forth in the Torah, God is committed by the covenant to reward it with peace and prosperity in the land in which it is to establish its political society and unique civilization. However, the covenant also contains a severe penalty clause: failure by Israel to fulfill its duties and obligations will result not only in the loss of peace and prosperity but also in its political decline and ultimate dispossession from its patrimony. This theme is sounded repeatedly in the Torah, one of the more explicit examples being the adjuration by Moses in his final address to the people, both collectively and individually, in which he effectively assigns responsibility for the welfare of the whole to every one of its constituents.

I command thee this day to love the Lord thy God, to walk in His ways, and to keep His commandments and His statutes and His ordinances; then thou shalt live and multiply, and the Lord thy God shall bless thee in the land whither thou goest in to possess it. But if thy heart turn away, and thou wilt not hear, but shall be drawn away, and worship other gods, and serve them; I declare unto you this day, that ye shall surely perish; ye shall not prolong your days upon the land, whither thou passest over the Jordan to go in to possess it. (Deut. 30: 16–18)

What Moses does not specify is what constitutes collective compliance. Does the covenant demand unanimity—that is, compliance by each and every individual member of the society? Or does the adjuration and penalty clause apply only if some critical mass of compliance is not attained? If the latter, what constitutes such a critical mass? Moses wisely leaves these questions unanswered. By so doing he places the burden of the entire community on each individual, since no one can be sure that he or she does not represent the final increment of compliance necessary. It would seem, in light of the vicissitudes of Israel's history from the perspective of the covenant, that its sorry record is to be perceived as tangible evidence of Israel's collective failure to conform to the standard of compliance set for it.

But what does "to love the Lord thy God, to walk in His ways and keep His commandments and His statutes and His ordinances" actually mean? It is this very ambiguity that compels Judaism and its exponents to struggle incessantly over the elaboration and specification of the appropriate norms of conduct and performance. It is thus the inherently open-ended nature of the biblical covenant that has both shaped the complex evolution of traditional Judaism and given it the ability to adapt as necessary to changing historical circumstances.

THE COVENANTAL HERITAGE

According to the biblical account, Judaic civilization has its earliest roots in what clearly, albeit implicitly, appears to be a divine covenant with Abraham, described at the very beginning of the biblical chapters devoted to the patriarch.[27] We are not informed in any explicit manner why such an initial covenant was deemed necessary or what it was intended to achieve. However, we may reasonably infer that the divine intent was to establish a contractual basis for the subsequent founding of a unique social and political entity. That entity would be instrumental in bringing to realization certain objectives of the divine plan for the universe and humankind. An essential component of this scheme was the establishment of a national territory in which such an entity might flourish.

This inference is based in part on the fact that the biblical account of the enactment of this special covenant with Abraham immediately follows the story of the tower of Babel. That saga depicts a vain attempt by the leaders of the dominant primeval civilization to establish a universal, but evidently godless, political society. The central ethos of that polity was to be manifested in the erection of "a tower, with its top in heaven" (Gen. 11:4), a structure that presumably would symbolize man's self-exaltation, perhaps even his self-apotheosis, thereby effectively challenging God's sovereignty over the universe. The consequence of this arrogant rejection of divine authority was the rapid decline of Babel into an increasingly corrupt and oppressive society, ultimately provoking divine intervention to bring about its political collapse and social dissolution.

A critical implication of the story is that while a universal political society may be a desirable goal for mankind, this is so only if such a society is based on the appropriate moral foundations. Otherwise, as seems to have occurred in the perhaps mythical primeval state of Babel, morally corrupt leaders might easily transform it into an instrument of universal oppression and injustice. Given the state of public and private morals in Babel at the time, the formation of a universal society was presumably considered to be premature and contrary to the best interests of mankind. The biblical writings suggest that it was the divine judgment that men would be better off living in distinct communities and nations until such time as they were better prepared morally to deal with the challenges of a universal society. The crucial question, of course, is how the diverse nations of the world and their leaders were to become aware of the morally desirable societal standards to which they should aspire.

The implicit biblical response is that this knowledge was to be obtained through the observation and emulation of a functioning model of a moral society, a model that was to be made available the nations of the world. Since no society deemed worthy of replication existed, it became necessary that such an entity be created for the purpose. Accordingly, the biblical narrative describes in some detail the processes by which a new and unique national society and civilization was to be fashioned to serve as an instrument of the divine plan for the moral advancement of mankind.

Abraham, a heroic figure endowed with exceptional moral qualities that evidently predisposed him for the role, was chosen to serve as the founding patriarch of the new model nation. Because that nation was to be based on a new paradigm of societal ethics, it was crucial that Abraham be adequately prepared for the challenges that lay ahead. To minimize residual influences, it was necessary that he be completely uprooted from the civilization into which he had been born and raised, thereby making it easier for him to dissolve the social and cultural ties with his past. Accordingly, Abraham was instructed to depart from the land of his birth and to sever his links with nation, clan, and family: "Get thee out of thy country, and from thy kindred, and from thy father's house, unto the land that I will show thee" (Gen. 12:1). The patriarch was ordered to abandon his place in the society and civilization in which he had been raised and educated, and to proceed to the strange and politically volatile land in which he was to begin building a new civilization. In return for his readiness to forsake such ties and to undertake the challenge of the unknown, a readiness that represented a dramatic demonstration of his faith in God, Abraham received an extraordinary promise: "And I will make of thee a great nation, and I will bless thee, and make thy name great; and be thou a blessing" (Gen. 12:2).

Under the implicit terms of this initial covenant, God would make good on his commitment if Abraham fulfilled the requirement that he terminate his relationship to the society and culture in which he had been nurtured and ventured into a completely alien environment. Only there could Abraham become the progenitor of a new and distinctive nation that was to emerge on the world stage as a direct result of divine intervention in the course of history.

Abraham accepted the challenge, turned his back on civilization as he knew it, and ventured into the unknown, solely on the basis of his faith in the covenant to which he thereby became a party. Having fulfilled his initial obligation under the terms of the agreement, upon his arrival in the designated land Abraham was reassured of the divine commitment to the covenant, which was now augmented with a territorial dimension: "Unto thy seed will I give this land" (Gen. 12:7). It is noteworthy that Abraham was not told that he himself would receive the land, for the reason mentioned earlier—that the time allotted to the nations then occupying the land had not yet run its course.

With renewed confidence in the viability of his enterprise, Abraham undertook the task of laying the foundations for a new religious civilization predicated on the implicit terms of his covenant with God. He built altars in diverse places "and called upon the name of the Lord" (Gen. 12:8), an activity that has been understood by numerous traditional commentators to mean the summoning of all men to the recognition of the one and only true God.[28] In other words, Abraham assumed the unprecedented role of apostle of the truly divine to the pagans of the land.

The partially explicit bilateral covenant originally struck between God and Abraham was subsequently extended into a unilateral and eternal covenant between God and all future generations of Abraham's descendants: "And I will establish My covenant between Me and thee and thy seed after thee throughout their generations for an everlasting covenant, to be a God unto thee and to thy seed after thee" (Gen. 17:7). One of the great challenges of Judaic thought has been that of defining and elaborating the intrinsic nature of this unceasing covenantal relationship and of all that it entails.

The rapid evolution of both a nation and a distinctive civilization from a single individual was, however, a rather complex and difficult process. The new nation, constituted as a unique political society, could not appear on the stage of history suddenly, miraculously, if it were to serve effectively as a model for emulation. It had to be perceived by others as a nation that was little different in most characteristics from themselves. For this reason, the divine intervention in the historical process could not be too obvious if it were not to prove counterproductive. It had to be accomplished in a manner that would permit the new nation to appear to have arisen naturally, in a way not intrinsically different from other nations, except with regard to its moral foundations, religious civilization, and political culture.

By following the natural process of social evolution, Abraham's progeny might ultimately have become a distinct group of people with a distinctive ethnic identity. But as the nineteenth-century commentator Samson Raphael Hirsch observed, "Numerous descendants do not yet constitute a nation. That any mass of people should become a *goy*, a nation, there must be some uniting bond. Everywhere else this is possession of a common land, where the people live together under the same influences and conditions. But the descendants of Abraham are also to become a nation, but not through a common land, but again only through God."[29] To emphasize the primarily theocentric character of the nation of Israel, it was necessary for it to emerge outside the land that was to be allocated to it as its patrimony. The nation was to be forged and tempered in a hostile environment that would give the people a common unifying experience of adversity, from which they would ultimately be delivered by the divine hand. The process of its formation as a nation and subsequent emergence upon the stage of history as a geopolitical entity would make it unique among the nations of the world.

Abraham is told, "Know of a surety that thy seed shall be a stranger in a land that is not theirs, and shall serve them; and they shall afflict them four hundred years. . . . And in the fourth generation they shall come back hither" (Gen. 15:13–16). Accordingly, the descendants of Abraham were to be constituted as the people of Israel outside the land destined to become theirs. That which would give them their initial self-identification as a people was their ethnic connection. Later, this essentially familial, or tribal, identity would play a progressively less significant role as the people become bound together through an indelible collective historical experience that transformed them into a nation, one that would be forged out of economic hardships and political oppression. This experience of collective adversity would prepare them for the challenges of their divinely assigned national mission.

THE NATIONAL MISSION

The nation that would ultimately emerge from the original covenant with Abraham was to be burdened with a national purpose that alone justified its autonomous existence. Moses, acting as interlocutor for the people of Israel, was explicitly informed of this just prior to the revelation of the Torah in the wilderness of Sinai: "Now therefore, if ye will hearken unto My voice indeed, and keep My covenant, then ye shall be Mine own treasure from among all peoples[,] . . . and ye shall be unto Me a kingdom of priests, and a holy nation" (Exod. 19:5–6). But what does it mean to be a "kingdom of priests" and a "holy nation?"

The answer to this crucial question brings us back to the concept of divine sovereignty, which pertains not only to Israel but also to all the nations of the world. One might suggest that perhaps the principal reason for Israel's continued existence is that the nations of the world have failed to acknowledge the truth of divine sovereignty and that it is therefore Israel's national mission to help bring them to this realization. However, this mission is to be accomplished not primarily through proselytism but rather by constituting and presenting the model of an ideal political society, one worthy of their emulation, a process that ultimately would lead the nations to the acknowledgment and acceptance of divine sovereignty. Israel's own acceptance of such a concept of the universal sovereignty of God is given clear expression in the words of the psalmist: "For the kingdom is the Lord's; and He is the ruler over the nations" (Ps. 22:29). This passage is recited as part of the annual liturgy for the New Year, which continues, "On this day it is decreed which countries are destined for the sword and which for peace, which for famine and which for plenty."[30]

To fulfill its assigned purpose, Israel was to be politically independent, free to pursue its national mission. Accordingly, the sages of the talmudic era also interpreted the divine reference to a "kingdom of priests" as meaning a "kingdom of princes." That is, they took the passage to mean, "I will allow only one of your own to be king over you, but not one from the nations of the world."[31] This should be understood as a reflection of their acute awareness that national autonomy and political self-direction are essential to the accomplishment of Israel's national aims. The political leader of the nation should therefore be someone who would most likely pursue these aims wholeheartedly and without conflicts of loyalties or interests.

Finally, the biblical passage refers to the prospect of Israel becoming a "holy nation." *Kadosh*, the Hebrew term for holy, means to be "set apart" or "consecrated." Accordingly, the sages understood the biblical phrase to refer to a nation that was "holy and sacred, separated from the nations of the world and from their abominations."[32] The intent of this interpretation appears to have been to provide a rationale for Israel's cultural distinctiveness from the surrounding nations and peoples. This would be achieved through the development of a unique set of religious rites and daily practices that would seriously impede extensive social interactions with alien cultures. Indeed, the dietary laws of Judaism alone would make social interactions with outsiders rather difficult. In essence, then, Israel was to become a nation wholly dedicated to God's purpose; it was to evolve into an autonomous and just political society, in which each member would conduct himself as though he were a priest or prince.[33]

The mission of Israel was to become, as Hirsch put it, "a nation to which other nations have only to look to become conscious of what their task is."[34] Israel was intended to be "a unique nation amongst the nations, a nation which does not exist for its own fame, its own greatness, its own glory, but the foundation and glorification of the Kingdom of God on Earth, a nation which is not to seek its greatness in power and might but in the absolute rule of the Divine Law."[35] Israel, as a political society, was to rise to a level that would inspire other peoples and nations to seek to emulate its constitutive principles. It would thereby serve as the "blessing" to the nations of the world alluded to in the original formulation of the covenant offered to Abraham. Martin Buber reiterated this concept in contemporary times with reference to his aspiration for the modern state of Israel. "For only an entire nation which comprehends peoples of all kinds can demonstrate a life of unity and peace, of righteousness and justice to the human race as a sort of example and beginning. . . . [A] true history can only commence with a certain definite and true nation[;] . . . the people of Israel was charged to lead the way toward this realization."[36]

The accomplishment of this national mission, however, is necessarily predicated on the prior establishment and continued existence of the nation as an independent political entity in its own land. It is only in the territory that was to be designated as the Land of Israel that the nation would be in a position to fulfill its assigned mission and reason for being. One would hardly expect the settled and independent nations of the world seriously to

consider emulating the political culture and mores of a nation that was itself homeless and without political form.

The model political society envisioned by the Torah was to be based on
social principles and behavioral norms that were radically different from
those prevailing in the other societies of the ancient world. "After the doings of the land of Egypt, wherein ye dwelt, shall ye not do; and after the doings of the land of Canaan, whither I bring you, shall ye not do; neither shall
ye walk in their statutes. Mine ordinances shall ye do, and My statutes shall
ye keep, to walk therein; I am the Lord your God" (Lev. 18:3–4). The Torah
thus clearly indicates that the ordered regime under which Israel is to function as a political society is to be based exclusively on a set of divinely legislated ordinances and statutes. Israel, as a nation and religious civilization
that is to be governed by the divine laws and precepts, both revealed and
implicit in the Torah, is not to emulate the practices, social or political, of the
morally and spiritually corrupt societies with which it comes in contact.

Moreover, Israel's human governors and leaders may make no claim to
sovereignty and are therefore also to be fully subject to this higher rule of
law. Indeed, the Torah makes it abundantly clear that that this requirement
applies to a king just as it does to every other Israelite. Accordingly, a king
of Israel, "when he sitteth upon the throne of his kingdom . . . shall write
him a copy of this law. . . . And it shall be with him, and he shall read therein
all the days of his life; that he may learn to fear the Lord his God, to keep all
the words of this law and these statutes . . . and that he turn not aside from
the commandment, to the right hand, or to the left" (Deut. 17:18–20). Even
with a monarch as its political head, Israel was to remain constituted as a
political society in which ultimate authority resided in the divine law and
not in man.

This, in brief, is the biblical legacy, as reflected and elaborated in traditional Judaic thought, that provides the raison d'être for the Judaic political
society and state. The chapters that follow will consider the political culture
of Judaism necessary to realize the biblical aspirations for Israel as a paradigm for the good and just society.

NOTES

1. Michael A. Fishbane, *Judaism*, p. 18.

2. *Sanhedrin* 59a.

3. Maimonides, *Hilkhot Melakhim* 10:9–10.

4. See discussion of Noahide Laws in Martin Sicker, *What Judaism Says about
Politics: The Political Theology of the Torah*, pp. 188–198.

5. *Sanhedrin* 56a; *Tosefta Avodah Zarah* 9:4.

6. *Nedarim* 28a; *Gittin* 10b; *Baba Kamma* 113a—b; *Baba Batra* 54b—55a.

7. Jacob ben Abba Mari Anatoli, *Malmad haTalmidim*, p. 72a.

8. See discussion in Isaac Husik, "The Law of Nature, Hugo Grotius, and the
Bible," *Hebrew Union College Annual*, vol. 2, pp. 381–417.

9. For an extensive discussion of the Noahide Laws and their relation to the Mosaic Law, see Aaron Lichtenstein, *The Seven Laws of Noah*.

10. *Sanhedrin* 59a.

11. Maimonides, *Hilkhot Melakhim* 10:9.

12. It should be noted that the connotations of the terms "civilization" and "culture" vary in the writings of different writers. Of particular interest here are the distinctions drawn by Leo Jung: "Civilization grew out of the instinct of self-preservation. . . . It reduces things to order, and multitudes and crowds to some form of system and discipline. . . . It stresses order and system, but not as ends. They are means for a larger, finer goal. That goal is culture, an affair of souls and hearts. Civilization brings rest; culture brings peace. Civilization familiarizes you with facts; culture raises you above them into a sphere of ideas and ideals. . . . Civilization is the foundation of culture, but culture is the consummation of civilization" (*Living Judaism*, p. 263).

13. Mordecai M. Kaplan, *Judaism as a Civilization*, pp. 218–219.

14. The term first appears in 2 Maccabees 2:21.

15. André Chouraqui, *A History of Judaism*, p. 9.

16. See Martin Sicker, *Judaism, Nationalism and the Land of Israel*.

17. Elijah of Vilna, *Aderet Eliyahu*, on Deut. 8:1, p. 390.

18. For a more extensive discussion of this issue, see Martin Sicker, "Reading the Pentateuch Politically," in *The Jewish Bible Quarterly*, vol. 27, no. 4, October—December 1999, pp. 251–258.

19. *The Complete ArtScroll Siddur*, p. 361.

20. Lawrence A. Hoffman, *The Art of Public Prayer*, p. 124.

21. Saadia Gaon, *The Book of Beliefs and Opinions*, p. 146.

22. Rashi, commentary on Deut. 6:18. Others derive the concept from Exod. 18:20. See discussion in R. Travers Herford, *Talmud and Apocrypha*, p. 140.

23. *Berakhot* 7a.

24. *Baba Metzia* 30b.

25. *Midrash Tanhuma*, Buber, ed., "Bereshit," 11. Also cited with some modification in *Yalkut Shimeoni* no. 187.

26. Rashi, commentary on Gen. 1:1.

27. Gen. 12:1–4.

28. Nahmanides, *Perushei haTorah*, commentary on Gen. 12:8, pp. 78–79. The divine promise of the land is reiterated in Gen. 13:14–17 and Gen. 15:18–21 in greater detail.

29. Samson Raphael Hirsch, *The Pentateuch*, on Gen. 12:2.

30. *High Holiday Prayer Book*, p. 131.

31. *Mekilta de-Rabbi Ishmael*, "Tractate *Bahodesh*" 2, vol. 2, p. 205.

32. Ibid., p. 206.

33. *Exodus Rabbah* 30:13. The sages cited the passage, "The king by justice establisheth the land" (Prov. 29:4), stating that "this refers to Israel, of whom it says, *And ye shall be unto Me a kingdom of priests*."

34. Hirsch, on Gen. 12:2

35. Ibid., on Exod. 19:6.

36. Martin Buber, *Israel and the World*, p. 187.

Chapter 2

Democratic Theocracy

How would one characterize a political society organized in consonance with the teachings of Judaism, as they are understood in traditional rabbinic thought? Because the contemporary vocabulary of politics does not seem to have an appropriate classification for such an entity, Samuel Belkin coined the phrase "democratic theocracy" to describe the proper Judaic state.

It is a theocracy because the animating force of Jewish morality is not the protection of the state or community in the abstract, or of any mundane form of government. The entire system of Jewish morality derives from, and is founded upon, the concept of the sovereignty of God. It is a *democracy* because, unlike any other legal system, the rabbinic code places all emphasis upon the infinite worth and sacredness of the human being. In Judaism, the recognition of the *demos*, the individual, and the infinite worth of his personality but a necessary outgrowth of the acceptance of God's *theos* (rulership), a relationship succinctly summed up in the phrase "democratic theocracy."[1]

Democracy and theocracy would normally be considered antithetical; Belkin is evidently employing these terms in a sense quite different from the manner in which they are commonly understood.

THEOCRACY

Although the term "theocracy" is generally used to describe government under the dominance of priests, mullahs, or other ecclesiastical authorities, such a system of government would more properly be termed a "hierocracy." Theocracy originally had a rather different connotation, one consistent with the way Belkin employs it. To the best of our knowledge, Josephus Flavius coined the term some two millennia ago to describe the unique political system of Judaism. "Some legislators have permitted their governments to be under monarchies, others put them under oligarchies, and others under a republican form; but our legislator had no regard to any of these forms, but he ordained our government to be what, by a strained expression, may be termed a Theocracy, by ascribing the authority and the power to God."[2]

In making this assertion, Josephus was reaffirming the long-standing traditional understanding of the political nature of the covenantal relationship between God and the people of Israel. The characterization of that relationship as a theocracy sought to help bridge the conceptual chasm between the transcendence of God and immanence of man. This was achieved by postulating the concept of divine sovereignty over the universe and history, a concept that was subsequently incorporated into the constitutional underpinnings of ancient Israel. As explained by Moses Mendelssohn more than two centuries ago:

In this original constitution, state and religion were not conjoined, but one; not connected, but identical. Man's relation to society and his relation to God coincided and could never come into conflict. God, the Creator and Preserver of the world, was at the same time the King and Regent of this nation; and his oneness is such as not to admit the least division or plurality in either the political or the metaphysical sense. Nor does this monarch have any needs. He demands nothing from the nation but what serves its own welfare and advances the felicity of the state; just as the state, for its part, could not demand anything that was opposed to the duties toward God, that was not rather commanded by God, the Lawgiver and Regent of the nation. Hence, in this nation, civil matters acquired a sacred and religious aspect, and every civil service was at the same time a true service of God. The community was a community of God, its affairs were God's; the public taxes were an offering to God; and everything down to the least police measure was part of the "divine service."[3]

The theory of divine sovereignty and its theocratic implications—notions so remote from the political experience of the people of ancient Israel—were very difficult for them to assimilate, as attested to repeatedly by the biblical authors. An early example of this is the account in which the Israelite leader Gideon was urged by the elders of several of the tribes to accept a crown and become their dynastic sovereign. Gideon responded by reminding them that sovereignty was neither his to take nor theirs to bestow: "I will not rule over you, neither shall my son rule over you; the Lord shall rule over you" (Judg. 8:23). As one commentator remarks with regard to this episode, "With prophetic insight he saw that Israel's destiny was bound up with God's Sovereignty and not with temporal kingship."[4] Nonetheless, and contrary to his explicit wish, Gideon's son Abimelekh did don the crown and rule over a tribal confederation, for three disastrous years.

Divine sovereignty, as so aptly pointed out by Mendelssohn, is by its inherent nature indivisible and therefore cannot be shared. Consequently, anyone who harbored pretensions to sovereignty could only do so in defiance of heaven. To lend weight to this point, the sages imputed a special layer of meaning to the biblical statement, "Ye shall be unto Me a kingdom of priests" (Exod. 19:6). Focusing on the words "unto Me," they asserted that God was stating, in effect, "I shall not appoint or delegate any one else, so to speak, to rule over you, but I myself will rule over you."[5] The idea that sovereignty over Israel rested entirely with God is also reflected in the rabbinic view that unconditional acceptance of "the yoke of the kingdom of heaven" constitutes a fundamental prerequisite for the adherence to Judaism.[6]

It is true that Scripture makes explicit provision for an organized priesthood, with important societal functions in addition to the sacerdotal. However, it also suggests that the idea of theocracy in its more modern connotation of rule by the clergy, ostensibly in the name or on behalf of God, was deemed highly inappropriate by the biblical authors. Although an explicit rationale for their objection is not given, it seems reasonable to conjecture that it had become evident to them that the fusion of political and spiritual authority in man was inherently undesirable, most probably because it might concentrate too much power in too few hands.

The biblical account thus informs us that when Moses took on the role of political leader of the nation, the sacerdotal and religious leadership was vested in his brother Aaron and the latter's descendants. This effectively established the principle of separation of powers, which is an underpinning of most subsequent constitutional thought. The rabbis elaborated on this idea by suggesting that Moses actually wanted to establish a system under which he and his descendants would serve as both kings and high priests, but that his request was denied.[7] It is also noteworthy that even though Moses seems to have exercised monarchical powers, he was never accorded regal status. This may well have been a consequence of his paramount role as prophet. Presumably, it was also deemed best to keep prophecy and supreme political power apart, vested in different bearers.

Similarly, the biblical authors undertook to ensure that there would be no usurpation of political power by the spiritual leaders of the nation. Thus, while the priesthood was made the exclusive province of the Aaronid branch of the tribe of Levi, the future royal prerogative was to be vested exclusively in the tribal line of Judah. This theoretical separation of powers is predicated on the last will and testament of Jacob, patriarch and progenitor of the Israelite tribes, stating in part: "The sceptre shall not depart from Judah, nor the ruler's staff from between his feet" (Gen. 49:10). Subsequently this statement was interpreted to mean that legitimate kingship in Israel was to be the exclusive perquisite of the house of David, a branch of the tribal line of Judah. As a practical matter, however, when the time became ripe for the several tribal confederacies to be forged into a unified kingdom,

Israel's first king, Saul, was chosen, for purely political reasons, from the tribe of Benjamin. Moreover, after the collapse of the unified state, the later rulers of the northern Israelite kingdom came from tribes other than Judah, which remained under the house of David to the end.[8] Although Israelite political practice, then, did not necessarily conform to the biblical theory of the separation of powers, the theory nonetheless continued to be treated as normative in subsequent Judaic thought. In any case, the biblical constraint was not considered to apply to lesser forms of governance than kingship.

Thus, for most of the nearly four centuries between the return of the remnants of Judah from the Babylonian Captivity to the rise of the Hasmoneans in Hellenistic times, Judaea was governed by a high priest serving as "ethnarch" but not as king of the Jews. The ethnarch was a functionary successively employed by the Persian, Ptolemaid, and Seleucid rulers of what would later be called Palestine. When Judaea ultimately reemerged as an independent state in 142 B.C.E., under the leadership of Simon the Hasmonean, a member of a priestly clan, Simon was proclaimed high priest and ethnarch of the nation, but not as its king. Even though he was a monarch in every sense of the term, Simon had to content himself with the lesser dignity of prince of his people in order to conform to the traditional ban against combining the authority of the high priest with that of the king.

Although this prohibition was violated by his grandson Judah Aristobulus, who declared himself both king and high priest about the year 105 b.c.e., even he was careful to employ the royal title only in the non-Jewish parts of his realm. The inscriptions on the coins he minted for use within Judaea proper referred to him only as high priest and ethnarch. It was only when his brother Alexander Jannai succeeded him in 104 and proclaimed himself both high priest and king, effectively exploiting the religious office for political purposes, that the impropriety of fusing the two roles became a matter of growing public concern. At the time, however, there was less concern about a priest being a king than about vesting both forms of authority in a single person. According to a tradition recorded in the Talmud, an elder of the community confronted him with the plea, "O King Jannai, let the royal crown suffice thee, and leave the priestly crown to the seed of Aaron"—notwithstanding that Jannai was himself an Aaronid.[9]

Rabbinic rejection of this fusion of roles is clearly reflected in the later teaching that effectively denied legitimacy to the combination of monarchic and ecclesiastical authority in a single person. Referring to the common ritual of anointing to resolve questions regarding the legitimacy of an incumbent to supreme office, the rabbis declared, "Priest-kings are not anointed"; they hoped thereby to preclude a repetition of the kind of tyranny imposed by Alexander Jannai.[10] Indeed, political scientist Milford Q. Sibley wrote in this regard, "Throughout most of their political experience and speculation, Hebrew thinkers repudiate the notion that the priestly and royal functions should be exercised by one man. No doubt this separation of functions is in part to be attributed to the very ambivalence with which Hebrews tended to look at kingship. It is also possibly rooted in a feeling that the priesthood must be independent of direct royal control if it is to be a critic of kingly government."[11]

The rabbinic restriction on the political roles open to members of the priesthood was held by some to be based on the traditional idea that legitimate kingship in Israel is reserved to the Davidic branch of the tribal line of Judah. Others grounded it in the biblical denial of any portion or inheritance in the land to the descendants of Levi, a severely limiting constraint in an essentially agricultural society, and one that was designed to restrict their activity to religious and cultural affairs. In either case, the evident intent of the sages was to base this dictum on unimpeachable biblical authority in order to delegitimate definitively hierocracy, or rule by a priesthood, as an acceptable model for government in the Judaic state. In his discussion of the talmudic rule, the eighteenth-century commentator Moses Margoliot suggested that the intent of the sages in setting forth this political restriction is clear and unequivocal: its meaning is not merely that the priest-king is not anointed but that "we do not *appoint* kings from among them [the priesthood]."[12] In other words, from a traditional rabbinic perspective, the Torah envisions Israel as a kingdom of priests but not as a priest-ruled kingdom.

With the destruction of the Temple of Jerusalem more than nineteen hundred years ago, the priesthood could no longer perform its sacerdotal functions and effectively became defunct. However, by the time of that cataclysmic event, the sages who now became the principal religious and cultural leaders of the people had long assumed the traditional pedagogic responsibilities of the priesthood. It therefore may be seen as somewhat anachronistic that in modern Israel, the rabbinate has begun to assume an institutionalized clerical role that tends to cross the line drawn by the biblical authors and the sages of the Talmud to separate clerical from political authority. There is no self-evident reason why the principle of the undesirability of concentrating too much power in too few hands should be disregarded by the contemporary rabbinate with respect to the modern State of Israel. This would suggest that the legitimacy of rabbinic or rabbinate-dominated political parties vying for power and influence in a representative democracy is highly questionable from a classical Judaic perspective.

It would seem that the more appropriate political role for the rabbinate would be that of disinterested public advocacy of moral responsibility and governmental conduct consistent with the traditional teachings of Judaism. In antiquity, this role was undertaken by the prophets, of whom the sages and rabbis claimed to be the heirs. "From the day that the Holy Temple was destroyed, prophecy was removed from the prophets and given to the sages."[13] Such a reorientation of the political role of the rabbinate would contribute significantly to alleviating concerns about rabbinic intentions to institute a theocracy in the modern, rather than ancient, meaning of the term. It seems quite clear that the Torah does not provide for, or desire, a clerical government in a Jewish state.

To recapitulate, Judaism is a theocracy only in the sense that it considers God alone as sovereign. Emanuel Rackman writes in this regard, "As in the case of so many other attributes of God we cannot say positively what His sovereignty is. We know better what it negates. It means that no one else is sovereign.... All created things have their place in that order which He ordained but none can exercise more power than He permitted. Indeed, it is precisely because Judaism was theocratic in the sense that it recognized only God's sovereignty that Judaism was able to inspire so much democratic thought."[14]

DEMOCRACY

Some modern traditionalist scholars are staunch advocates of the proposition that the roots of democratic thought are firmly grounded in biblical and rabbinic teaching. Simon Federbusch went so far as to assert that democracy is the natural organizing principle of human society and that this can be seen clearly reflected in the formative stages of the nation of Israel, as that history is recounted in the biblical writings.[15] Robert Gordis similarly argued that in premonarchic times Israel was governed as a "primitive democratic order," in which the assembly of the community "exercised political and juridical functions."[16]

According to Federbusch, the original tribal structure of the ancient Israelites was fundamentally democratic. It was not very different in this regard from many, if not most, early family and clan-based social groups with comparable characteristics. The Israelite tribe was essentially a classless society, one in which social and economic distinctions among its members were of little practical importance. With the exception of women, children, and others who suffered from traditional social disabilities, all members of the tribe were held to be intrinsically equal.

This perhaps oversimplified perspective on Israelite tribal society was apparently also maintained by Meir Leibush Malbim, who argued that during its initial sojourn in the desert following the Exodus, Israel consisted essentially of a single economic and social class and was therefore at peace with itself. Because of this, he suggested, Moses was able to defer introducing a hierarchical leadership structure to govern the tribes. "While they were at Horeb the people did not have any matters of conflict requiring adjudication, since they had no houses, landholdings, or vineyards that might cause litigation to take place, nor did they have any commerce; moreover all received equal shares of the *manna*," the divine gift of food for their nourishment. However, the situation was to change radically, as soon as it became clear that the Israelites were about to enter, occupy, and settle the land of Canaan, "because when they enter the land and take possession of it, conflicts [would] break out among them."[17] In other words, Malbim intimated that intrasocietal conflict is naturally at a minimum in a social system in which there are no significant class distinctions, where intrinsic social and economic equality prevails. Viewed from this perspective, the initial tribal structure of Israel may be considered to have been inherently democratic, in that no artificial and divisive class distinctions had emerged as yet. The implicit corollary to this argument is that the societal arrangements subsequently called for in the biblical texts, such as monarchy, which deviated from the practice of democracy, were driven by expediency rather than principle.

What was true of the individual tribes is presumed by some to have held for the tribal confederacies as well. Each of the tribes considered itself fully equal to every other. As a consequence of this strongly maintained belief, it was only with great difficulty that the tribes were ultimately welded into a broader, cohesive national political unit. There is substantial textual evidence that during the early formative period of the nation, the tribal confederacy was governed by an assembly composed of the "elect of the congregation, the princes of the tribes of their fathers; they were the heads of the thousands of Israel" (Num. 1:16). As noted by Gordis, "As the supreme authority, representing the entire people, the assembly has an important role to play in the allocation of the land to the various tribes, since the decision is regarded as a kind of social contract in which all the tribes are equal."[18] Each tribe strenuously resisted any diminution of its virtually unlimited autonomy, as would inevitably result from the imposition of a central authority.

This persistent concern about preserving autonomy helps account for the biblical reports of challenges to Moses' authority by tribal leaders. The biblically reported rebellion of Korah and his associates against assertions of the political and religious authority of Moses and Aaron may be understood as but one egregious example of the reluctance of the tribal leaders to surrender any of their traditional independence and equality of status. Korah and his colleagues, according to Scripture (Num. 16:2–3), "were princes of the congregation, the elect men of the assembly, men of renown; and they assembled themselves against Moses and against Aaron, and said to them: 'Ye take too much upon you, seeing all the congregation are holy, every one of them, and the Lord is among them; wherefore then lift ye up yourselves above the assembly of the Lord?' " These tribal leaders were evidently unwilling to concede any of their autonomy to Moses and therefore challenged his claim to authority derived from a unique divine grant. They predicated their counterclaim on the presumed equality of all before God.

For some, however, the fact that Scripture specifically calls for the establishment of societal structures and institutions that are essentially incompatible with the egalitarian presumptions of democracy raises serious questions about the extent to which Scripture may be understood as the source of other apparently democratic ideas. In contrast to the position taken by Federbusch, others argue that "the way of life envisaged for the Israelites in the Bible cannot properly be termed a democracy." They acknowledge that the development of democratic ideas in seventeenth- century England and eighteenth-century America was influenced heavily by the Bible and that the constitution of the ancient Israelite tribes may also be considered to reflect a primitive form of democracy. Nonetheless, they insist, "a system which provides for both an hereditary monarch and an hereditary priestly caste cannot be so termed, even though kings often ruled by popular consent."[19]

It might be argued, however, that this position is somewhat overstated. At most, the Torah can be construed as mandating only that leadership of the Israelites is to be vested in the tribe of Judah, and even this constraint was evidently put aside by the prophet Samuel, when he appointed Saul of Benjamin to take up the scepter. Moreover, as argued by Yoel Bin-Nun, in reference to the debate in religious circles about the nature of the state in contemporary Israel, "Even the term 'king of Israel' does not necessarily connote a monarchy or an absolute authority. In my judgment, most of those who assert that democracy is an alien cultural influence and advocate the rule of 'a kingdom of Israel' in its place, are thinking of totalitarian rule, which is in opposition to the Torah more than anything else. Even a monarchy does not have to be totalitarian; it can be democratic, just as a republic can be a dictatorship."[20] Milton Konvitz also takes issue with those who assume that the priesthood constituted a privileged class, a hereditary aristocracy—"But this is due to a misunderstanding. The priests were not permitted to consider themselves the heads of the community: they were a class whose status was determined by function; they were servants of God in a special sense; but being such servants, they carried obligations rather than privileges. People were not to stand in superstitious fear of them; they had no superior spiritual powers."[21]

The notion of describing the Judaic state as a democracy was first suggested by the ancient Jewish philosopher Philo of Alexandria, who believed it to be the best possible constitutional framework for any political society. Philo considered democracy to be the political extension of the fundamental principle of equality, which he held to be intrinsic to the proper order of the universe and everything encompassed within it. "All that goes amiss in our life is the work of inequality, and all that keeps its due order is of equality, which in the universe as a whole is most properly called cosmos, in cities and states is democracy, the most law-abiding and best of constitutions, in bodies is health and in souls virtuous conduct. For inequality on the other hand is the cause of sicknesses and vices."[22]

For Philo, the "democratic theocracy" of the Judaic, or Mosaic, state represents the ideal form of the polity because it is based on a divinely revealed system of laws, the Torah, which applies equally to all members of the society. The divine author of this legislation is therefore the ultimate sovereign of the political society and state organized around its precepts. All legitimate authority in the state derives from that legislation and must be exercised in compliance with both its prescriptions and proscriptions. In this scheme, the roles of the king and high priest, or their surrogates, are limited to the interpretation, application, and administration of that legislation on behalf of the society. The Judaic king is not sovereign, nor is the high priest a supreme pontiff. Their word becomes civil or religious law only in a very limited sense. As citizens of the state, they have the same obligation as all others to conduct themselves in compliance with the precepts of the Torah, which they are not free to interpret as they please; they may construe it only in a manner consistent with the normative tradition transmitted through the generations.

While this sets forth the *nomocratic* concept of the Judaic state, the *democratic* aspects of this scheme are not immediately self-evident. In this regard, it has been suggested that Philo's political vocabulary must be understood in the context of the time in which he lived, a time when democracy was not understood to refer to popular government. As one interpreter of the philosopher put it, "Philo describes the Mosaic state as combining the best features of kingship, aristocracy, and democracy, the term democracy being used by him not in the sense of government of the many but rather in the sense of a government in which each one enjoys his own in accordance with law."[23] Other scholars have struggled long and hard to understand precisely what Philo had in mind when he used the term "democracy" in juxtaposition with kingship and aristocracy, systems of government that would appear to be incompatible, if not mutually exclusive.[24]

The original meaning of democracy was rule by the *demos*, referring not to the people as a whole but rather those living in the countryside. The *demos* stood in contrast with the *polis*, the citadel that effectively controlled the surrounding countryside. In ancient Greece, where the term originated, democracy therefore referred to rule by the residents of the countryside, the common farmers and fishermen, who constituted the largest social and economic classes in the society. The institution of democracy in the world of antiquity represented a radical change from traditional rule by the warrior and other elite classes that had dominated the city-state from the *polis*. Democracy therefore had its greatest appeal to those who chafed under the dominance of societal elites, as well as to those who sought to manipulate the *demos* to further their own political ambitions. Because of its corruptibility, democracy soon came to be seen as simply a form of political of pandering to the lowest common denominator. This devalued it in the eyes of the educated elite, which therefore did not consider it an appropriate organizing principle for bringing the good society into being.

In the opinion of such political thinkers as Plato and Aristotle, the principal flaw of democracy resided in the notion of human equality, on which it was predicated. The idea that all citizens of the state were to be considered and treated as equals was seen as subverting the traditional concepts and sources of political and moral authority. The principle of equality thus came to be perceived as a popular but nonetheless ill-conceived justification for eliminating existing culture-based constraints on the public conduct of the common people, constraints that were deemed essential to bringing about the betterment of society. The manipulation of the general public by demagogues and charlatans for partisan purposes was endemic, making society subject to wide swings of popular mood. As a result, democracy always seemed to be on the verge of transformation into *ochlocracy*, the rule of the mob.

From a theoretical standpoint, democracy, based on the presumed intrinsic equality of all members of the society, may be held to constitute the appropriate organizational framework for governing a classless society. As a practical matter, however, Greek democracy, like all other ancient political systems, was based on the domination of the society by a single class. In this instance, however, the ruling class included the vast majority of a city-state's citizenry—which itself constituted but a portion of the overall, disenfranchised population—not just a small, elite minority. In practice, Greek democracy tended to produce regimes that were quite intolerant of nonmembers of the dominant class, as well as of those who deviated from its vulgar norms.

Given these considerations, it seems rather improbable that classical Judaism would have found much of interest or value in such an approach to government. The Greek concept of democracy would not appear to be supportive of a religious system and way of life dedicated to the elevation of the society of Israel to the highest moral plane, to its transformation into "a kingdom of priests, and a holy nation" (Exod. 19:6). The adoption of Greek democratic ideas would quite likely have produced results diametrically opposed to those intended by the biblical authors. Greek-style democracy surely would have rejected the concept of divine sovereignty and the nomocratic authority of the Torah. It would have been inhospitable to the moral teachings of Judaism and intolerant of its presumptions.

Accepting the argument that Judaism is ideologically incompatible with classical democratic theory, it may still be asked whether this also holds true for democracy in its more modern forms and variations, both liberal and nonliberal. Many traditionalists take issue with the notion of any compatibility with, or even affinity between, Judaic and democratic values. Some suggest that the principal disjunction between the two systems lies in the source of societal norms. In a democracy, in which the people are held, at least in theory, to be sovereign, the majority determines what constitutes acceptable behavior. In Judaism, on the other hand, where sovereignty is ascribed to God, basic societal norms reflect the traditional understanding of the precepts of the Torah, which are not subject to popular approval. The medieval philosopher Joseph Albo observed in this regard, "If we should follow the consensus of the majority of mankind, we should have to say that we must keep away from the acts of prophets and pious men, for the majority of mankind act differently from them."[25] As one contemporary writer put it, "In the Jewish view, there can be no worse moral system than one in which man, rather than God, decides on proper moral and ethical behavior. . . . To state that Judaism is a democracy, therefore, is a perversion not only of Jewish history, but also of Jewish religious belief."[26]

The critical issue here, as Shalom Rosenberg points out in his discussion of the question as addressed in the work of Joseph B. Soloveitchik, is the crucial distinction between a society based on a social contract and one predicated on a divine-human covenant.[27] Rosenberg writes, "Contract forms the basis for liberal democracy, which is predicated implicitly on a minimalist principle"; that is, the social contract sets forth the minimum requirements for an ordered society. "The covenant, on the other hand, is maximalist, and is based on the attempt to introduce the model of a more perfected existence into society, obligated to a joint goal. This obligation may at times even bring us into conflict with principles deriving from our minimalist outlook."[28] Presumably, then, it is this distinction between social contract and divine-human covenant that is the basis of the tension between Judaism and democracy concerning the principles that are to govern conduct in an ordered society.

It has been pointed out by many writers that the social contract is essentially hypothetical, that the evidence for its very existence is hard to come by. The notion of the contract is that of a group of people saying, in effect, "Let us assume for ourselves the principles of governance we would have arrived at had we been in the position to formulate such a contract from the start." As such, the social contract is constantly available for review and improvement in accordance with a general meeting of minds. By contrast, the covenant, at least for those who accept it, is historical, not hypothetical. It does not lend itself to review and modification. The contract being conceived as a covenant between God and Israel, there are no means by which negotiations can take place with God to alter its content. Thus, as one contemporary observes, "The idea of the hypothetical contract exemplifies the freedom of people to choose governmental arrangements for themselves. By contrast, the historical covenant was concluded once and for all time, and we are not at liberty to nullify or improve it."[29]

Sol Roth, addressing the same issue, suggests some important distinctions between contract and covenant that are directly relevant here. For one thing, he argues that a political right derived from a social contract "confers a privilege," whereas a covenantal right "affirms a promise." The import of this is that a person who possesses a privilege may or may not exercise it;

however, "since the covenantal right is not a privilege but a promise, it may, with consistency, be construed as imposing obligations." Accordingly, "the covenant does not require the Jew to assume obligations to man. It does require that he shall, in many instances, fulfill obligations to God by behaving in specified ways to man."[30] Another distinction is that a contract may be conditional, whereas the covenant is unconditional. "Some philosophers have regarded the contract as the basis of political community in the same manner as Judaism viewed the covenant as the foundation of the religious community. These philosophers explicitly declared that the political community is dissolved when the terms of the contract are violated. It is otherwise with a covenant. There are no conditions in which the covenantal obligation may be suspended or annulled."[31] Finally, a democratic polity that sees its basis in a social contract is essentially rights oriented. Because of its need to ensure that all equally enjoy their rights, the obligations imposed on its members derive from its grant of rights to all. "In the covenantal society, on the other hand, obligations are derived, not from rights, but from commitment; it is accordingly obligation-oriented."[32] But as already observed, that obligation, in principle, is to God and not to society or its institutions. In other words, the terms of the social contract can never, in principle, override the demands of the covenant—which makes the compatibility of Judaism and democracy potentially tenuous at best.

Immanuel Jakobovits, going beyond religious considerations, sees the democratic order as posing a challenge to fundamental moral principles. "Basically, democracy represents a mere extension of the maxim 'might is right.' What, if not power necessarily the result of superior numbers, should otherwise give the majority the prerogative for having its views and decisions turned into law and imposed by force upon the minority[?]" After all, "wisdom does not inevitably bear any relation to numerical strength. Only might does."[33] Indeed, if democracy, populist rhetoric aside, ultimately reduces to a variety of "might makes right," what moral as opposed to merely pragmatic claim can it make for our allegiance?

Eliezer Berkovits suggested that the critical question to be answered is whether a religious moral system predicated on the Torah can function effectively within a modern democratic political society. In his opinion, the two may prove compatible, but only for as long as the democratically governed state confines its field of activity to the prosaic problems confronting the public. "The moment a society attempts to rule over the conscience of its members, determining their religious faith and dictating their personal value system, it becomes immoral, and it ceases to be a democracy."[34] That is, when the majority exploits the democratic legislative process to impose its values on the society, demanding in effect that the minority conform to its moral and religious preferences, democracy forfeits its legitimacy and takes a step on the slippery slope toward totalitarianism. If this danger exists with regard to a democratic society, how much more does it threaten other, more authoritarian approaches to governance?

Confronted by this dilemma, the early third-century sage Samuel, whose pronouncements on civil matters was considered authoritative by subsequent generations, set down the rule that for the Jewish community, "the law of the government is the law."[35] That is to say, the law of the land was to be considered binding on all residents, whether or not it was predicated on the covenant. The rule, however, was understood as being hedged by a number of prior constraints.[36] In general, it was considered to apply only to matters of civil law. It was not considered binding if obedience to the government's will involved transgression of a prohibition prescribed by the higher law of the Torah. Many rabbinic authorities extended this exemption to resorting to non-Judaic courts on matters of family law.[37] Moreover the rule was considered to be binding only where there was specifically enacted legislation that required compliance; it was not held to apply to matters of customary law.[38] Finally, it was held to apply only in the case of a legitimate government acting legitimately according to its own laws.[39] Interestingly, there is a dispute among rabbinic authorities over whether Samuel's rule also applies to the government of modern Israel, or whether the latter embodies the biblically derived authority granted to the earlier kings of Israel.

The issue thus takes on additional complexity in a Judaic democratic theocracy, in which—in contrast to the secular democratic mode of governance—the Torah is held to reflect divine guidance, the validity of which is not subject to review by the majority of those for whose benefit it is believed to have been revealed. Because of their unequivocally authoritative origin, truth, and legitimacy, the precepts of the Torah cannot be abrogated or amended by some democratic political process. The authority of the divine word is not an appropriate matter for decision by majority vote, nor is its acceptance optional. The Torah demands conformity with its prescriptions by all adherents of Judaism, without exception. The problem, then, is how to reconcile such an unwavering requirement with the deliberative and consensual character of democracy.

According to Berkovits, the value system of the Torah may well be able to function in a democratic society, but only if "all its members freely and unanimously accept the authority of the Torah."[40] That is, a value system based on the Torah can be compatible with a democratic political society only if the democratic process itself operates within the parameters established by the precepts of the Torah. This condition becomes critical to the preservation of the democratic character of the society. For if the condition is not met and there is no unanimous acceptance of the value system of the Torah, and it becomes necessary to impose the discipline of the Torah on a reluctant minority, the society will cease to have legitimacy as a democracy. This will be the case even if the imposition reflects the conscious will of the majority of the citizens. As Jakobovits put it, "Moral leadership cannot assert itself or its authority through the ballot box until the elector, no less than the elected, is guided by the dictates of righteousness, not expediency."[41] This would require a level of moral education among the general public that, although highly desirable and worth striving for, does not really appear achievable in society as we know it. Short of that, the will of the majority alone, whether expressed or inferred, cannot claim the requisite moral authority to make democracy the ideal system that many of its advocates would like it to be. It therefore seems reasonable to conclude that there is little prospect of a Torah-derived value system's functioning effectively within a democratic society; however, there may be greater latitude for a democratic political process within a Judaic society predicated on the value system of the Torah.

In essence, as Berkovits points out, there is a significant difference in the basic organizational principle of a democratic, as opposed to a Judaic, society. "In a democracy the people's representatives frame the laws by which a given society wishes to live," laws that are subsequently administered by the executive and judiciary branches of the government. However, according to the teachings of the Torah, "the law as such was revealed by God at Sinai. The people appoint the judges and officers to administer a system of laws over which they have no control, about whose formulation the people's representatives have no right to vote; a law that is unchangeable."[42] Within such a framework, the democratic political process might deal with the election of those judges and officers, and with the prosaic practical choices and decisions that all governments must routinely make. However, it would always remain subject to a higher law that it can neither abrogate nor modify.

The problem, of course, is how a Judaic government would deal with citizens who reject the authority of the Torah. Should it exercise its power of coercion to ensure conformity with halakhah? This issue is far from hypothetical in the contemporary State of Israel, where there is strong opposition to, and resentment of, legislation that effectively imposes religious values and practices on a largely secular public. Moreover, it has created a chasm between conservative and liberal traditionalists that has yet to be bridged. As Eugene Korn observed, "Modern religious Israelis and their political parties repeatedly agonize over how much they will support legislation that imposes Orthodox standards upon the Israeli populace."[43]

It is especially noteworthy that Avraham Y. Karelitz—popularly known by the name of his first published work, the *Hazon Ish*, and one of the principal halakhic authorities of the twentieth century—actually laid the groundwork for a liberal resolution of the coercion problem. He wrote:

It seems to me that the law of throwing [the heretic] into a pit [to be left to die] applies only to those periods when the Blessed Lord's Providence is apparent, such as when miracles took place, or the Heavenly Voice functioned, or the righteous men of the generation lived under a generalized Divine Guidance visible to all. At such times, those who commit heresy are acting with deliberate perversity, allowing their evil impulse to lead them into passion and lawlessness. . . . But when Divine Providence is concealed, when the masses have lost their faith, throwing [heretics] into a pit is no longer an act against lawlessness, but on the contrary, it is an act which would simply widen the breach; for they would consider it an act of moral corruption and violence, God forbid. And since our entire purpose is to remedy the situation, the law does not apply to a period when no remedy would result. Rather, we must bring them back through the bonds of love and enlighten them to the best of our abilities.[44]

In other words, religious coercion does not provide an acceptable halakhic solution in contemporary times, because it is essentially counterproductive in a society where the overwhelming majority of people do not accept religious norms as authoritative. This is not to say, however, that halakhic norms are no longer to be considered the ideal toward which the society should strive. As Korn reminds us, "When one confuses legal tolerance with pluralistic value equivalence he departs from both the halakha and religious Jewish thought."[45] Although this approach does not resolve the fundamental problem of the intrinsic incompatibility of Judaism and the libertarian aspects of democracy, it does go a long way toward a pragmatic accommodation.

When one considers these various views and arguments from the perspective of political theory, it soon becomes apparent that much of the underlying problem is essentially semantic in nature. The protagonists in the discussion about democracy in Judaism often seem to be confusing the two distinct senses in which the term is usually employed. Referring back to the views of Philo, it may be seen that in his own way he appears to have been drawing the critical distinction between political and social democracy.

At issue is the distinction between an equal right to participate in government and an equal right to benefit from such government. Political democracy is concerned primarily with the allocation of public power and authority. Accordingly, there is an obvious incompatibility between a modern representative democracy, in which the people as a whole exercise a degree of political power, and an aristocracy and an oligarchy, under which political power is the exclusive perquisite of a small social or economic group. Social democracy, by contrast, is concerned with the institutionalization of the principles of equality and justice within the society. From its standpoint, the fundamental political incompatibilities between democracy, aristocracy, oligarchy, or monarchy may be set aside as long as the ruling group or individual strives to make social justice for all members of the society a reality.

Judaic thinkers have also been divided over the question of whether equality is the basis of justice, or the converse. Following the ancient Pythagoreans, to whom he referred as "the masters of natural philosophy,"

Philo asserted that "the mother of justice is equality."[46] That is, he held that the idea of equality was inherent in the natural order of things and that the concept of justice was therefore derived from it. In contemporary times, however, Louis Finkelstein has challenged the validity of this assertion. Because God is characterized in Judaism as being intimately bound up with the idea and profession of justice, Finkelstein suggested, "artificial inequalities, unless necessary for fulfillment of a transcendent purpose set by God, are abhorrent to Him, and a violation of His will." Therefore, he insisted, "Because God demands that communities, being His servants and agents, act justly toward their individual members, these members have a right to equal standing. The concept of equality thus derives from justice; not, as is often asserted, justice from equality. Men clearly are born with varied gifts, but such inequalities have no relevance to God's concern with His creatures nor, therefore, with the community's duty to do justice to every man."[47]

The Judaic concept of man does indeed begin with the presumption of a certain intrinsic human equality. As Simon Greenberg put it, "The basic characteristic of the Biblical-Rabbinic concept of man is its *indivisibility*. The concept cannot tolerate any limiting modifiers," such as those related to race and gender.[48] This idea is held to be implicit in the biblical concept of the equality "of all men" before God, a consequence of each equally being descended from the one created in the divine image, as Scripture informs us: "And God created man in His own image" (Gen. 1:27). For Finkelstein, this and other biblical passages provide clear evidence of the fundamentally democratic underpinnings of biblical teaching. "The most significant contribution in literature to democratic thought is probably that in the early chapters of Genesis. In the first, we are told that God made man in His image. In the fifth, we are informed that the descendants of Adam were born in his image, and consequently in the image of God. This assertion that all men—all descendants of Adam—are alike bearers of the image of God, are the possessors of supreme dignity, and that all are equal in this dignity, sets the goal toward which all democratic thinking must strive."[49]

This thesis is exemplified in a curious discussion that takes place between two of the sages of Israel, R. Akiba and Ben Azzai. R. Akiba pointed out that one of the great principles of the Torah is encapsulated in the "golden rule"—"But thou shalt love thy neighbor as thyself" (Lev. 19:18). Ben Azzai demurred and asserted that an even greater principle was established by the verse, "This is the book of the generations of Adam. In the day that God created man, in the likeness of God made He him" (Gen. 5:1).[50] As explained by the traditional commentators on this text, what is at issue here is Ben Azzai's perception of a fundamental flaw in the golden rule: that, seemingly, if a person is put to shame by another, he may retaliate against that other, because the rule does not require a person to love his neighbor *more* than he loves himself. By contrast, the passage adduced by Ben Azzai as being of greater weight would preclude such retaliation, because of its stress on the sanctity of man. Man, including all of mankind, is created in the image of God, and an affront to any man is therefore an affront to God. Thus, as Greenberg put it, "The Biblical-Rabbinic doctrine of the equality of man is rooted, therefore, not in the Fatherhood of God but rather in the common descent of all men from Adam. *Actual consanguinity is thus assumed for men of all races and creeds.*"[51] Viewed from this perspective, the fundamental idea of human equality before God, as opposed to such alternative conceptions as equality of right or privilege, serves as the true basis for the development of the ideal democratic society.

It has often been pointed out that the principal focus in Judaic thought is not on one's rights but rather on one's duties and obligations. All men are considered to be equal with respect to God, but this relationship of equality only involves duties and obligations; it does not convey any concomitant rights. Paul Eidelberg argues: "The modern non-Jewish view emphasizes equality of *rights* secured by heteronomous laws which balance and serve personal or egoistical interests. The Jewish view emphasizes an unequal distribution of *duties* . . . defined by autonomous laws which, while securing individual freedom, would unite mankind in the service of God."[52]

This proposition does not make any argument whatsoever concerning the existence of human rights, whether conceived as deriving from natural or from positive law. It merely asserts that in the scale of Judaic values, individual rights are necessarily subordinate to obligations to God. Finkelstein thus quite properly maintains that the essence of the idea of equality of rights has a legitimate place in biblical and rabbinic thought. He argues that this is so even though the idea is not explicitly articulated in propositional formulations and is not directly predicated on the assumed equal mutual and reciprocal obligations of individuals to each other. The source of such rights, Finkelstein insists, is to be found in the equal obligations of all men to God and in the divine dispensation of equal justice to all.

But just what is it that we seek to convey in the proposition that all humans share an intrinsic equality before God? In what manner is such equality manifested? It has been suggested that in order to grasp fully the egalitarian implications of the biblical conception of man's having been created in the divine image, it would be helpful to adopt and employ the mathematical concept of a "range property." John Rawls has described this in the following manner: "The property of being in the interior of the unit circle is a range property of points in a plane. All points in this circle have this property although their coordinates vary within a certain range. And they equally have this property, since no point interior to a circle is more or less interior to it than any other interior point."[53] A "range property," which defines a common qualitative property relationship, is therefore not subject to quantitative distinctions and may be said to be possessed equally by all who are similarly positioned within its boundaries. In essence, the idea of a range property is an elaboration on the concept of equality articulated ear-

lier by Alfred North Whitehead, who wrote, "The relation of equality denotes a possible diversity of things related by an identity of character
qualifying them."[54] In other words, if we view the divinely created universe of man as circumscribed by a circle, everyone within that circle has
the range property of having been created in the image of God. Regardless
of any other qualities they may have that distinguish one from the other,
they are all absolutely equal in this one basic regard.

Another example of a range property that exemplifies the principle of
equality in Judaism concerns man's moral potential. Although men may
differ radically in their physical and mental attributes, and though they
may be clearly distinguishable and unequal in their individual capacities
for moral attainment, they are nonetheless considered to be essentially
equal with respect to their potential for moral development. The moral potential of the common person is considered completely equal to that of the
societal elite. As Maimonides put it, "Every man is capable of being righteous like Moses our teacher or a scoundrel like Jereboam."[55] In effect, morality constitutes what might be called an equal opportunity field of
endeavor, where the emphasis is not exclusively on outcomes but rather on
one's intentions and degree of commitment. In this regard, Sol Roth observes that "there are two ways in which the descriptive judgment of equality may be made. First, human beings possess equally some trait which
derives from their possession of the image of God, though they differ in the
degree to which they possess it. Second, all men have equal potential for
commitment to moral precept, though they differ in the extent of moral
achievement."[56]

Categorizing the idea of man's creation in the divine image as a defining
range property may help clarify the Judaic concept of human equality before God. It is important to recognize, however, that in no way does it touch
upon the notion of the civic equality that is so fundamental to the "one man
one vote" concept of political democracy. As Eidelberg notes, "Judaic
equality does not involve the leveling of distinctions that is so characteristic
of democratic equality and moral equivalence or relativism."[57] In other
words, there is no necessary or self-evident linkage between the two concepts of equality.

While Judaism may be compatible with democracy, under the conditions stipulated by Berkovits, there does not seem to be any conclusive evidence that political democracy, in contrast to social democracy, is intrinsic
to the political theory of the Torah. Nonetheless, as Yoel Bin-Nun recently
stated, "The concept of democratic rule does not provide for an all-power-
ful human authority, it separates power between different authorities, and
it does not have room for a personality who is identified with the state, either fully or partially. Such a system is closer than any other system or
model to a correct solution from a Torah perspective. It is a proper and desirable solution that distinguishes between human government and the

Kingdom of Heaven."[58] In a perhaps more cautious formulation, Gerald Blidstein offered a similar observation: "I would say . . . that democracy is profoundly coherent with much of the structure of the Jewish world-view, and that we find in our commitment to democracy a concrete, specific expression of ideals that are central to our view of ourselves as Jews."[59]

NOTES

1. Samuel Belkin, *In His Image*, p. 18.
2. Josephus, *Against Apion* 2:17.
3. Moses Mendelssohn, *Jerusalem*, p. 128.
4. Judah J. Slotki, commentary on *Judges*, p. 229.
5. *Mekilta de-Rabbi Ishmael*, vol. 2, "Tractate Bahodesh" 2, p. 204.
6. *Berakhot* 13a–14b.
7. *Zevahim* 102a; *Exodus Rabbah* 2:13.
8. Some critical scholars of the biblical writings resolve these contradictions by suggesting that the statement attributed to Jacob was inserted in the text of Genesis much later, to attest to the exclusive legitimacy of the royal line of David. An extensive analysis of the statement from a traditional perspective may be found in Manasseh ben Israel (1604–1657), *The Conciliator*, vol. 1, pp. 93–99.
9. *Kiddushin* 66a. It has also been suggested that this statement reflects a concern over Alexander Jannai's fitness to serve as a priest. It was rumored that his mother had been taken captive shortly before his birth, thereby casting a cloud over his lineage, something that would have disqualified him.
10. *J. Shekalim* 6:1; *J. Horayot* 3:2; *J. Sotah* 8:3. Maimonides does not refer directly to this rabbinic dictum in his codification of rabbinic law, but the principle is subsumed under the categorical statement that we do not anoint as king any one other than a descendant of the house of David (*Hilkhot Melakhim* 1:10). Moreover, if a king is in fact selected from other than the line of David, such appointment is considered as an expedient that does not confer dynastic legitimacy (ibid. 1:9).
11. Milford Q. Sibley, *Political Ideas and Ideologies*, p. 20.
12. Moses Margoliot, *Pnei Moshe*, commentary on *J. Sotah* 8:3.
13. *Baba Batra* 12a. See also the chain of tradition in *Avot* 1:1.
14. Emanuel Rackman, *Modern Halakhah for Our Time*, p. 18.
15. Simon Federbusch, *Mishpat haMelukhah beYisrael*, p. 33.
16. Robert Gordis, *Judaic Ethics for a Lawless World*, p. 150.
17. Meir Leibush Malbim, *HaTorah vehaMitzvah*, on Deut. 1:9.
18. Robert Gordis, "Democratic Origins in Ancient Israel: The Biblical *Edah*," p. 385.
19. R. J. Zwi Werblowsky and Geoffrey Wigoder, *The Encyclopedia of the Jewish Religion*, p. 112.
20. Yoel Bin-Nun, Interview, pp. 134–135.
21. Milton R. Konvitz, "Judaism and the Democratic Ideal," p. 127.
22. Philo, *The Special Laws* 237.
23. Harry Austryn Wolfson, *Philo*, vol. 2, pp. 427–428.
24. See F. H. Colson, Appendix to vol. 8 of his *Philo*, pp. 437–439, and Erwin R. Goodenough, *The Politics of Philo Judaeus*, pp. 86–90.
25. Joseph Albo, *Sefer Ha-'Ikkarim*, 3:6, p. 54.

26. Michael Kaniel, "Judaism: 'Godocracy,' rather than Democracy," *Jerusalem Post International*, week ending April 20, 1991.

27. The ideas discussed by Rosenberg are found in Joseph B. Soloveitchik, "The Lonely Man of Faith," *Tradition*, vol. 7, no. 2 (Summer 1965), pp. 21–33. Soloveitchik uses the two descriptions of the creation of man in Scripture to define what he calls "majestic man," as distinct from "covenantal man"—the former being a member of a "natural community," formed by contract or other arrangements, and the latter a member of the "covenantal faith community." Although he does not discuss the issue of democracy explicitly, the issue is addressed implicitly throughout the paper.

28. Shalom Rosenberg, "Demokratia veHalakhah—Perspectivah Filosofit," p. 194.

29. Elazar Weinryb, *Dat uMedinah*, p. 98.

30. Sol Roth, *The Jewish Idea of Community*, pp. 80–81.

31. Ibid., pp. 86–87.

32. Ibid., p. 88.

33. Immanuel Jakobovits, *Journal of a Rabbi*, p. 107.

34. Eliezer Berkovits, *Not In Heaven*, p. 116.

35. *Gittin* 10b; *Nedarim* 28a; *Baba Kamma* 113b. An comprehensive discussion of this rule and its ramifications may be found in Shmuel Shilo, *Dina deMalkhuta Dina*.

36. For a brief discussion of these constraints and related considerations, see Gidi Frishtik, "Dina deMalkhuta vehaMinhag haBeinleumi: LeKeviat Hogenet Din haMalkhut," *Sinai*, no. 110, 1992.

37. See, with regard to divorces, *Gittin* 88b.

38. Shilo, *Dina deMalkhuta Dina*, p. 186.

39. Maimonides, *Hilkhot Gezeilah veAveidah* 5:13.

40. Ibid.

41. Jakobovits, *Journal of a Rabbi*, pp. 109–110.

42. Berkovits, *Not In Heaven*, p. 114.

43. Eugene Korn, "Tradition Meets Modernity: On the Conflict of Halakha and Political Liberty," *Tradition*, vol. 25, no. 4 (Summer 1991), p. 31.

44. Cited by Korn, p. 38.

45. Ibid., p. 42.

46. Philo, *The Special Laws* 231.

47. Louis Finkelstein, "Human Equality in the Jewish Tradition," pp. 179–180.

48. Simon Greenberg, *Foundations of a Faith*, p. 118.

49. Finkelstein, "Hebrew Sources: Scripture and Talmud," p. 27.

50. *Sifra* "Kedoshim" 4:12.

51. Greenberg, *Foundations of a Faith*, p. 120.

52. Paul Eidelberg, *Jerusalen vs. Athens: In Quest of a General Theory of Existence*, p. 37n.

53. John Rawls, *A Theory of Justice*, p. 508.

54. Alfred North Whitehead, *The Principle of Relativity*, p. 42.

55. Maimonides, *Hilkhot Teshuvah* 5:2.

56. Sol Roth, *Halakhah and Politics*, p. 55.

57. Eidelberg, *Judaic Man*, p. 138.

58. Yoel Bin-Nun, Interview, p. 134.

59. Gerald J. Blidstein, "Halakha and Democracy," *Tradition*, vol. 32, no. 1 (1997), p. 6.

Chapter 3

The Idea of Consent

The essence of the democratic spirit that is reflected in the principle of government by consent is held by some to be manifest in the biblical account of the institutionalization of the covenant between God and Israel through the voluntary adoption of the Torah as the constitution of the nation. This view is exemplified in the rabbinic tradition relating that the Torah was first offered to the various nations of the world, all of whom rejected it, because of the incompatibility of fundamental precepts that it propounded with their existing societal norms. As affirmed by Scripture, Israel responded positively and accepted it without hesitation.[1] "And Moses came and called for the elders of the people, and set before them all these words which the Lord commanded him. And all the people answered together, and said: 'All that the Lord hath spoken we will do' " (Exod. 24:3). If the nations of the world were able to reject the covenant, Israel's acceptance may be assumed to have been optional and therefore consensual.

The sages took pains to stress that the affirmative answer of the people to the divine offer made through Moses was not the result of a mass hysteria resulting from the drama of the moment but represented a carefully thought-out response to the presentation of the covenant. "They did not give this answer with hypocrisy, nor did they get it from one another, but all of them made up their mind alike."[2] It was, in other words, a conscious and deliberate decision on the part of each of them to place themselves under the regime of the covenant. The sages affirmed this in a homily, in which God purportedly responds to Moses' inquiry as to why He is so concerned to give instruction to Israel: "I keep giving them commands through thee because they took upon themselves the yoke of My kingship at Sinai."[3]

To emphasize this point even further, some sages suggested that the response of the people—"All that the Lord hath spoken we will do"—was found to be insufficient by Moses. They asserted that Moses was concerned about the reliability of a commitment to action that had not been preceded, or at least accompanied by, a commitment to obedience—that is, internalizing the precepts of the Torah so that they became in effect self-generating imperatives for action. These sages visualized Moses remonstrating with the people: "Is it possible to do without obeying? It is obeying that leads to doing!"[4] According to this homiletic interpretation, the people corrected themselves and restated their commitment in the manner in which it appears in a later biblical passage: "And he took the book of the covenant, and read in the hearing of the people; and they said: 'All that the Lord hath spoken will we do, and obey'" (Exod. 24:7).

These texts clearly propound the view that the covenant was consciously and freely accepted by the people and therefore became binding upon them by their explicit consent. As Joseph B. Soloveitchik put it, "The giving of the law on Mt. Sinai was a result of free negotiation between Moses and the people who consented to submit themselves to the Divine Will. The Halakhah treats the Sinai and Moab covenants in categories and terms governing any civil agreement."[5] We thus find at the very threshold of the development of Judaic law the fundamental principle that government and law should be based on the consent of the governed.

It should be noted, however, that there is an interpretive tradition recorded in the Talmud that challenges this contention and argues that the Torah was imposed on the people of Israel unilaterally and without their consent. As R. Abdimi commented on the text "And they stood under the mount" (Exod. 19:17): "This teaches that the Holy One, blessed be He, overturned the mountain upon them like an [inverted] cask, and said to them, 'If ye accept the Torah, 'tis well; if not, there shall be your burial.' "[6] That is, the original covenant having been made with Abraham and reaffirmed to the patriarchs Isaac and Jacob, representing divine intervention in the course of history, God would not permit the generation of the Exodus to repudiate it without incurring severe and unacceptable penalties. According to this view, the people had no viable or even plausible alternative to accepting unconditionally the nomocratic regime of the Torah. Under such circumstances, the popular consent indicated by the biblical texts was more nominal than real.

This perspective evidently was highly troubling to at least some sages, not because they found fault with the underlying logic of the argument but because it challenged the legitimacy of the Torah as the authoritative guide to observance of the covenant. Once one acknowledges that the regime of the Torah was imposed on the people by duress, not adopted by popular consent, the rationale for subsequent adherence becomes rather question-able. If the covenant was not accepted freely by the nation, its moral foun-dation would be seriously undermined, making conformity with the precepts of the Torah more a matter of habit than conviction. Indeed, the sages felt that this view provided the basis for a strong protest against the existence of any moral or contractual obligation to observe the Torah at all.

The sages did not reject R. Abdimi's view outright, apparently prefer-ring to find a way to circumvent the implications of his position. Presum-ably, they took this approach to avoid a major split among the sages, though the argument they employed seems rather problematic from a historical perspective. Thus, in an attempt to mitigate the undesirable implications of R. Abdimi's position, the sage Raba invoked a biblical passage concerning the origins of the festival of Purim. This was presented to demonstrate that there had been popular acceptance by Israel of the yoke of the Torah, if not at Sinai then at some subsequent time. He interpreted the passage "The Jews undertook and irrevocably obligated themselves and their descen-dants, and all who might join them" (Esther 9:27) as clear evidence that "they confirmed what they had accepted long before."[7] That is, even though there may have been an element of compulsion involved in the original ac-ceptance of the covenant immediately following the Exodus, that accep-tance was later reaffirmed voluntarily by the nation. As explained by Raphael Chiyya Pontremoli, "Although the Jews had accepted the Torah on Shavuoth [Pentecost] when it was given on Sinai, they were actually under duress at that time. Their lives were in God's hand and they knew it. If they did not accept the Torah, they knew that their graves would be right there in the desert. But on the first Purim the Jews were already victorious, and un-der no duress. In the midst of their great celebration, they reaffirmed their acceptance of the Torah without reservation."[8]

Soloveitchik suggested that the difficulty might be resolved by assum-ing that two sequential commitments were required of the community of Israel. The first was a general commitment to abide by the will of God, even though the community had as yet no specific knowledge about what that entailed. This is reflected in the passage that states:

Thus shalt thou say to the house of Jacob, and tell the children of Israel: Ye have seen what I did unto the Egyptians, and how I bore you on eagle's wings, and brought you to Myself. Now there fore, if ye hearken unto My voice indeed, and keep My covenant, then ye shall be Mine own treasure from among all peoples; for all the earth is Mine. . . . And Moses came and called for the elders of the people, and set be-fore them all these words which the Lord commanded him. And the people an-swered together, and said: All that the Lord hath spoken we will do. (Exod. 19:3–7)

The second commitment (cited above), which took place afterward, was the agreement to abide by the specific laws that were to be imposed on them. Once the community acceded to the first, it had no effective alternative to accepting the second as well.[9]

Reverting to the position of the rabbinic majority on the question, Simon Federbusch asserted unequivocally that the acceptance of the covenant by Israel had clearly been an informed act of popular consent, based entirely on the free choice of the people. The decision had been articulated by them either directly or through their traditional representatives, the elders of the tribes. Moreover, Federbusch urged that one bear in mind that it was only subsequent to the popular acceptance of the covenant that the political and social order ordained by the Torah first took effect. The implications of this sequence of events are twofold. First, Federbusch insisted, "The fact that the covenant preceded the giving of the Torah teaches us that there is no moral right to impose a political regimen upon the people to which they have not agreed." Second, it also suggests that the biblical description of the popular consent to the covenant represents the earliest known documented formulation of a social contract, a fundamental agreement by which the political society of Israel became established.[10]

In essence, Federbusch is arguing that the theocracy of Judaism—using the term in its original sense of divine rule and not in its later meaning as rule by a religious hierarchy—was itself given legitimacy through a popular democratic process. "In agreeing to the covenant, the children of Israel did not waive their rights to a human regime, but transferred their rights to God." In other words, at least in the case of Israel, Scripture teaches that democracy preceded theocracy in Israel. Elaborating this point, Federbusch insisted that the theocracy of Judaism "requires democracy in all aspects of the political and spiritual life of the people." Accordingly, the Torah merely sets forth the authoritative guidelines for achieving the divine ends of society, leaving their implementation to the people. Federbusch concluded that under the implicit terms of the basic covenant between God and Israel, the people "retained the right to govern themselves, and did not transfer this right to any ruler."[11] Consequently, the establishment of a political regime requires an additional agreement between the people and those designated to govern on their behalf, an agreement that some political theorists refer to as a "governmental compact."

Under such a compact, those who govern do so in accordance with pre-established principles and ground rules of government that bind the regime, and that alone give it legitimacy. The Torah promulgates these constitutional principles of governance as part of the divine guidance to Israel. Thus, the Torah demands of every prospective ruler of the nation:

And it shall be, when he sitteth upon the throne of his kingdom, that he shall write him a copy of this law in a book, out of that which is before the priests and the Levites. And it shall be with him, and he shall read therein all the days of his life; that he may learn to fear the Lord his God, to keep all the words of this law and these statutes, to do them; that his heart be not lifted up above his brethren, and that he turn not aside from the commandment, to the right hand, or to the left; to the end that he may prolong his days in his kingdom, he and his children, in the midst of Israel. (Deut. 17:17–20)

The profound political implications of this passage seem evident. The king is as bound to the nomocratic regime of the Torah as are his subjects. Any deviation therefrom on his part would constitute an unacceptable violation of the governmental compact, placing his very legitimacy as monarch in question, and in jeopardy of popular revolt. Any such lapse on the part of the ruler would surely curtail rather than prolong his days in his kingdom. In essence, then, the scope of the ruler's legitimate authority and his freedom of action are severely circumscribed by the governmental compact to which he is a party.

Federbusch argued further that this inherently democratic conception of political authority subsequently was carried over into the political thought of the talmudic period. For one thing, as R. Isaac taught, "We must not appoint a leader over a community without first consulting it."[12] For another, the essential idea of democracy is reflected to some degree in the rabbinic principle that "we should not impose a restriction upon the community unless the majority of the community will be able to stand it."[13] That is, the authorities may not impose binding regulations on the public that run contrary to the demonstrated will and interests of the people. To do so would be to impugn the legitimacy of such rule making. Moreover, the rabbis also established the general principle that for purposes of law, "a majority is regarded as the whole."[14] However, it is important to recognize that this restatement of the classical democratic principle of determining whether shoes pinch by deferring to the judgment of those who wear them is limited exclusively to rabbinic legislation; it does not apply to laws of biblical origin. The obligation of obedience to the latter, as already indicated, cannot be made subject to popular approval.

The democratic principle under discussion relates to either an enactment designed to improve the society (*takkanah*) or to legislated restriction (*gezerah*) that is specifically introduced for the purpose of limiting the probability of widespread unintentional transgressions of certain biblical laws. The rabbis viewed the imposition of such restrictions as an awesome responsibility, one that placed them in the awkward position of violating one legal principle in order to preserve the integrity of another. Scripture declares unequivocally, "All this word which I command you, that shall ye observe to do; thou shalt not add thereto, nor diminish from it" (Deut. 13:1). This would appear to preclude any additional legislation in a Judaic society. As pointed out by Maimonides, this constraint on legislation was considered necessary because if the law was amended frequently, "this might have led to the corruption of the rules of the Law and to the belief that the latter did not come from God."[15]

Nonetheless, the sages felt obligated to resort to extraordinary measures to protect the divine law, both written and oral, from inadvertent transgression, because its application was ambiguous or uncertain under some circumstances. They taught that it was both permissible and desirable to "make a fence for the Torah."[16] By this they meant that the authorities were empowered to institute regulations that exceeded the strict requirements of the Torah, as long as such regulations were designed to prevent unintended violations of its precepts by placing constraints on behavior that was likely to result in such transgressions. The later sage R. Kahana asserted that the source of this principle was implicit in the scriptural text, "Therefore shall ye keep My charge" (Lev. 18:30), which he interpreted as meaning, "provide a charge to my charge."[17] As Maimonides put it, the authorities may "take precautions with a view to consolidating the ordinances of the Law by means of regulations in which they innovate with a view to repairing fissures, and to perpetuate these precautionary measures."[18] However, these fences for the Torah were made subject to the principle that the majority of the community must give its tacit consent to their imposition. Indeed, the sages R. Simeon b. Gamliel and R. Elaezar b. Zadok asserted that "all public affairs are conducted on the condition that that the majority of the community accepts the decisions made."[19]

This principle was extended by some sages to provide that should such an arbitrary regulation in fact be promulgated, it would be legally invalidated by the mere fact of popular noncompliance.[20] Maimonides codified the halakhic rule governing the imposition of such restrictions on the public:

Before instituting a decree or enacting an ordinance or introducing a custom which it deems necessary, the court should calmly deliberate (the matter) and make sure that the majority of the community can live up to it. At no time is a decree to be imposed upon the public that the majority thereof cannot endure. If the court has issued a decree in the belief that the majority of the community could endure it, and after the enactment thereof the people made light of it and it was not accepted by the majority, the decree is void and the court is denied the right to coerce the people to abide by it.[21]

Based on Maimonides' authoritative restatement of the halakhic principle, Federbusch concluded that the legitimacy of any nondivine legislation was dependent upon the effective consent of the majority of the people or their representatives. That is, conventional rules and regulations may not be imposed upon the public against its will. Once enacted, such legislation is subject to invalidation by the people if the circumstances that precipitated its promulgation change significantly. Moreover, if the majority of the people no longer observe a law or regulation in practice, it becomes unenforceable and therefore defunct.[22] In effect, common disregard of an enactment is taken as tantamount to tacit rejection and delegitimatization.

GRASSROOTS DEMOCRACY

It seems clear that representative democracy was never considered the ideal form of Judaic government. However, historical circumstances, particularly the loss of national independence at the beginning of the first century, appear to have conspired to assign progressively greater political authority to the community and ultimately to its members. This latter development began to take shape as early as the latter part of the tenth century. For some eight hundred years, until the Age of Enlightenment, the *kehillah*, the internally autonomous local Jewish community found throughout Europe and the Middle East, served as the dominant political institution in Jewish life. It dealt with both religious and secular matters; it regulated ritual as well as commercial activities. Enforcement of its decisions rested primarily in its ability to excommunicate those who defied its authority, a threat that was extremely potent for members of a minority community who could not expect to find support from a frequently hostile external political and social environment. In effect, it reflected an early form and model of grassroots democracy and representative government.

Perhaps the earliest implicit statement suggesting the legitimacy of communal authority dates from the fifth century b.c.e. We are told in the biblical book of Ezra that an assembly of all the people was proclaimed and that those who failed to attend risked excommunication and forfeiture of their assets (Ezra 10:7–8). In early talmudic times, the sages also stated explicitly—along with such other things as requiring the members of the community to build synagogues and to purchase copies of Scripture—that "the townspeople may fix market prices, weights and measures, the wages of laborers, and they may enforce their regulations."[23] Although this statement is limited in scope and does not in itself establish communal authority for general legislation, it and the biblical verses were so understood by the religious authorities of the Babylonian Jewish community in the tenth century. "From these verses and statements we learn that the elders of the town are permitted to enact legislation for the people of their town and to force the townspeople to [obey] what was legislated."[24] This marks a major turning point, because in talmudic law the authority to enact laws is granted exclusively to a national court; applying that authority to a local communal institution thus represents a dramatic development.

Moreover, as pointed out by one contemporary writer, the teaching of the sages, notwithstanding its limited scope, "does assume that a kind of social contract exists, according to which individuals submit to the authority of the collective in order to enjoy the benefits of uniform commercial standards in the marketplace. In other words, the townspeople are viewed as forming a kind of cooperative or partnership, the authority of which derives directly from its membership."[25] In effect, the talmudic dictum suggested the notion of citizenship and its prerogatives. However, as Gerald J. Blidstein points out, "This concept was not deeply rooted in Talmudic Judaism; it is not a Jewish value, and does not bestow an authority based on the values and mission of Judaism. To be a 'citizen' is not a Jewish (but rather a Hellenistic) ideal. Thus many rabbis treated this concept as a secondary tradition, an institution which must seek appropriate axiological support."[26]

The medieval rabbis therefore proceeded to enlarge the scope of the legislative and enforcement authority of the kehillah by analogizing it to a *bet din*, or court of law, which the halakhah endowed with more extensive powers. "R. Elaezar b. Jacob stated, 'I heard that even without Scriptural authority for their rulings, a *bet din* may administer flogging and other penalties; not, however, for the purpose of transgressing the words of the Torah but in order to make a fence for the Torah."[27] Using this statement and the one previously cited regarding the authority of the kehillah to regulate commerce, the medieval rabbis conflated the concepts of the *bet din* and the kehillah. They thus assigned to the kehillah the halakhic authority to govern its members as though it was a court of law.

An example of this is the responsum of the eleventh-century Joseph Bonfils, in which he almost equates the two institutions. "From this we learn that the *bet din* in each and every kehillah has the right to enact legislation for its own kehillah as it sees fit according to the needs of the time."[28] Similarly, the twelfth-century Joseph ibn Migash explained the authority of the kehillah to regulate commerce and to impose severe penalties for violations on the basis that a *bet din* had the inherent authority to do so.[29] However, Ibn Migash also drew between the two institutions a distinction that effectively denied the community the legal right to impose penalties that went beyond those prescribed by halakhah, because the community did not have the same legal standing in this regard as a *bet din*.[30] Another responsum of the same period issued by Eliezer b. Joel haLevi, dealing with the power of a community to enforce a tax against the will of a dissenter, also blurred the distinction between a kehillah and a *bet din*. "Once the legislation has been passed, given that the court has power to confiscate [property, therefore,] in a matter involving communal legislation . . . as long as the majority consent to the legislation of their representatives, they may legally compel the minority to be bound by their regulation."[31]

Although a few dissenting voices rejected the analogy between kehillah and *bet din*, arguing therefore that the authority and power of the former were contingent on the unanimous agreement of the members of the community, the majority view of rabbinic scholars viewed this as impracticable. They clearly understood that the effective granting of veto power to every member of the community would make it well nigh impossible to legislate or regulate anything in the interest of the overwhelming majority, which could be made hostage to the whims of an individual.[32] As the important medieval halakhic authority Solomon b. Adret put it, "In every community, the individuals are subject to the will of the majority. They are obligated to comport themselves in all matters according to its direction. The majority in each city is to the individuals within it as is the high court is to all Israel."[33] Accordingly, a sort of grassroots democracy emerged as a pragmatic means of dealing with the needs of the Jewish community, notwithstanding its tenuous intellectual roots in the classical literature of Judaism.

However, it would be a gross error to assume that the system of governance that emerged provided for equal access to the reins of communal power. This was far from the case. It did not provide a vehicle for equal participation in government. Even local legislation had to be in conformity with halakhic norms, and there was no presumption that every member of the community was competent to render such judgment. Indeed, this becomes quite clear in Maimonides' codification of the relevant halakhah. Thus he points out that it is perfectly permissible for the "townspeople to fix the price of anything they choose," and for tradesmen to regulate their own activities, and to lay down that "whoever violates their stipulation will be punished in this or that manner." However, he writes:

Where does this apply? Only in a city without a prominent scholar to order civic affairs and to facilitate the activities of its residents. If, however, there is such a prominent scholar there, their stipulation is without effect and they cannot punish and cause loss to anyone who does not accept their conditions, unless the latter has joined in it and it [the stipulation] was made under the scholar's auspices. And anyone who causes a loss [to another] in accordance with a stipulation that is not adopted under the scholar's auspices must pay compensation.[34]

Later rabbinic authorities sought to extend Maimonides' application of the concept of the civic role of the "prominent scholar" beyond the marketplace and apply it to the complete range of ordinances enacted by a community.

Moreover, there was no suggestion of government by the people as a whole, through plebiscite or referendum. Executive and legislative responsibility was vested in the community's leadership. Thus, although the leadership of the community had to be broadly acceptable to the majority—and in this regard the system may be considered as constituting a representative democracy—its membership was not really open to all that expressed an interest in public affairs.[35]

An in-depth analysis of how the Jewish communities of the medieval world actually functioned and the numerous issues that arose over the application of the principles discussed above, while extremely interesting in themselves, are beyond the purposes of this discussion. Suffice it to note that a society structured in consonance with the teachings of Judaism, as pointed out in the preceding chapter, does not fit well into the prevailing political terminology and is perhaps best described as a democratic theocracy, as proposed by Samuel Belkin.

NOTES

1. *Mekilta de-Rabbi Ishmael*, Tractate "Bahodesh" 5. See also *Exodus Rabbah* 52:1.

2. Ibid., "Bahodesh" 2. See *Midrash Sekhel Tov* on Exod. 19:8 for a slightly different version.

3. *Pesikta de-Rab Kahana*, Piska 2:7. See also *Sifre Deuteronomy*, Piska 344.

4. *Midrash haGadol*, "Shemot" 24:7, p. 554; *Mekhilta de-Rabbi Simeon bar Yohai*, p. 221.

5. Joseph B. Soloveitchik, "The Lonely Man of Faith," *Tradition*, vol. 7, no. 2 (1965), p. 29n.

6. *Shabbat* 88a; *Avodah Zarah* 2b.

7. *Shabbat* 88a.

8. Raphael Chiyya Pontremoli, *Yalkut MeAm Lo'ez: The Book of Esther*, p. 195.

9. Soloveitchik, "The Lonely Man of Faith," p. 29n.

10. Federbusch, *Mishpat haMelukhah beYisrael*, p. 34.

11. Ibid., pp. 34–35.

12. *Berakhot* 55a.

13. *Baba Kamma* 79b; *Baba Batra* 60b; *Avodah Zarah* 36a; *Horayot* 3b. The basis for this principle, according to R. Adda b. Ahaba, is the prophetic verse: "Ye are cursed with the curse; for ye rob Me, even this whole nation" (Mal. 3:9). That is, "when the whole nation has [accepted an ordinance, then the curse which is the penalty of its infraction] does apply, otherwise it does not" (*Avodah Zarah* 36b).

14. *Horayot* 3b; *Nazir* 42a; *Hullin* 70a; *Niddah* 29a.

15. Maimonides, *The Guide of the Perplexed*, 3:41, p. 563.

16. *Avot* 1:1.

17. *Yevamot* 21a.

18. Maimonides, *The Guide of the Perplexed*, 3:41, p. 563.

19. *Tosefta Sanhedrin* 2:13.

20. *Jer. Avodah Zarah* 2:8; *Jer. Shabbat* 1:4. See also *Jer. Horayot* 1:5.

21. Maimonides, *Hilkhot Mamrim* 2:5–6.

22. Federbusch, *Mishpat haMelukhah beYisrael*, p. 35.

23. *Tosefta Baba Metzia* 11:23.

24. Cited by Eli D. Clark, " '*After the Majority Shall You Incline': Democratic Theory and Voting Rights in Jewish Law*," p. 126, n. 9.

25. Clark, "After the Majority Shall You Incline," p. 99.

26. Gerald J. Blidstein, "Individual and Community in the Middle Ages: Halakhic Theory," in *Kinship and Consent*, ed. Daniel J. Elazar, p. 223.

27. *Yevamot* 90b.

28. Cited by Menahem Elon, *HaMishpat haIvri*, p. 567.

29. Clark, "After the Majority Shall You Incline," p. 100.

30. Blidstein, "Individual and Community in the Middle Ages: Halakhic Theory," p. 222.

31. Cited by Clark, "After the Majority Shall You Incline," p. 101.

32. For an extensive discussion of the question of the limits of communal authority over the dissenting individual, see Samuel Morell, "The Constitutional Limits of Communal Government in Rabbinic Law," pp. 87–119.

33. Cited by Menahem Elon, *HaMishpat haIvri*, p. 570.

34. Maimonides, *Hilkhot Mekhirah* 14:9–11.

35. See discussion of the question of who should rule in Michael Walzer et al., eds. *The Jewish Political Tradition*: Vol. 1 *Authority*, pp. 421–424.

Chapter 4

Nomocracy, or the Regime of Halakhah

The central concept upon which Judaic society is based is the idea of divine sovereignty, manifested in the revelation of God's guidance in the Torah. The Torah, in effect, serves as the constitutional blueprint for the structure and functioning of the political society and its central institutions. Because of the central role played by the Torah, Judaic political society may be characterized as a *nomocracy*, wherein divine law, mediated by competent human authority, is normative and indefeasible. As pointed out by Maimonides, this is what makes the nomocratic regime of Judaism fundamentally different from the government of other political societies. "The government of a city is a science imparting to its masters a knowledge of true happiness. . . . It also lays down laws of righteousness for the best ordering of the groups. The sages of the peoples of antiquity made rules and regulations, according to their various degrees of perfection, for the government of their subjects. These are called *nomoi*; and by them the people were governed. . . . But in these times we do not need all these laws and *nomoi*; for divine laws govern human conduct."[1]

Moses Mendelssohn suggested that the normative import of the last sentence of this passage is simply that "the Torah commanded to us by Moses is that which corrects our ways in divine matters and in the ways of honesty in matters between man and man. We have but to reflect on it and learn from it those things that a man should do and therefore enhance his life."[2] In other words, the normative underpinnings of the Judaic political society are given effective expression through the *mitzvot* (literally, commandments or demandments)—that is, the principles and precepts set forth in the Torah.

The means by which the eternal principles and precepts of the Torah are given practical effect is the system of *halakhah*, an Aramaic term that generally denotes the normative prescriptions and traditions followed by the nation of Israel throughout the ages.[3] In the broadest sense, the halakhah constitutes a system of operational principles, informed and hallowed by Judaism's oral tradition, which serves as the principal intellectual instrument for translating the teachings of the written Torah into feasible applications under the circumstances and conditions of a particular time and place. In other words, there is a significant distinction between the *mitzvah* and the halakhah.[4] As pointed out by Hayyim Z. Reines, "The halakhah is a faithful expression of Judaic ethics," and the primary concern of the Torah is the moral improvement of man. Accordingly, "the precepts (*mitzvot*) may not impinge in any way on ethics. Therefore, the halakhah does not hesitate on occasion to constrain a precept because of an ethical consideration."[5] From the standpoint of Rabbinic Judaism, the halakhah is the law of the Torah as it is to be carried out in practice. One can no more determine appropriate Judaic constitutional practice directly from the precepts of Scripture than one can determine the law of the land from direct reference to the Constitution of the United States. In both instances, the operative constitutional law is determined by how the source documents have been interpreted in practice by competent judicial authority.

The halakhah, as applied law, gives a good deal of attention to psychological and sociological factors that have significant influence on the lives of the public, as well as to objective ethical considerations. A case in point is the matter of capital punishment. According to Scripture, there are a number of transgressions the penalty for which is death; according to the halakhah, however, there are extraordinary evidentiary requirements, nowhere mentioned in the Torah, that must be met for inflicting capital punishment, virtually eliminating it as a practical matter.[6] Nonetheless, there is no hint in the halakhic literature of humanist arguments for the abolition of capital punishment. On the contrary, the sages taught: "You might say, 'since the victim has already been slain, why should we become responsible for the blood of the slayer?' Therefore the verse says, Thine eye shall not pity him, but thou shalt put away the blood of the innocent [Lev. 19:13]—put those who do evil out of Israel."[7] How is this anomaly to be explained? Abraham H. Rabinowitz wrote in this regard, "It is due to the inherent spirit of halakhah which on the one hand stressed the gravity of the infringement by declaring the extreme penalty, whilst at the same time it tempered usage by means of a legal framework that tended to render the threat innocuous in all but the extremest of cases because of both the possibility of human error and the irreversibility of the punishment once executed."[8]

In the narrower and more technical sense in which it is often used in the Talmud, the halakhah specifies the norm to be followed in the event of an apparent conflict of laws, or of a disagreement regarding the appropriate application of the law under a given set of circumstances. In other words, the halakhah is the normative outcome of a deliberative process carried out by competent authorities. It is through the halakhah that the biblical command "Mine ordinances shall ye do, and My statutes shall ye keep, to walk therein" (Lev. 18:4) is made operative in Judaic society. As Eliezer Berkovits put it, the halakhah "is the bridge over which the Torah moves from the written word into the living deed."[9]

In sum, then, as one contemporary writer put it, "The source of the Halacha's [sic] authority is divine legislation and its validity is limited neither in time [nor] in space. Nevertheless, according to Jewish religious conception, the Halacha having been divinely revealed was delivered into human custody of the sages versed in the Torah. Ever since the high point of the Revelation, the exclusive authority to determine the Halacha has rested in human beings."[10] The halakhah, once settled, was considered so authoritative that, according to R. Ishmael, in three instances it overruled the explicit teachings of Scripture.[11] Moreover, it is clear that the halakhah "relates itself to the changing social reality but in so doing is guided by transcendental prior values. Human interests are certainly of great importance among the legitimate considerations for laying down the Halacha, but these interests are subject to the supreme value, the worship of the Creator."[12]

It is important to note, however, that the halakhic decision-making process is considered to apply only to matters of practice. The rabbinic authorities of the post-talmudic period specifically rejected its application to matters of theoretical speculation or ethical judgment.[13]

BIBLICAL ORDINANCES AND STATUTES

A question of some importance for understanding the political concept implicitly reflected in the biblical text of Lev. 18:4, just cited, concerns the theoretical and practical differences between ordinances (*mishpatim*) and statutes (*hukim*). The sages of the talmudic period generally understood these categories of legislation to reflect the distinction between precepts of the Torah that are considered to be in accord with human reason and those that are not.

Following this classification scheme, the sages asserted that the biblical "ordinances" proscribing idolatry, immorality, bloodshed, robbery, and blasphemy are the sort of "commandments which, if they were not written [in Scripture], they should by right have been written."[14] That is to say, these prohibitions are the kinds of constraints that would be placed by any ordered society on conduct negatively affecting the public welfare.

"Statutes," on the other hand, were considered by the sages to be the sort of "commandments to which Satan objects." The statutes, which have no evidently rational bases—at least none that are accessible to the unaided human intellect—presumably would be found objectionable by persons inclined to reject the legitimacy of any rule or regulation that does not serve as a rational response to a societal need. Assuming such a position obviously places one in direct opposition to divine authority—a posture the sages considered satanic.

Nonetheless, it seems clear that the notion that one was obliged to observe nonrational commandments or precepts was considered highly problematic to many. The sages sensed that such persons might be tempted to discount the importance of this type of law. Accordingly, the sages admonished them, "And perhaps you might think these are vain things, therefore Scripture says: 'I am the Lord,' i.e., I, the Lord have made it a statute and you have no right to criticize it."[15] That is, while a precept may not seem rational, we are obligated to assume that it does make sense to God and to accept that we are not competent to sit in judgment of divine reason. As observed by Jon D. Levenson, "The presence of apodictic laws between man and God serves as a warning against identifying the Lord of the covenant with any rational principle. Reason is not the suzerain. This category of laws, the least palatable to people of a philosophic cast of mind, stands guard against any effort to depersonalize God. It is because the covenant relationship is founded upon personal fidelity that there can be laws whose only 'explanation' is the unfathomable decree of God."[16]

Nonetheless, a number of sages, as well as later rabbinic teachers, sought relentlessly to uncover a rational purpose for statutes as a whole, even though most despaired of discovering the specific rationale behind the individual prescriptions and proscriptions. Such purpose may be inferred to some extent from Scripture itself, which emphatically admonishes Israel not to adopt the norms and mores of the surrounding societies, which it evidently considered to be degenerate. "After the doings of the land of Egypt, wherein ye dwelt, shall ye not do; and after the doings of the land of Canaan, whither I bring you, shall ye not do; neither shall ye walk in their statutes" (Lev. 18:3).

The society of Israel was to be governed exclusively in accordance with the ordinances and statutes of the Torah. It is therefore easy to understand that the biblical author wished to supplant the societal norms that condoned the corrupt "doings of the land of Egypt" with an alternate set of normative ordinances that would reflect a higher standard of morality. But, we may ask, what role do the statutes, which deal principally with sacral matters, play in this regard? The answer appears to be that the behavioral discipline imposed on the children of Israel, requiring unqualified compliance with a set of divinely ordained statutes for which they are unable to discern a rational purpose, will serve to predispose them to comply faithfully with the ordinances. In other words, if they comply with requirements that defy rational explanation, they will surely comply with those that are fully in accord with reason. This suggests that the mere fact that a constraint or requirement of human conduct may be rationally conceived is no guarantee that it will be observed in practice.

The biblical author is evidently only too well aware of the foibles and follies of mankind, and of the oppression and immorality that are perpetrated by nominally rational persons. What Scripture suggests instead, as the sages understand it, is that man has a profound need for moral discipline; the free exercise of his will must be constrained within morally acceptable bounds in order to prevent his reason from becoming subverted into rationalization of arbitrary and unreasonable conduct. From this perspective, it becomes essential that even those precepts of conduct that are consonant with reason, the ordinances, be divinely ordained. This point is well illustrated in a talmudic homily in which the ministering angels are described as raising objections to the divine revelation of the Torah to Moses. The response of Moses to their challenge was, "What is written therein? Thou shalt not murder. Thou shalt not commit adultery. Thou shalt not steal [Exod. 20:13–15]; is there jealousy among you; is the Evil Tempter among you? Straightway they conceded."[17]

The point of the homily is that angels, who are not subject to the passions and emotions that drive man, have no need of the Torah; men, on the other hand, have a desperate need for it. The rational precepts, notwithstanding man's ability to adduce them by reason alone, require the divine imprimatur to prevent men from succumbing to their passions and inclinations and then rationalizing their failings. In the final analysis, man is to follow the precepts not so much because they are reasonable and of intrinsic value but because it is the divine wish that he do so.

Moreover, if this is so with regard to the ordinances, which may be grounded in self-evident reason, it certainly applies for those disciplinary precepts, the statutes, that do not appear to have any such basis. This point is made clear in another rabbinic homily on the essence of the statutes, a homily based on a play of words: "They are called *hukkim* [statutes] because they are engraved (*hakukim*) as a safeguard against the Evil Inclination; thus it is written, Woe unto them that decree (*hahokekim*) 'unrighteous decrees' [Isa. 10:1]."[18] The "evil inclination" (*yetzer harah*) refers to a person's tendency to follow his urges rather than objective reason. It is that tendency that must be overcome by disciplining one's will, and this is conceived as the purpose of the statutes. This view is also reflected in the teaching of R. Eleazar of Modi'im: " 'statutes' means the laws against incestuous practices, as in the passage: That ye do not any of these abominable customs [*mehukkot*]" (Lev. 18:30).[19]

Expanding on this theme, the sage Rab, using the statute concerning *shehitah* (the ritually prescribed procedure for slaughtering an animal for food) as a case in point, stated: "The precepts were given only in order than man might be refined by them. For what does the Holy One, blessed be He, care whether a man kills an animal by the throat or by the nape of its neck? Hence its purpose is to refine [try] man."[20] In this instance, the refinement presumably derives from the requirement to follow an exacting procedure before one can satisfy one's appetite for meat. By effectively sublimating the prosaic act of food preparation, the ritual procedure serves as yet another reminder to man of his relationship to the divine. According to Aharon Lichtenstein, the essential point of Rab's teaching is not really whether God cares about how the animal that is to be used for food is slaughtered. It is that God "wants man to care, wants him to be aware of His commanding presence in every area of life. By forbidding one type of behavior, permitting a second and requiring a third, Halakhah engages man's conscious mind and will at every point." A person who sits down to a steak dinner may be characterized as merely a carnivorous biped. However, should the same person insist upon a kosher steak, an additional and most significant dimension is added to the activity. It involves that person's spirituality in the exercise of a purely physical action. It effectively transforms the elemental act of eating into a religious rite. "Halakhah makes the service of God part of a total life which is suffused with religious significance, harmoniously organized into a divinely ordained whole and gives man a sense of purpose and a sense of divine purpose."[21]

THE HALAKHIC CORPUS

The biblical superstructure of ordinances and statutes is thus conceived as serving the distinctive purpose of creating a uniquely moral society. These ordinances and statutes, which rabbinic tradition numbers at 613, constitute the basic corpus of Mosaic Law. Not surprisingly, the rabbis sought to discover within this canon central principles for comprehending the purpose of this imposing array of rules and regulations. This search is clearly evidenced in the classic talmudic discussion of the essence of the numerous precepts of the Torah.

R. Simlai preached, "Six hundred and thirteen precepts were communicated to Moses, three hundred and sixty-five negative precepts . . . and two hundred and forty-eight positive precepts. . . . David came and reduced them to eleven [principles], as it is written, 'A Psalm of David. Lord, who shall sojourn in Thy tabernacle? Who shall dwell in Thy holy mountain? He that walketh uprightly, and worketh righteousness, and speaketh truth in his heart; that hath no slander upon his tongue, nor doeth evil to his fellow, nor taketh up a reproach against his neighbour, in whose eyes a vile person is despised, but he honoureth them that fear the Lord, He sweareth to his own hurt and changeth not, He putteth not out his money on interest, nor taketh a bribe against the innocent. He that doeth these things shall never be moved'" (Ps. 15:1–5).[22]

According to this classic interpretation of the halakhah, the essential purposes of the traditional 613 precepts of the Torah, including statutes that are clearly sacral in nature, can be summarized in the eleven principles of ethical conduct suggested by the psalm. The Talmud attempts to illustrate the application of these norms by offering historical examples, where available, of individuals who exemplified them in practice. Thus, one who "walketh uprightly" is identified as a person who patterns his general demeanor and conduct after the patriarch Abraham, who is considered to be the exemplar of one who is "wholehearted" (Gen. 17:1).

A person who "worketh righteousness" is one who, like the sage Abba Hilkiahu, is exceptionally scrupulous in his work and other aspects of his behavior. The Talmud records a story that illustrates why this particular sage was chosen as the model of one who "worketh righteousness." It appears that some of the rabbis believed him to have the ability to induce rain by means of prayer. During a period of drought, a delegation of rabbis came to seek his assistance; the rabbis found him working in a field. When they greeted him, however, he failed to return the courtesy or even visibly acknowledge their presence. Questioned later about his strange silence, he responded that he had been hired as a day laborer and that for him to divert his attention from his contractual obligation even for an instant would have been ethically improper.[23]

One who "speaketh truth in his heart" is understood to be a person who conducts himself with the same pristine honesty as the sage R. Safra. The Talmud relates that while traveling between cities, Mar Zutra ran into Raba and R. Safra. Believing that the sages had come to meet him, Mar Zutra inquired why they had taken the trouble. R. Safra responded that in fact they had not gone out of the city to meet him; if they had known that he was coming they would have organized an entourage in his honor. This precipitated an exchange with Raba, who did not believe that R. Safra had acted appropriately, since his remark apparently offended Mar Zutra. R. Safra responded that to have done otherwise would have been to deceive him into believing that the sages had come out to do him honor when such was not the case. Raba insisted that if a deception had been involved, it would have been a matter of Mar Zutra deceiving himself.[24] However, it is made clear in the Talmud that the rabbis attributed greater merit to the position of R. Safra than to that of Raba, by pointing to the former as a model of one who "speaketh truth in his heart."

Similarly, the medieval commentator Samuel b. Meir (Rashbam) cites another tradition about R. Safra, who was a businessman as well as a scholar. It describes how a buyer made him an offer while he was engaged in silent prayer. Misconstruing the sage's silence as a rejection of his offer, the buyer raised the price he was willing to pay. Upon concluding his prayer, R. Safra insisted upon taking the original, lower offer, because he would have accepted it if he had been free to respond.[25]

The patriarch Jacob is singled out by the rabbis as an example of the person who "hath no slander upon his tongue." Jacob's mother insisted that he deceive his father Isaac by pretending to be his brother Esau; Jacob demurred, because "My father peradventure will feel me and I shall seem to him as a deceiver" (Gen. 27:12). The rabbis understood this to mean that if Isaac had discovered the deception, Jacob could have justified his behavior only by asserting that Esau was unfit for the blessing Isaac intended to bestow on him, and Jacob was unwilling to slander his brother.[26] Although Jacob ultimately went through with the deception, out of devotion to his mother, the rabbis apparently considered his reticence to slander his brother, even if it meant loss of the birthright that he had wished to become his, as exemplary and noteworthy.

The rabbis considered someone that does no "evil to his fellow" to be a person "who does not set up in opposition to his fellow craftsman."[27] That is, it refers to a person who does not enter into competition with another (who is already established in his business or professional practice) in a manner that will detract from the latter's income. Put in more contemporary terms, a person who sets up a business that will divide an existing market rather than cater to an expanding one might be considered as one who does "evil to his fellow." Similarly, a person who "taketh [not] up a reproach against his neighbour" is considered to be a person who avoids bringing discredit on a neighbor and instead makes a point of befriending him, in order to increase social harmony.[28]

As an example of a person "in whose eyes a vile person is despised," the Talmud chose King Hezekiah of Judah, who had his deceased father's remains dragged through the street on a pallet made of ropes. Even though it might be perceived as a public slight to the monarchy and to his own honor, Hezekiah denied his father a royal burial in order to emphasize that the deceased king merited public contempt because of his collaboration in spreading pagan beliefs and practices in Israel.[29] As an exemplar of one who "honoureth them that fear the Lord," the rabbis chose Jehoshaphat, king of Judah, who is reported by tradition to have risen from his throne to accord personal honor to every scholar, addressing each as his teacher and master.[30]

A person who "sweareth to his own hurt and changeth not" was understood by the rabbis as one who remained faithful even to a self-imposed restriction known only to himself. R. Johanan was identified as just such a person, one who was known to have observed scrupulously such vows even when it clearly was disadvantageous for him to do so.[31] The virtues applauded here are steadfastness and consistency.

The Bible expressly states, "Unto a foreigner thou mayest lend upon interest; but unto thy brother thou shalt not lend upon interest" (Deut. 23:21). Nonetheless, the rabbis interpreted the psalmist's statement "He putteth not out money on interest" as praising one who refuses to do so on the basis that lending money on interest even to foreigners is a demoralizing business practice.[32]

Finally, the psalmist extolled the man who will not "taketh a bribe against the innocent." As the exemplar of such a person, the rabbis referred to R. Ishmael b. R. Jose. The Talmud relates that he had a gardener-tenant on his land who used to bring him a basket of fruit as rent each Friday. Once, his tenant deviated from his routine and brought the fruit to him a day earlier; R. Ishmael inquired as to the reason for the change. The tenant replied that he had come early because he was participating in a lawsuit that was to be heard by R. Ishmael, his landlord, and thought he would take advantage of the circumstance to pay his rent at the same time. R. Ishmael refused to accept the early rent payment and immediately disqualified himself from serving as a judge in his tenant's case. He took these steps to avoid even the slightest suggestion that his impartiality as a jurist might have been impaired. Indeed, even after he recused himself, he found himself conjuring up arguments in his mind that would have assisted the case of his tenant. This led him to exclaim, "Oh, the despair that waits for those who take bribes! If I, who have not taken [the fruit at all], and even if I had taken I would only have taken what is my own, am in such [a state of mind], how much more [distressing would be the state of] those who accept bribes."[33]

These eleven fundamental principles of ethical conduct, as understood by the rabbis, were considered to reflect the essence of the entire canon of biblical law, as reflected in the 613 precepts of the Torah. However, another view suggested that the essence of the Mosaic Law might be encompassed by an even smaller number of ethical principles. Advocates of this approach made reference to the teaching of Isaiah: "He that walketh righteously, and speaketh uprightly, he that despiseth the gain of oppressions, that shaketh his hand from the taking of bribes, that stoppeth his ear from hearing of blood, and shutteth his eyes from looking upon evil; he shall dwell on high" (Isa. 33:15–16).

Once again the rabbis chose Abraham as the model of one "that walketh righteously," and R. Ishmael b. R. Jose as the exemplar of one "that shaketh his hand from holding of bribes." Moreover, they singled out R. Ishmael b. Elisha as one who "despiseth the gain of oppressions," as evidenced by his behavior in a situation very similar to that confronted by R. Ishmael b. R. Jose, on which occasion he had responded in an identical manner.[34] As one who "speaketh uprightly" they envisioned a person who studiously avoids affronting another in public, while one "that stoppeth his ear from hearing of blood" was understood to refer to a person who would not listen in silence to aspersions cast against a colleague.[35] In the latter instance, the rabbis drew a negative example from a tradition about R. Eleazar b. R. Simeon relating how his widow discovered a worm in her dead husband's ear. According to the story, R. Eleazar appeared to his widow in a dream and explained the worm as a result of his having once heard aspersions against a colleague without his rising to the man's defense, as he should have done.[36] Finally, the Talmud cites R. Hiyya b. Abba as an exemplar of one that "shutteth his eyes from looking upon evil." The rabbis evidently had in mind here a specific kind of immorality, namely, that which results from succumbing to temptation. Thus, R. Hiyya taught that the prophet's phrase refers to a man "who does not peer at women as they stand washing clothes [in the court-yard]" and thereby avoids arousing immoral desires within him.[37]

Certain sages, evidently not fully satisfied with having reduced the 613 precepts to six principles of ethical and moral conduct, suggested that the prophet Micah had effectively reduced them to three. The prophet wrote, "It hath been told thee, O man, what is good, and what the Lord doth re-quire of thee: only to do justly, and to love mercy and to walk humbly before thy God" (Mic. 6:8). The sages considered the first two of these principles as self-evident and did not take the trouble to elaborate them further. They did, however, attribute a special meaning to the admonition to "walk hum-bly." R. Eleazar asserted that this "refers to attending to funerals and dow-ering a bride for her wedding," a type of assistance that, like acts of mercy or loving-kindness, should be given humbly and privately so as not to em-barrass the recipient.[38] Clearly, the observance of this latter principle would contribute to social harmony by deemphasizing the economic and social distinctions among members of the society.

Taking the reductionist argument even farther, the Talmud states: "Again came Isaiah and reduced them to two [principles], as it is said, 'Thus saith the Lord, Keep ye justice and do righteousness' [Isa. 56:1]. . . . But it is Habbakuk who came and based them all on one [principle], as it is said, 'But the righteous shall live by his faith' " (Hab. 2:4).[39]

It seems reasonably clear that the intent of this remarkable set of state-ments is to teach that all of the precepts of the Torah, the seemingly esoteric statutes as well as the obviously rational ordinances, serve a common moral imperative: they are designed to constrain man's behavior and guide him toward the good life. This same thought may be seen as lying behind a saying of R. Meir cited in the context of a homily on the text: "For the com-mandment is a lamp, and the teaching [Torah] is light . . . [t]o keep thee from the evil woman" (Prov. 6:23–24). R. Meir is quoted as having taught, on the basis of this passage, "Happy is the person who has obtained the Torah. Why? Because it protects him from the path of evil."[40] The medieval com-mentator Menahem Meiri later amplified this notion. He argued that the biblical idea of a precept "alludes to the perfection of the attributes, by means of which the precepts establish order and direction among men, pre-vent one from harming another, and promote conduct in consonance with good traits while cautioning against the opposite."[41] Similarly, Isaac Arama suggested that the meaning of the biblical phrase "Torah [teaching] is light" is that "the Torah is the light that illuminates the paths that bring one to those appetites and desires."[42] That is, by exposing that which causes one to lose his moral bearings and to go astray, the Torah redirects one to the proper path. Once again, the point being made is that the entire Torah, with its elaborate corpus of precepts, is informed by a pervasive ethical imperative.

THE NATURE OF HALAKHIC AUTHORITY

While it is clear that Judaism encompasses both political and religious elements, these two elements must be separated for the purpose of determining their respective authority. However, as pointed out by Aharon Lichtenstein, "Judaism has consistently regarded the sacral and the mundane as distinct but not disjunct. Pervasive halakhic norms relate to all areas of personal and communal existence, even as objective categories demarcate the sacred and the profane."[43]

As shown in the preceding chapter, there is an implicit bias in the biblical writings against the concentration of political and ecclesiastical power in a single body. Moreover, because Judaism as a civilization has been subjected to the vicissitudes of history, its patterns and processes of governance have changed over time in accordance with circumstances. Given the fundamental concept of divine sovereignty, all human authority must ultimately be divinely derived to have any legitimacy. The manner of derivation of such authority is well established in the traditions that describe the two chains of authority through which the Written and Oral Torahs are supposed to have been transmitted from Moses to succeeding generations. These traditions seem to demarcate a clear separation of powers within Judaic society.

With regard to the Written Torah—that is, the Pentateuch—we are told by Scripture, "And Moses wrote this law, and delivered it unto the priests the sons of Levi, that bore the ark of the covenant of the Lord, and unto all the elders of Israel" (Deut. 31:9). Accordingly, the unchanging written legacy of divine legislation was entrusted to the safekeeping of the priests, although it was also made available to the tribal elders. By contrast, the transmission of the Oral Torah—the principles and precepts for the application of the Written Torah within the context of historical circumstances and conditions—is described in a markedly different manner. The tradition teaches, "Moses received Torah from Sinai and transmitted it to Joshua; Joshua to the elders; the elders to the prophets; and the prophets transmitted it to the Men of the Great Assembly."[44] The latter, an institution about which we have little historically reliable information, transmitted the oral tradition to subsequent generations of sages and rabbis, who disseminated it to their disciples and the public at large. The sages appear to have derived their binding legislative authority from the biblical adjuration, "According to the law which they shall teach thee, and according to the judgment which they shall tell thee, thou shalt do; thou shalt not turn aside from the sentence which they shall declare unto thee, to the right hand, nor to the left" (Deut. 17:11). As explained by R. Kahana, "All the ordinances of the Rabbis were based by them on the prohibition of 'thou shalt not turn aside.' "[45]

The title "Rabbi," which is equivalent to "master," or "doctor of the Law," was a designation granted to only a limited number of persons considered capable of bearing the burden of transmission of the tradition, persons entrusted with substantial responsibilities for the future of the Judaic society. The original investiture of rabbinic authorities appears to have involved a form of vicarious consecration, based upon the biblical procedure of transferring the sins of the community to an animal whose sacrifice would atone for society's transgressions. "The elders of the congregation shall lay their hands upon the head of the bullock" (Lev. 4:15), thereby effecting the transfer of the sins of the community to the bullock. Although the evidence is inconclusive, it has been assumed by some that the early sages subsequently adopted the "laying on of hands" for the ordination of elders.[46] This practice was evidently discontinued by the fourth or fifth century C.E., for reasons that are not entirely clear. The cessation of the practice may be related to the need for a different procedure in the commercial towns of Babylonia as contrasted with the principally agricultural society of Palestine, when the center of rabbinic scholarship moved from the latter to the former. Thus, the son of Raba asked R. Ashi: "Is ordination effected by the literal laying on of hands? [No,] he answered; it is by the conferring of the degree. He is designated by the title of Rabbi and authorized to adjudicate cases of kenas [involving the imposition of fines]."[47]

The chains of authority for the transmission of the written and oral traditions of Judaism were ultimately interrupted by historical events having dramatic repercussions in the subsequent history of Judaic civilization. The sacerdotal role of the priests, including their guardianship of the Written Torah, came to an end with the destruction of the Temple in 70 C.E. The ordination of the rabbis continued for another four centuries before it too came to an end in its formal juridical sense at about the time of the final redaction of the Talmud, about 500 C.E. At that time, juridical ordination, or *semikhah*, was replaced by the *hattarat hora'ah*, the authority to instruct—an academic device designed to ensure the perpetuation of the rabbinic tradition through formal certification of those responsible for the education of the community. Since then, there has been no operative central authority in Judaism, even though rabbis throughout subsequent history, including the present, have in some instances sought to fill this lacuna by acting as decisors in certain matters of Jewish law.

In contemporary times, however, rabbinic rulings often do not enjoy the status of enacted law, because they are not necessarily accepted as authoritative outside a particular fellowship or group within the wider Jewish community. Although the various streams of contemporary Judaism all have seminaries that grant the degree of rabbi to their graduates, there are no common standards for the degree, and in most cases, the halakhic rulings of one stream are not accepted by the others. Moreover, to compound the problem further, a good deal of private ordination takes place, on occasion producing rabbis with highly dubious qualifications.

Even the codified halakhah of the venerable Maimonides, almost universally recognized as the greatest halakhist of the post-talmudic period, although it was widely followed, failed to be accepted as the ultimate authority—because of his omission of the sources on the basis of which he determined the operative halakhah. It took another four hundred years before a broad consensus accorded authoritative recognition to the sixteenth-century halakhic code of Joseph Caro, annotated by Moses Isserles, as serving the long-standing traditions of segments of the broader traditional community. Since that time, numerous codes have appeared to collect decisions—based on the principles set forth in the Caro's code, the *Shulhan Arukh*—required by changing times, circumstances, and technology. However, none of these ever achieved even nearly universal acceptance as the authoritative expression of halakhah. In any case, halakhic rulings are generally judicially unenforceable as public law outside the context of a Judaic political society. In the absence of a recognized central authority, such as the ancient *Sanhedrin*, rabbinic law in contemporary times has only moral force and authority, and only for those who accept its burden.

An attempt to reestablish juridical ordination by consensus, as a first step toward a resurrection of the Sanhedrin, was initiated by Jacob Berav in 1538. However, this effort met with the strenuous opposition of most rabbinic authorities of the period and was soon abandoned.[48] Four centuries later, a similar effort was mounted by Judah L. Maimon to reestablish the Sanhedrin as the central judicial institution of the modern Jewish state; his attempt met the same kind of opposition from rabbinic authorities.[49] A less ambitious project, initiated by Kalman Kahana, was to have Jewish civil law—that is, the civil law and procedure of the rabbinic codes—adopted by the Jewish state. Kahana argued, "The more we delve into Jewish law and into its history the more we find there the reflection of the creation of our own national ideas. . . . This plea for the acceptance of Jewish law is not based only on the idea of tradition; it is an appeal for the recognition of our people's instinctive feeling that our law is founded on ethics and justice."[50] While Kahana's proposal also failed to gain much support, it is by no means inconceivable that such efforts might succeed in the not too distant future. It would be premature to rule out the long-term possibility that halakhah might be considered as the basis for a reordering of the internal legal framework of the State of Israel. Moreover, such an approach would not in itself necessarily transform the state into a theocracy—using that term in its contemporary sense of an ecclesiastical state—although one might anticipate strong opposition to it from secularist circles.

THE PRINCIPLE OF MAJORITY RULE

The halakhic regulatory process, generally speaking and subject to a number of qualifications that we will not go into here, is governed by a well-established rabbinic procedural rule that essentially corresponds to the democratic principle of majority rule. The classic expression of this rule is: "Where there is a controversy between an individual and a group, the halakhah follows the group."[51] With regard to the group, "Throughout the Torah there is an established rule that a majority is like the whole."[52]

Nonetheless, one must not leap to the conclusion that the incorporation of this procedural rule in the public decision-making process reflects an intrinsically majoritarian or democratic thrust in fundamental Judaic political thought. The application of the principle of majority rule in the halakhic process appears to have been primarily a practical expedient, given the difficulty of attaining unanimity among a group of otherwise autonomous halakhic scholars and decisors. This may be clearly seen in Maimonides' description of the decision-making process employed by the high court of the early rabbinic period, the Sanhedrin. "If they were not certain of the law, they ... discussed it until they either reached a unanimous decision or put it to a vote and decided in accordance with the majority opinion."[53] Presumably, if the scriptural basis for the law or a strong precedent for its application were known, the majority-rule process would be inapplicable. In other words, according to Maimonides, the process was employed as a matter of expedience rather than of democratic principle.

As Paul Eidelberg points out, "In Judaic law the meaning of majority rule is rational rather than volitional. ... Although the Hebrew word *rov* can be translated literally as 'majority,' the term 'probability' conveys its cognitive meaning. What is decisive is not the will of the majority so much as the judgment of the majority. It is the judgment of the majority—reached by thorough examination of diverse evidence and diverse opinions—that carries moral authority, for it is more likely to be in accord with truth on matters of law."[54]

Legislative and judicial functions are fused in Judaic jurisprudence, making halakhic decisors also the adjudicators and administrators of the law. Because of this, a number of prominent rabbinic authorities of the post-talmudic period challenged the validity of the majority-rule principle with regard to halakhic rule making (although not with regard to judicial proceedings, where decisions are made on the evidence). The essence of their view was that the determination of the halakhah is an essentially intellectual process; it cannot be assumed that a majority opinion necessarily reflects sagacity, wisdom, and knowledge appropriate to the task. They suggested that the majority-rule principle is intended to apply only where the members of the majority and minority are of equal competence in the Torah. However, some argued, a minority opinion that reflects the views of more competent authorities is to be preferred to the opinion of a less competent majority: "It is not to be claimed that a small group of sages shall not be decisive over a large group of ignoramuses."[55] Joseph Albo also argued in this regard, "We must not therefore abandon the general rule, which is to follow the majority and ignore the individual or the minority, provided, however, that the majority consists of learned men and not ignoramuses, for the masses and the ignorant people are easily persuaded of a thing that is not so, and strenuously insist that it is."[56]

Moreover, because the decision-making process was pragmatic in nature, a majority decision was not presumed to establish the truth of the position espoused, only its practicality given a particular set of circumstances. As Berkovits points out, "That an opinion is held by a majority of scholars is no proof at all that it is true. A majority may be no less mistaken than a minority. Therefore, always follow the opinion that is based on logically valid reasoning."[57] In other words, where there is doubt, the rule of reason should prevail.

Other sages took the position that a minority of the highly competent should be considered equivalent to a majority of the less competent, leaving it up to the individual to choose freely which opinion to follow. Thus, as noted by Berkovits, "When there is no reason to prefer the minority view to that of the majority, when logically the two hold the balance to each other, only then follow the majority."[58] Nonetheless, there is a substantial body of rabbinic opinion that maintains that the principle of majority rule continues to apply even where the minority is better qualified.[59]

It is noteworthy that minority opinions are treated with remarkable deference in the talmudic literature and are duly recorded. This is because under different circumstances, the minority view may become the majority position. As stated by the sages, "Why do they record the opinion of the individual against that of the majority, given that the halakhah may only be in accordance with the opinion of the majority? Because, if a court approves the opinion of the individual it may rely upon him"—provided that the court in question is greater in both number and wisdom than the court whose opinion it wishes to annul.[60]

There is a degree of uncertainty as to the precise criteria as to number and greater wisdom for overriding a previous majority opinion. The notion of a court of greater number and wisdom is problematic, because the size of the high court, the Sanhedrin, was fixed in number; how could there have been a court of greater number? Some halakhic commentators suggested that the notion of being "greater in number and wisdom" related to the age of the members of the court, deference being given to seniority, or to the age of the president of the court. Maimonides dealt with this problem by asserting that the notion referred not to the actual court but to the number of qualified sages of the generation who "agreed and accepted the word declared by the High Court and did not challenge it."[61] In other words, it would appear that in Maimonides' opinion, the decisions of the high court were expected to reflect the majority opinion of the entire legal community and receive tacit validation therefrom, presumably because the membership of the court was continually drawn from that body. Rabinowitz suggests that Maimonides' argument implies a further, generally concurred-in, concept of halakhic authority and its organization: "On the one hand, there is the Sanhedrin of seventy-one[,] . . . on the other that of the sages of Israel acting together in matters not declared absolute by the decision of the seventy-one. When no formal Sanhedrin of seventy-one exists, but all the sages of the generation gather together, their decision is binding[,] as was that of the seventy-one who sat in the Sanhedrin. The direct, absolute authority of the Beth Din Hagadol [High Court], passes to the collective body of the sages of Israel."[62]

Once a majority decision was reached in the Sanhedrin, the principle of democratic centralism came into effect. That is, once the deliberative process concluded, the holders of the minority opinion became obliged to accept the majority view in practice, if not in theory. Any publicly recognized authority who violated this principle and encouraged people to follow his own dissenting opinion in practice was to be designated as a "rebellious elder" and indicted for a capital offense.[63] Such a harsh position toward the "rebellious elder" was justified on the pragmatic basis that it was necessary in the public interest, so that "contention might not increase in Israel."[64]

It is important to recognize, however, that the notion of the "rebellious elder" has application only with regard to the decisions of the central high court, that it does not necessarily apply to the decisions of lower, local courts.[65] An elder who dissents against the ruling of the majority of a lower court is entitled to maintain his view publicly until the issue is decided on appeal by a high court. "They would go to the court at the entrance to the Temple court and say, 'Thus have I expounded, and thus have my colleagues expounded. Thus have I taught, and thus have my colleagues taught.' If they had a tradition on this matter, they would relate it, but if not, they would all go to the great court in the Chamber of Hewn Stone, from which Torah used to be dispensed to all Israel."[66] Once again, it needs to be emphasized that the issue is one of practice and not opinion. Even after the high court rendered its decision, the "rebellious elder" was permitted, indeed even expected, to maintain his point of view and to profess it. However, he was precluded from opposing the majority view in practice or from encouraging others to do so.

NOTES

1. Maimonides, *Treatise on Logic*, p. 64.
2. Moses Mendelssohn, *Biur Millot haHigayon*, p. 67b.

3. Nathan of Rome, *Sefer haArukh*, "halakh," p. 182. See also Ephraim E. Urbach, *The Halakhah: Its Sources and Development*, pp. 2–3.

4. Michael Chernik, "HaHevdel bain Mitzvah veHalakhah beTorato shel haRambam," *CCAR Journal: A Reform Jewish Quarterly* (Spring 1997), p. 122ff.

5. Hayyim Z. Reines, *Torah uMusar*, p. 192.

6. *Tosefta Sanhedrin* 10 and 11; *Sanhedrin* 8b.

7. *Sifre on Deuteronomy*, *Piska* 187. Maimonides writes in this regard that it is forbidden for the court to say, "The victim is already dead, what profit will accrue from killing another[?]" Nevertheless, the murderer must be executed (*Hilkhot Sanhedrin* 20:4).

8. Abraham H. Rabinowitz, *The Jewish Mind*, pp. 73–74.

9. Eliezer Berkovits, *Not in Heaven*, p. 1. Berkovits also observed that "Halakha is the wisdom of the application of the written word of the Torah to the life and history of the Jewish people" (ibid., p. 71).

10. Izhak Englard, "The Problem of Jewish Law in a Jewish State," in *Contemporary Thinking in Israel*, ed. Avner Tomaschoff, vol. 1, *Halacha*, p. 60.

11. *J. Kiddushin* 1:2. See also *Sotah* 16a: "R. Johanan said in the name of R. Ishmael: In three places the halakhah crushes the Scriptural text under the heel."

12. Englard, "The Problem of Jewish Law in a Jewish State," p. 63.

13. See *Teshuvot haGeonim: Shaarei Teshuvah* 23; Samuel haNagid, *Mavo haTalmud*, last sentence; also Maimonides, *Perush haMishnaiot on Sotah* 3:5 and *Sanhedrin* 10:3.

14. *Yoma* 67b. See also *Sifra* "Aharei Mot," 13:9 (13:10 in some editions).

15. Ibid.

16. Jon D. Levenson, *Sinai and Zion*, p. 53.

17. *Shabbat* 89a.

18. *Leviticus Rabbah* 35:5.

19. *Mekilta de-Rabbi Ishmael*, vol. 2, p. 182 (on Exod. 18:20).

20. *Genesis Rabbah* 44:1.

21. Aharon Lichtenstein, "R. Joseph Soloveitchik," in *Great Jewish Thinkers of the Twentieth Century*, ed. Simon Noveck, p. 292.

22. *Makkot* 24a.

23. *Taanit* 23a–b.

24. *Hullin* 94b.

25. Rashbam commentary on *Baba Batra* 88a.

26. Samuel Eidels (Maharshah), *Hiddushei Agadot* on *Makkot* 24a.

27. *Makkot* 24a; *Sanhedrin* 81a.

28. *Makkot* 24a; *Sanhedrin* 76b.

29. *Makkot* 24a; *Sanhedrin* 47a. See *Sanhedrin* (Soncino Talmud edition), n. 3, p. 310.

30. *Makkot* 24a; *Ketuvot* 103b.

31. *Makkot* 24a; *J. Nedarim* 8:1.

32. *Makkot* 24a; *Baba Metzia* 70b–71a.

33. *Ketuvot* 105b.

34. Ibid.

35. *Makkot* 24a. The expression, "hearing of blood" is treated as the equivalent of causing someone shame, since the person subjected to such abuse is likely to turn red.

36. *Baba Metzia* 84b.

37. *Makkot* 24a; *Baba Batra* 57b.

38. *Sukkah* 49b. See also *Makkot* 24a, where the teaching is cited without reference to R. Eleazar.

39. *Makkot* 24a.

40. *Midrash Mishlei*, Buber ed., p. 56.

41. Menahem Meiri, *Perish haMeiri al Sefer Mishlei*, p. 65.

42. Isaac Arama, *Sefer Mishlei im Perush Yad Avshalom*, 21b.

43. Aharon Lichtenstein, "Religion and State," in *Contemporary Jewish Religious Thought*, ed. Arthur A. Cohen and Paul Mendes-Flohr, p. 774.

44. *Avot* 1:1

45. *Berakhot* 19b.

46. For an extensive discussion of the matter of ordination of rabbis, see Lawrence A. Hoffman, "The Origins of Ordination," in *Rabbinic Authority*, ed. Elliot L. Stevens, pp. 71–94.

47. *Sanhedrin* 13b.

48. Jacob Berav, *Sefer Sheilot uTeshuvot*, pp. 199–209.

49. Judah L. Maimon, *Hiddush haSanhedrin beMedinatenu haMehudeshet*.

50. Kalman Kahana, *The Case for Jewish Civil Law in the Jewish State*, p. 14.

51. *Berakhot* 9a, 37a, and numerous other places. See also *Eduyot* 1:5: "The Halakhah must be in accordance with the majority." This principle is predicated on rabbinic exegesis of Exod. 23:2.

52. *Horayot* 3b.

53. Maimonides, *Hilkhot Mamrim* 1:4.

54. Paul Eidelberg, *Judaic Man*, p. 130

55. Aaron haLevi of Barcelona, *Sefer haHinukh* 67, p. 120.

56. Joseph Albo, *Sefer Ha'Ikkarim* 3:23, pp. 205–206.

57. Berkovits, *Not in Heaven*, p. 7.

58. Ibid.

59. See discussion and citation of sources in *Entziklopedia Talmudit*, vol. 9, "halakhah," cols. 258–259.

60. *Eduyot* 1:5. This rule applies only if the former court adopted a majority opinion. However, if that court had ruled in accordance with a minority opinion, its ruling may be set aside by a court that does not meet the criterion of having both greater number and greater wisdom.

61. *Maimonides*, Hilkhot Mamrim 2:2.

62. Rabinowitz, *The Jewish Mind*, p. 201.

63. *Sanhedrin* 86b. The notion of the "rebellious elder" is based on an extrapolation of Deut. 17:12, which prescribes capital punishment for one who deliberately contravenes the authority of the court.

64. *Sanhedrin* 88b.

65. For a comprehensive discussion of the "rebellious elder," see Haggai Ben-Artzi, "HaYahid mul haMemsad beHevrah Halakhatit," *Sinai*, vol. 94 (1984), pp. 79–94.

66. *Sifre on Deuteronomy*, Piska 152.

The Individual and Society

It is a striking feature of the intellectual history of the world that only in modern times has the idea of the person as an integral individual become prominent. This development took place notwithstanding that it was and remains the universal human experience that all persons necessarily exist within the context of some society. With the dubious exception of a few scattered hermits, who pursue solitary lives only by the tolerance of the surrounding society, individual man is in fact nowhere to be found outside the framework of a more or less organized society. Even the outlaw is defined by the society he defies. It is therefore not surprising that when Aristotle addressed himself to the question of the nature of political society, he considered the elemental human unit to be the natural family rather than the individual. Indeed, even a cursory review of the Bible will reveal that it too seems to place principal emphasis on society. To the extent that there is a focus on individuals, they are almost always considered within the context of the society of which they are integral parts.

One contemporary writer asserts, "The goal of Judaism is to teach men how to live together in harmony and in peace, and it stresses man's need of society in which to realize his potential. Any doctrine that advocates a shunning of society or withdrawal from it is deemed pernicious."[1] Indeed, the great sage Hillel adjured, "Do not separate yourself from the community."[2] The individual and the community of which one is a part have a reciprocal relationship. "Man owes society his allegiance, respect, and his active participation in its endeavors. Society owes the individual the protection of life, and property under its laws and by its collective power to maintain a stable community that will afford him the opportunity to live a free and productive life, and assist him in time of need."[3]

Nonetheless, there appears to be a certain deliberate ambivalence in Scripture about the question of the individual in relation to society, an ambivalence that may be seen as reflected in the two disparate versions of the origin of man that it offers. Thus, in one text, the biblical author states, "And God created man in His own image, in the image of God created He him; male and female created He them" (Gen. 1:27). Assuming that the word "man" is used in its generic sense, the text seems to be describing the origin of primeval society, the simultaneous creation of two persons bound together with the ties of common origin, experience, and condition. But several verses later, the biblical author seems to affirm man's creation as a single solitary being: "Then the Lord God formed man of the dust of the ground, and breathed into his nostrils the breath of life; and man became a living soul" (Gen. 2:7). In this second version of the creation saga, the woman is not formed until later. Needless to say, the traditional commentators sought to reconcile these two versions. The explanation offered by Rashi in this regard seems quite serviceable. He suggests that the common sense understanding of the texts indicates that in the first version we are simply being told that the creation of the first man and woman—in effect, human society—took place on the sixth day of creation; we are told nothing about the process itself. The second version, by contrast, specifies that the creation of the prototype male and female was sequential rather than simultaneous.[4]

However, this still leaves us with the question of the significance of the second version, since the events it describes all take place the same day. Why is it important for us to know that man was created as a solitary creature? Is Scripture trying to tell us that although the person is defined by his role in society, the individual precedes society and as such is naturally autonomous? If one assumes that the second account of the creation of man intends to make such a point, the implications of the text are far-reaching.

Scripture emphasizes the distinctiveness of man within the order of creation in a number of ways, of which one is particularly relevant to our present discussion. In stark contrast to the rest of the animal world, which is created in pairs—male and female, presumably to ensure natural reproduction and the perpetuation of the species—man is depicted in this version as clearly having been created alone. An implicit analogy is suggested here between man and his Creator. Just as God is conceived as singular and unique, man is held to reflect a singularity. Accordingly, the sages derived a vital message from this biblical description of the uniqueness of paradigmatic man. They suggested that the reason why man is depicted as having been created alone, even though it is evident that without a mate he would be incapable of perpetuating human existence, is to promulgate a central principle of morals. "Therefore but a single man was created in the world, to teach that if any man has caused a single soul to perish Scripture imputes it to him as though he had caused a whole world to perish."[5] That is, the individual is not merely one out of the billions of living human beings and therefore a creature of little if any significance. To the contrary, man is a complete and self-contained microcosm.

Moreover, Judaism conceives of man as having a direct and unmediated connection to God, affirming not only his individual significance but also his intrinsic equality to all others, regardless of relative power or station. Emphasizing this point, R. Levi taught with regard to the revelation of the Torah at Mount Sinai, "When the Holy One spoke, each and every person in Israel could say, 'The Divine Word is addressing me.' Note that Scripture does not say, 'I am the Lord your [the plural pronoun] God,' but I am the Lord THY [singular] God."[6] The individual human being is thus conceived as having inestimable intrinsic value, a concept with important implications for the moral basis of Judaic society and government. Samuel Belkin asserts in this regard, "Judaism is based upon the fundamental concept that in our national and individual lives we can continue to function properly only so long as we believe in the dignity of every individual, in the inviolability, infinite worth and sacredness of each human being."[7] It has also been pointed out that Judaism's conception of the singularity of the individual person is exemplified by the Hebrew language's inability to render the word for "man," *adam*, in the plural.[8]

There is also implicit in this view of man the idea that it is the individual alone—not generic man, but particular man—that is the concrete reality, whereas the society of which he may be a member is essentially an abstraction that man reifies whenever it serves his purpose. As such, society has practical relevance for the individual only insofar as he is a living being and can have recourse to it for whatever benefit it may provide. However, once the individual is faced with the threat of oblivion, society becomes a meaningless metaphor for him. His obligations to society pale in significance when confronted with the principle of self-preservation, except as will be discussed later with regard to certain categories of war.

The question of the responsibility one has to oneself is reflected in the following ethical dilemma discussed by the sages. The hypothetical situation is that two people are traveling in the desert, far from civilization, and one of them has a pitcher or container with only enough water to enable one person to survive until he can reach safety. It is taken as a given that if they share the water, both will surely die. Ben Batira taught: "[I]t is better that both should drink and die, rather than that one should behold his companion's death.'" This opinion evidently was accepted until R. Akiba refuted it on the basis of his exegesis of the biblical teaching "that thy brother may live with thee" (Lev. 25:35). The sage read this as emphasizing "with thee"— that is, if there was enough water for both—but not to the extent that the one who originally had the water should effectively throw away his own life out of a misguided sense of propriety. In other words, he may elect to die so that another may live, for some unspecified altruistic reason, but is in no way morally obligated to do so. Accordingly, R. Akiba asserted, in a proposition later generally accepted as normative, "Your life takes precedence over his life."[9]

This proposition is restated in its maximalist form in the halakhic principle, "If a man comes to kill you, rise early and kill him first."[10] Implicit in this dictum is the idea that the life of another is of no greater importance than one's own and that the principle of self-preservation takes precedence over the prohibition of taking another's life, if necessary to remove the threat to one's own. However, this does not apply to taking the life of an innocent third party to protect oneself from a second party.[11] David Novak writes in this regard, "There are no priorities in the value of human lives unless a person . . . forfeits his right to protection by denying this equality of value in his own favor. The function of society is to make this de jure equality de facto in the affairs of men. What society and any of its citizens do in the case of the pursuer [rodef] is to re-establish the equality of persons which the pursuer is upsetting. To protect or ignore the true rodef would be to deny along with him this very basis of law and right."[12]

This perspective on the relationship of the individual to society, and most particularly to the state, is perhaps nowhere stated more incisively than in the writing of Abraham Hen.

Every government in the world, since the foundation of the earth, and especially since the flowering of civilization, is based on society, on the state, on the majority, that is to say, on the sacrifice that the individual must bring to the altar of the many. In actuality, the individual is always sacrificed on the altar of some tyranny, of some dictator or some accepted slogan which we are too lax to examine and recognize as a mere fabrication. . . . The individual by himself, in his independent and private life, is nothing but an expendable quantity—such is the secular state. The Jewish state is designated to be the very antithesis to this sanctified viewpoint; it must be based only on the individual man, on the three 'qualitative aspects of existence': the truth of being, the right to exist and the sanctity of existence; simply, the existence of each individual.[13]

Echoing these thoughts, Eugene Korn writes that Judaism "insists on the unique spiritual integrity of each human being and can never lose sight of his immeasurable value. . . . The divine character of every human being demands that each person be considered an end in himself. He may never be used as a means within some larger system, and must never be dominated completely by any form of totalitarian political or legal authority."[14]

However, there is a concern that the notion that the individual is inherently of ultimate importance in the divine scheme may lead to an unbridled egotism that makes each individual the ultimate measure of what is or is not appropriate action with respect to any or all other individuals. The Judaic ethos categorically rejects such an approach. As Israel Mattuck correctly puts it, the Judaic "conception of community lays on its every member and individual share in the responsibility for the ethical quality of its collective life—for the justice in its social order."[15] Ideally, Judaism demands that the egotism of the individual be bridled in the interest of his fellow man. It rejects the notion that self-interest is the proper motivation for social responsibility, whether such self-interest is manifested by simply feeling good about assisting others or by the expectation of some social benefit such as public recognition and honor for one's beneficence,[16] or where, as in such countries as the United States, the philanthropist is rewarded by significant and tangible tax benefits.

But, one may ask, is not self-interest natural to man? If it is natural, why does Judaism denigrate it as a motivation? Emanuel Feldman writes in this regard, "The fact is that man is basically a creature of instinct, and the most natural instinct of all is to look out for number one—which often results in hurting others. When Genesis 8:21 says that 'the inclination of man's heart is evil from his youth,' it means to say that man, left to his own devices, is going to be selfish, greedy, and quite unconcerned about his fellow human beings."[17] Accordingly, he argues, "A genuine human being is not one who merely does everything that comes naturally. The fact that something is natural or instinctive is not reason enough for us to give it full reign." He suggests that "society today is destroying itself because we have allowed the 'natural' to dominate." The consequence of this is that "the sacredness of human life has lost all meaning. Permissiveness is the order of the day, and as a result the weakest members of society are at risk." Such a situation "represents a corrosion of moral values, and it is the inevitable result of a society living according to instincts that are unbridled and unchanneled."[18]

Nonetheless, Judaic ethics does recognize, people being as they are, that aiding others for the wrong motivation is clearly better than not doing so at all, and that the donor of charity, even acting for the wrong reason, receives greater ultimate benefit than the recipient of charity. This argument is made somewhat elliptically in a talmudic parable. It is related that the Roman governor of Judaea, Tineius Rufus, put the following question to R. Akiba: "If your God loves the poor, why does He not support them?" R. Akiba replied, "So that we may be saved through them from the punishment of Gehinnom."[19] The point being made is that poverty is not a natural state, and the "haves" should disabuse themselves of the notion that their well-being is equally natural. Accordingly, their philanthropy serves as a corrective to excessive egotism, which is abhorrent to God. In other words, all men, regardless of condition, are intended by their nature to be equal in certain respects, including their personal dignities, and it is incumbent upon each to sustain that dignity by rendering such assistance as they can. Indeed, the opportunity to assist others should be viewed as an even greater opportunity to restore one's own balance. This is reflected in the teaching of R. Joshua: "The poor man does more for the master of the house than the latter does for him."[20]

THE DIGNITY OF MAN

Scripture relates that the prophet Ezekiel beheld an awesome vision of the likeness of the glory of God: "And when I saw it, I fell upon my face, and I heard a voice of one that spoke. And He said unto me: 'son of man, stand upon thy feet, and I will speak with thee'" (Ezek. 1:28–2:1). Milton R. Konvitz writes, "In this stirring passage in the Bible, God asks man to neither fall on his knees nor grovel in the dust nor cringe in fear in the presence of His glory."[21] As a creature created in the image of God, Man has dignity, and God insists that he reflect it. Judaic tradition sees the dignity of man as a critical component in the intrinsic equality of men, regardless of station in life. Thus the Talmud tells us, "A favorite saying of the Rabbis of Yavne was: I am God's creature and my fellow is God's creature. My work [as a scholar] is in the town and his work [as a laborer] is in the country. I rise early for my work and he rises early for his work. Just as he does not presume to do my work, so I do not presume to do his work. Will you say, I do much and he does little? We have learnt: One may do much or do little; it is all one, provided he directs his heart to heaven."[22]

Putting the matter in philosophical perspective, Joseph B. Soloveitchik argued that "man is a dignified being and to be human means to live with dignity.... The brute's existence is undignified because it is a helpless existence. Human existence is a dignified one because it is a glorious, majestic, powerful existence." However, "there is no dignity without responsibility, and one cannot assume responsibility as long as he is not capable of living up to his commitments. Only when man rises to the heights of freedom of action and creativity of mind does he begin to implement the mandate of dignified responsibility entrusted to him by his Maker."[23] Although Soloveitchik was writing primarily with regard to man's relation to the external physical environment, his words are applicable to man's social environment as well.

Because the individual is assigned inestimable value in Judaic tradition, maintenance of the dignity of man, as a being created in the image of God, becomes a normative imperative. Thus, the sages declared, "Great is human dignity, since it overrides a negative precept of the Torah." The question, of course, is how human dignity can be given priority over the divine dignity, which requires compliance with the precepts of the Torah. Accordingly, the sages suggested that this principle did not actually apply to any specific negative precept set forth in the Torah but rather to rabbinic enactments, both positive and negative. That is, as explained by the sage Rab b. Shaba, maintaining the dignity of a person overrides the rabbinic authority to impose binding obligations, an authority derived from the negative biblical precept, "Thou shalt not turn aside from the sentence which they shall declare unto thee" (Deut. 17:11). R. Kahana taught in this regard, "All the ordinances of the Rabbis were based by them on the prohibition of 'thou shalt not turn aside' but where the question of [human] dignity is concerned the Rabbis allowed the act."[24] At the same time, however, the normative imperative concerning human dignity could be held to apply with regard to the fulfillment of the positive precepts set forth in the Torah. For example, one would be required to give priority to the burial of a corpse, if there were no one else able to do it, over the positive Torah requirement to circumcise one's son on the eighth day. The rationale for this is the principle that "abstention from the performance of an act is not regarded as an abrogation of the law," as would be the case (in the opposite sense) with regard to a negative commandment of the Torah to desist from some act.[25]

The concern for human dignity is given vivid expression in the rabbinic teachings about philanthropy, which should be practiced in a manner that takes into most serious consideration the effect on the dignity of the recipient. The Talmud relates a story about R. Jannai, who saw a man give a coin to a poor person publicly. He said to the donor, "It had been better that you had not given him, than now that you have given him publicly and put him to shame."[26] In this same regard, R. Eleazar said, "A man who gives charity in secret is greater than Moses our Teacher."[27] During the period of the Temple, this concern about causing embarrassment to a recipient of charity was institutionalized. The Mishnah reports that there was a special room, "the Chamber of Secrets," in the Temple where charitable transactions could be undertaken anonymously. "Into the Chamber of Secrets the devout used to put their gifts in secret and the poor of good family received support therefrom in secret."[28]

Moreover, as pointed out by Jacob Z. Lauterbach, "This consideration for personal dignity must, according to the Halakhah, be extended even to those who have apparently lost their sense of dignity and degraded themselves by committing a crime."[29] This principle is reflected in the biblical rule, "If a man steal an ox, or a sheep, and kill it, or sell it, he shall pay five oxen for an ox, and four sheep for a sheep" (Exod. 21:37). Why the difference in penalty for stealing an ox or a sheep? "R. Johanan b. Zakkai said: Observe how great is the importance attached to the dignity of man, for in the case of an ox which walks away on its own feet [while the thief steals it] the payment is five-fold, while in the case of a sheep which was usually carried on the thief's shoulder only four-fold has to be paid."[30] The fine for the sheep is smaller because even in the act of stealing man's dignity is diminished by the probable need to carry the animal on his shoulders. It is this humiliation that the law takes into consideration in reducing the fine, demonstrating that God himself respects the dignity and honor of every person, even of the thief.

Maimonides applied this principle to the discretionary power vested in the judge. He asserted in his codification of the halakhah, "Let not human dignity be light in his eyes; for the respect due to man supersedes a negative rabbinical command. . . . The judge must be careful not to do anything calculated to destroy their self-respect."[31] As Israel's present chief justice, Aharon Barak, put it, "The concept 'human dignity' is not new with us. Its roots are imbedded in our Judaic tradition. . . . The dignity of man derives from the dignity of the Creator because man was created in His image. 'Human dignity' means not to shame the image of God that is inherent in man." On the basis of this rationale, Israel's high court rejected involuntary body searches by police because it violated the principle of "human dignity."[32]

The sages went so far as to suggest that "one who publicly shames his neighbor is as though he shed blood," because he causes the person suffering the indignity to become pale.[33] They therefore considered it "better that a man throw himself into a fiery furnace than publicly put his neighbor to shame."[34] An affront to human dignity was considered in Jewish law to be one of the principal categories of damage that one person may cause to another.[35] Thus, in addition to other damages, a seducer must pay for the indignity he causes his victim, the amount to be determined by the status of the one who inflicts and of the one who suffers the indignity.[36] Maimonides devotes an entire chapter in his code of laws to the subject of how offenses to human dignity are to be assessed.[37]

On the other hand, human dignity was considered so important that the self-abased were halakhically disqualified from serving as witnesses in a civil proceeding. The sages also applied this principle to an ignoramus. Moreover, their concern for human dignity was such that they considered that one "who eats in the marketplace is like a dog"[38]—the rationale being that a person who has lost his sense of dignity may not hesitate to give false testimony. That is, they would have looked askance at the eating of hot dogs and corn on the cob while walking in the street as an infraction of the dignified behavior expected of a responsible human being. Maimonides wrote in this regard, "The self-abased are disqualified on the authority of the Rabbis. These comprise men who walk in the street eating in the sight of the public, and those who walk about naked in the street while they are engaged in a repugnant occupation, and those who do similar things indicative of a lack of a sense of shame."[39] It should be noted, however, that the self-abasement that Maimonides refers to in a repugnant occupation applies only to the way one is dressed in public while pursuing such occupation. The sages did not consider any kind of legitimate work as beneath a person's dignity. In fact, they preferred it to a reliance on public welfare. Rab stated, "Flay carcasses in the market place and earn wages and do not say, 'I am a priest and a great man and it is beneath my dignity.' "[40]

THE INDIVIDUAL IN SOCIETY

As a solitary being existing in an assumed state of nature, man's physical powers are entirely subordinate to his own individual will and intellect; he constitutes a veritable microcosm. In his original solitude, he is completely at liberty to exercise his will as he chooses in response to the imperative to master his environment and satisfy his elemental needs, his survival being dependent upon his ability to exploit existing natural opportunities for the support of life.

In effect, in such a primal state of nature man finds himself in a condition of absolute liberty. He is completely free to act as he sees fit, there being no external constraints on his conduct other than those imposed by the natural order of things. Nor is there any intrinsic reason implicit in the nature of things why there should be any fundamental change in this condition even after the eventual appearance of other humans, who presumably would be comparable to him in all fundamental respects. In other words, any other human being would also be characterized as existing in a natural condition of absolute personal liberty. Assuming that the actions of one did not impinge on the unfettered freedom of action of the other, there is no reason for one to consider imposing any constraints on his conduct. Under ideal circumstances, such an assumption would be valid. However, the predication of ideal circumstances does not comport with the political economy of even primeval man.

This consideration may be seen as reflected in the biblical story of the Garden of Eden. The primeval man is placed in the protected environment of Eden, where his needs are satisfied without significant exertion on his part. However, once man is evicted from this sanctuary, he becomes subject to the ravages of nature and must earn his bread through arduous toil. In other words, he is subjected to a radical change in his economy. He must now seek the best possible land for agriculture if he is to minimize his labors. He must now confront the fundamental problem of scarcity. Under conditions of scarcity, it becomes virtually impossible to sustain the absolute liberty of the individual once there is more than one person vying for the same resources.

In addition to the problem of fulfilling his basic physical needs, man's recognition that he possesses special attributes generates an additional need that is unique to the species. He has a compelling need for leisure in order to be able develop and hone those very attributes that distinguish mankind from other created beings. In the biblical view, man is endowed with these attributes in order to carry out an assigned role in the divine plan for the universe. He therefore must not be compelled to expend all his time and energy in a relentless competitive struggle for survival in a world under the inhospitable regime of brute nature. As noted by Obadiah Sforno, "He will be unable to achieve the purpose implied by his being created 'in the image' and 'in the likeness' of God, if he must personally attend to satisfying all of his life's needs."[41] Moreover, his being endowed with attributes that distinguish man from the rest of creation also implicitly create certain disabilities for him. Whereas the other living creatures are guided by innate instincts, man learns survival skills only by training. Because of this, the processes by which he is required to satisfy his essential needs are quite difficult for him to master. His requirements for food, clothing, and shelter therefore present a far greater challenge for him than they do for other created beings. Indeed, generally speaking, the individual human being is surprisingly ill equipped to satisfy those needs independently and adequately.

As a consequence, man is driven to seek to augment his own skills and capacities with those of his fellow humans. It is only by acting in cooperation with others that the individual can realize the economic efficiency necessary to permit the diversion of one's attention from the essential tasks of physical survival to creating opportunities for the leisure that is so critical to personal growth and cultural development. This notion may be seen as implicit in the scriptural statement that "it is not good that the man should be alone" (Gen. 2:8)—that is, without human association. Moreover, as Emanuel Rackman points out, the "sages saw in this verse the suggestion that it is not good for man to be like God—independent—self-sufficient, alone. Adam had to be reduced to size: he had to be made a dependent creature[,] and a dependent creature he would always be."[42]

The efficient satisfaction of man's fundamental physical needs ultimately imposes a demand for specialization and a division of labor. An appreciation of this and of the benefits to be derived from such cooperative economic endeavor is clearly reflected in the talmudic description of the musings of a typical beneficiary of such an economy: "How much labor Adam must have expended before he obtained bread to eat! He ploughed, sowed, reaped, piled up the leaves, threshed, winnowed, selected the ears, sifted the flour, kneaded and baked and after that he ate; whereas I get up in the morning and find all this prepared for me. And how much labor must Adam have expended before he obtained a garment to wear! . . . All artisans attend and come to the door of my house, and I get up and find all these things before me."[43]

The implications of this passage are evident. Man benefits immeasurably from cooperative association with others. Indeed, without such leisure-producing association, man is condemned to a life of monotonous struggle for mere survival. Under such conditions, he is denied the opportunity of even developing an appreciation of more elevating pursuits.

To facilitate the formation of such a prototypical societal environment, the Creator provides man with an *ezer kenegdo*, a counterpart, or "helpmate." The latter is another complete individual human, endowed with a personality comparable in every essential respect to that of the man. Intended to complement man's efforts, the "helpmate" will be a person who partakes in the tasks he must perform and who augments his capabilities, providing strength where he is weak. The "helpmate" will assist the man in maintaining the critical balance between his passions and his reason, helping him to develop and flourish as a human being endowed with moral personality. Together they will constitute the original primeval society, possessed of a basic social structure calculated to satisfy man's intrinsic social and economic needs in a manner that will nurture his self-development.

Finding himself in the most fundamental of societal structures, association with another integral human being, man is compelled to develop a pattern of relationships that will enhance and promote the viability and practical utility of that association. The essential principle that is to serve as the foundation for this uniquely human social structure is that of the inherent equality of all its members. Just as the first man is created in the image of God and is therefore special, reflecting ultimate value, so too is his counterpart and companion, as well as all subsequent human beings. It becomes essential that the "helpmate" be considered equal to the man in all respects if his social and economic needs are to be met fully. If such were not to be the case, the important element of complementarity would be defective.[44] Samson Raphael Hirsch, in his discussion of the essential character of man's "helpmate," argued most forcefully that the biblical passage implies the complete equality of the woman. "Even looked at quite superficially this designation expresses the whole dignity of Woman. It contains not the slightest reference to any sexual relationship, she is placed purely in the realm of Man's work, it was there that she was missing, she is to be *ezer kenegdo*. And *ezer kenegdo* certainly expresses no idea of subordination, but rather complete equality, and on a footing of equal independence. Woman stands to man *kenegdo*, parallel, on one line, at his side."[45]

It also seems clear that the general condition of unlimited individual freedom can last only as long as there are sufficient natural resources to satisfy everyone's total needs. However, once demand exceeds supply, abundance being replaced by scarcity, men will inevitably enter into competition with one another to satisfy their needs and wants, as long as each is absolutely free to pursue his interests as he pleases. As a result, the human condition must necessarily undergo a radical revision. Once man enters into association with others, it readily becomes evident that his personal freedom of action can no longer be considered absolute. The very notion of absolute individual liberty is essentially incompatible with the concept of human equality. Theoretically, as well practically, it is simply not possible for all the members of a society to be considered as equal to one another, and at the same time for each to act as if the others did not exist. If all are equally free to behave as they please, inevitably one will encroach on the interests of another, precipitating conflict. Moreover, the claim of a right to such encroachment on the basis of one's absolute freedom of action would entail a basic denial of the ultimate worth and comparable right of another human, thereby negating the principle of essential human equality.

R. Simeon b. Yohai expressed this concern in the following homily: "It is comparable to a group of men who found themselves seated in a boat. One of them took hold of an augur and began to bore a hole beneath him. His companions challenged him: What are you doing? He retorted: What concern is it of yours? Am I not doing it under my own seat?"[46] The message is clear. One may directly affect the lives of others in an unacceptable manner even through an indirect act.

One implication of this is that certain acts that a person might deem as entirely private may in fact be public acts. Moreover, the sages held that private transgressions may have public consequences, and therefore that "all Israelites are guarantors for one another."[47] In other words, the transgression of one person may impact on another, placing a degree of responsibility on the individual for the well-being of his fellow. This dictum is of wide-ranging import, demanding that the individual acknowledge that in his life and conduct he bears a responsibility not only for himself but also for the community and nation—and by extension, for the universe of which he is a part. In the rabbinic worldview, the actions of men and nations are ultimately measured on a divine balance scale, with merit and fault being assigned in accordance with the behavior of the majority. Because of this, if an individual "performs one good deed, happy is he for turning the scale both for himself and for the whole world on the side of merit; if he commits one transgression, woe to him for weighting himself and the whole world in the scale of guilt."[48] Moreover, the dictum that "all Israelites are guarantors for one another" also confirms the biblical principle that the community bears a share of the responsibility for the transgressions of the individual. This is particularly so in instances where, as the sages put it, "it was in their power to prevent it, and they did not prevent it."[49]

Scripture admonishes, "Thou shalt surely rebuke thy neighbor and not bear sin because of him" (Lev. 19:17). The implication, of course, is that failure to do so makes one, or perhaps the entire community, culpable. It was taught in the name of R. Hanina, "Jerusalem was destroyed only because they did not rebuke each other: for it is said, Her princes are become like harts that find no pasture [Lam. 1:6]. Just as the hart, the head of one is at the side of the other's tail, so Israel of that generation hid their faces in the earth, and did not rebuke each other."[50] In other words, a society in which the idea of corporate dependence is dormant is fundamentally dysfunctional and will ultimately prove unviable. The principle is clear; the question is how to apply it without creating conflict by intruding into the conduct of another's life and, worse, putting someone to shame. The dilemma is patent, and was so in antiquity.

R. Tarfon, who witnessed the destruction of Jerusalem, is reported to have said, "I wonder whether there is any one in this generation who accepts reproof." R. Eleazar b. Azariah, who lived shortly thereafter, replied, "I wonder if there is one in this generation who knows how to reprove."[51]

Indeed, the question of how far one should go in reproving another was a matter of contention among the sages. "R. Eliezer said: Until he [the reprover] be beaten. R. Joshua said: Until he be cursed. Ben Azzai said: Until he be rebuked."[52] Referring to the biblical demand, Maimonides wrote, "By this injunction we are commanded to rebuke one who is sinning or is disposed to sin, to forbid him to act so and to reprove him. A man may not say: 'I am not going to sin; and if another sins, that is a matter between him and God.' Such an attitude is repugnant to the Torah. We are commanded not to sin and not to permit any of our nation to sin. If one chooses to sin, it is every man's duty to reprove him and to prevent him, even though there be no supporting evidence of his liability to punishment."[53] However, the injunction was not held to apply when it became apparent that the person being reproved was not prepared to listen and that his continual harassment would prove counterproductive.[54]

The application of the principle of corporate dependence is clear, particularly if one's transgression is likely to lead another to do likewise. However, this principle is held to apply even where the possibility of emulation is not at issue. A case in point is that of suicide, which is strongly condemned by the halakhah as an act of murder, for which God will hold the perpetrator accountable.[55] As argued by Lauterbach, the extraordinary significance attached to human life by the halakhah is predicated on two interdependent principles. The first is that the essential purpose of the Torah is "the furtherance of the cause of humanity"; the second is that every human being is capable of contributing to that cause and thereby working toward the realization of the divine purpose. "Since potential usefulness for the cause of humanity determines the value of life, it follows that the imperative duty of preserving human life applies to all without distinction." A person therefore has the same responsibility for the preservation of his own life and health as he does for another's. Accordingly, "A man has no right to dispose of his life without consideration of his fellow-man. For he does not belong to himself alone. He belongs to humanity at large in whose cause he is to work. . . . He has, therefore, no right to withdraw from his post of duty and deprive humanity of his service." Even if one considers himself to be a burden on society, he may still be able to contribute something and has no right to deprive society of this benefit, no matter how small it might be.[56]

This same responsibility of the individual to be concerned about the public consequences of his private behavior is extended by the halakhah to the use and disposition of one's personal property. The owner of private property is presumed to have inherent rights therein, but these do not extend to its wanton destruction. In the Judaic view, man is merely the guardian of his economic assets and as such is obligated to guard and not destroy them, since others may be able to benefit from them. This notion is encapsulated in the halakhic principle of *bal tashkhit*, which denies a person the freedom to vandalize or destroy his own property, let alone that of another. The sages considered a person who acts in this way as one who is on the slippery slope to spiritual self-destruction, perpetrating rebellion against God, who entrusted him with the assets he has in his care. R. Simeon b. Eleazar taught, "He who rends his garments in anger, he who breaks his vessels in anger, and he who scatters his money in anger, regard him as an idolater, because such are the wiles of the Tempter: Today he says to him, 'Do this'; tomorrow he tells him, 'Do that,' until he bids him, 'Go and serve idols,' and he goes and serves them."[57]

The sages even extended this principle to the giving of charity. "If a man desires to spend liberally he should not spend more than a fifth, [since by spending more] he might himself come to be in need [of the help] of people."[58] That is, although there is great merit in being charitable to those in need, there is no merit in impoverishing oneself and thereby become a burden on the public. Thus, although one has the right to dispose of his property as one sees fit, the exercise of that right should not result in immediate or potential harm to others.

Under the conditions of even the most rudimentary society, it becomes readily apparent that man's individual freedom of action can no longer be absolute, if the society is to remain stable. The assertion of a claim by one to a right to uninhibited freedom of action entails a simultaneous implicit denial of the identical right to all others, thereby negating the principle of essential human equality.

Within the context of society, man is thus confronted by a fundamental conflict of values, absolute liberty versus intrinsic equality. Since these values, each held to be absolutely inviolate, are essentially irreconcilable, a principled compromise must be reached if the society is to remain viable. One approach to such a compromise is to establish a balance between the conflicting principles, a balance that is clearly tilted in favor of sustaining the concept of the intrinsic equality of men at the expense of absolute freedom of action. This seems eminently reasonable, since it is the latter, rather than equality as such, that leads to social strife. Accordingly, it becomes necessary to impose certain constraints on the liberty of the individual. The principle of human freedom is thus effectively reformulated in negative terms. That is, within certain specified limits the individual is to be left at liberty to act as he wishes, without regard to the effects of his actions on others. Beyond these bounds, however, he is enjoined from such acts that are likely to have detrimental effects on others.

THE INDIVIDUAL AND PROPERTY RIGHTS

The issue is compounded when one considers the relationship between an individual and the community of which he is a part. In the Judaic system the community—at the national, local, and communal levels—has certain residual rights to the property, both real and mobile, of the individual, and it may exercise those rights when appropriate and necessary in the public interest. One of the more complex problems that the halakhah addresses in this regard is the clash of interests between individual industrial and commercial developers and the host community. At issue is the cost versus benefit to the community as a whole, with benefits to individuals being only a secondary consideration.

Exemplifying an early approach to ecological planning, halakhah may require an entrepreneur to establish or relocate his establishment in order to limit the environmental impact on the community. Thus the sages stipulated that because of the chaff that pollutes the air, "a permanent threshing-floor may not be made within fifty cubits from the city." Similarly, because of the stench, "carcasses, graves, and tanneries may not remain within a space of fifty cubits from the town." Moreover, because of the prevailing winds, "a tannery may be set up only on the eastern side of the town."[59] Moreover, if the residents of a community give their tacit or even explicit consent to the establishment of an environmentally unsound installation, halakhic authorities permitted those affected to demand that the installation be removed at a later date; this was held to apply even where the original permission was granted by formal agreement.[60] An example of this is the ruling rendered by a halakhic decisor in sixteenth-century Italy. The case brought to him concerned a group of butchers who had purchased the right from their neighborhood to establish an abattoir there. However, once the facility went into operation, the people of the neighborhood found the odors it emitted unacceptable. The decisor wrote as follows:

At the outset it would seem that because they have purchased this right from the neighbors, the neighbors have given their consent to its construction and may not be allowed to retract their consent. However, we see that all the authorities argue that, with regard to damages of smoke and bad odors, a man is not really able to bear them, and therefore we may suppose that even if one agreed at the beginning we may not see this as forgoing their rights in the future. They agreed at the outset, since they thought they would be able to live with the damage. However, now, when they see and smell it in practice, they see that they cannot do so. Even if, as in our case, they actually sold this right, they may retract their consent, and therefore the abattoirs have to be closed.[61]

The cost-versus-benefit approach of the halakhic authorities led them to conclude that in cases where the trade-off was between economic and environmental damage to the community, concern about economic loss would not be permitted to take precedence over concern for the health and safety of the people. However, for this principle to apply, the environmental damage actually had to cause bodily harm, as opposed to inconvenience or unpleasantness. Where this was not the case and it was impractical to move the offending facility to another site, the economic well-being of the community was given precedence. As one decisor put it, "This is an enlargement of the principle that where a person is doing work that is essential to his livelihood and that it is not possible to do elsewhere, the neighbors do not have the right to prevent it."[62]

Moreover, since the fundamental value that is to be sustained intact is the intrinsic equality of all members of human society, this principle must also be applied to the individual's negatively defined freedom of action. In other words, a properly constituted society is to be characterized by an equality of "negative liberty" among its members. That is, the limits on individual freedom of action are to be the same for all persons within the society, irrespective of the differences in natural endowments that may exist among them.

The principle of equality of negative liberty was set forth as a principle of proper human conduct in antiquity. It is to be found in the ethical teachings of Confucius, Isocrates, and in the Indian classic the *Mahabharata*, and it was reflected in early pharisaic times in the apocryphal teaching, "Do that to no man which thou hatest."[63] It was subsequently given expression by the sage Hillel in the form of an epigram that has become a classic expression of Judaic ethics: when asked to summarize the central teachings of the Torah in a very concise statement, Hillel responded, "What is hateful to yourself, do not do unto your fellow man. That is the whole of the Torah, and the remainder is only commentary. Go and learn it!"[64]

There is evidently more here than meets the eye. Hillel's purpose was not merely moral exhortation to desirable conduct. The question with which he was concerned was how to operationalize the principle of equality of negative liberty as an effective guide to human action. Given the natural and substantial differences of character and temperament among people, it seems quite evident that the threshold of acceptability of particular actions by other persons is likely to vary widely in accordance with individual idiosyncrasies. Without externally established behavioral parameters, such variations in acceptable conduct would effectively nullify the possibility of establishing meaningful society-wide norms, thereby placing the practical application of the principle in jeopardy. Accordingly, Hillel proceeded to indicate that while the principle of equality of negative liberty, as reflected in his formulation, was indeed the central teaching of the Torah, it was not self-implementing. The formula itself provided no guidance as to how to apply it in practice. This, he asserted, was to be gleaned from the teachings of the Torah that constituted, in effect, a commentary on the central principle. That is, it is only in the teachings of the Torah that one will discover the parameters of desirable—or at the very least, acceptable—conduct that are to be used as guidelines in the practical application of the fundamental principle of equal negative liberty. He therefore concluded his dictum with the exhortation, "Go and learn it!"

The application of the principle may perhaps best be illustrated by the rabbinic treatment of the biblical injunction "Thou shalt not remove thy neighbor's landmark" (Deut. 19:14). This is understood by Maimonides and others to mean that "we are forbidden to alter land boundaries fraudulently, that is, to shift landmarks between ourselves and our neighbors, so as to be able to claim another's land as our own."[65] In his codification of the law, Maimonides condemned the practice unequivocally. "If one moves his neighbor's boundary mark and brings some of his neighbor's land inside his own border, even if this be only a finger's breadth, he is deemed a robber if he does so by force and a thief if he moves it secretly."[66] This specific biblical injunction subsequently became the prooftext for a general prohibition of encroachment upon the rights of another. Thus, in one talmudic source, the injunction is extrapolated to include a prohibition against planting so close to a neighbor's property line that the roots of one's crop necessarily draw sustenance from the neighbor's land, thereby impoverishing it without the owner's consent.[67] By extension, this has been taken to apply to encroachment on another's livelihood as well. However, it was not applied in such a manner as to eliminate economic competition—that is, the restriction on economic competition applied primarily to instances where encroachment involved the complete destruction of another's business, not where only the margin of profitability was at issue. Even in the case of destructive competition, the limitations imposed were usually for a limited time only, to allow for a readjustment of the market.[68]

The principle also was extended to include intangible property, in addition to material property. Thus the sages considered the principle of "encroachment" to prohibit the misattribution of ideas and opinions and to require proper acknowledgment of sources.[69] After the introduction of printing, issues regarding copyright soon came under its sway. The medieval codifier of Jewish law Jacob ben Asher further extended the principle to give customary practices the force of law. That is, he saw it incumbent upon the individual not to encroach on another's property, as such might be defined by local custom; he argued on the basis of the qualifying clause of the biblical precept, "Thou shalt not remove thy neighbor's landmark, which they of old time have set."[70]

THE QUESTION OF CIVIL DISOBEDIENCE

One of the knotty problems faced in a just society is whether an individual has the moral right to disobey lawful authorities as a matter of conscience, and how the society should deal with such a challenge. Judaic tradition accords great authority to legitimate governance. R. Simeon stated, "Whoever rebels against the [legitimate] king is subject to the death penalty."[71] Maimonides extends the obligation for political obedience to the extent that virtually any infraction of the legitimate ruler's command is subject to extreme sanction. Thus, if the king ordered an individual to go to a certain place and that person did not comply, or not to leave his house and he did anyway, the violator could be subject to capital punishment.[72] This sweeping authority originally assigned to the monarchy is deemed to have devolved to communal authorities at the national or local level, where decisions are reached on a majoritarian basis.

However, the opinions and legislative actions of the majority may not always be consistent with the general principles of justice and equity advocated by the Torah. What avenues of redress are open to those who assert that the legitimate authorities have acted improperly? Is the citizen bound by the will of the majority regardless of his own sense of what justice requires? The dilemma, as Basil Herring points out, is this: "When the Halakhah gave sweeping powers to the king and other forms of properly constituted government, Jewish or otherwise, it did not empower the citizen to surrender the use of his moral conscience. He remains responsible for his actions at all times, unless physically coerced to act against his will."[73] Indeed, the sages stipulated circumstances under which one had the moral obligation to suffer martyrdom rather than follow the demands of the authorities blindly. It was taught that "By a majority vote, it was resolved . . . that in every [other] law of the Torah, if a man is commanded: 'Transgress and suffer not death' he may transgress and not suffer death, excepting idolatry, incest [which includes adultery], and murder." With regard to the latter, the Talmud reports that a person came to the sage Rabbah and told him to go and kill so and so, and that if he refused he himself would be slain. The sage responded, "Let him rather slay you than that you should commit murder; who knows that your blood is redder? Perhaps his blood is redder." [74]

The problem is illustrated in the biblical story of King David and his general Joab, who unhesitatingly contrived to bring about the death of Uriah at the king's instruction, David having become enamored of Uriah's wife (2 Sam. 11:14–16). There was no issue of national security here; it was clearly a morally indefensible act on the part of the king, but Joab suspended his own moral judgment and simply carried out the king's orders. Contrast this with the biblical story of King Saul, who saw David as a threat to his reign and sought retribution against those who aided him, directly or indirectly. "And the king said unto the guard that stood about him: 'Turn, and slay the priests of the Lord; because their hand is also with David, and they knew that he fled, and did not disclose it to me.' But the servants of the king would not put forth their hand to fall upon the priests of the Lord" (1 Sam. 22:17). In this case, the soldiers defied the orders of the king and would not carry out what they perceived to be an arbitrary and improper command.

The sages dealt with the basic issue of disobedience to the orders of one's superior by considering it from the aspect of the halakhah governing the principle of "agency," particularly with respect to an agent commissioned to perform an improper act. The general principle of agency asserts that an one acting on behalf of another has no independent status; the consequences of his actions relate back to the person who commissioned him. However, in the view of the halakhah, the principle is modified when what the agent is commissioned to do is in itself illegal or improper. The principle established in the Talmud is that there is no agency for wrongdoing; if an agent is commissioned to do something improper and does it, he is to be held liable and not the person who commissioned him. The rationale for this is, "When the words of the master and the words of the pupil conflict, whose are obeyed?"[75] That is, when God requires one thing and the person who commissions the agent requires something else, one must give preference to the divine command. Accordingly, the majority position in the halakhah is that there is no agency to do wrong, that the agent therefore must bear the full responsibility for his acts.[76]

Given this principle, it becomes evident that the halakhah requires that one disobey improper orders regardless of who issues them, a principle finally adopted as universally normative at the Nuremberg trials following World War II. Milton Konvitz writes, regarding

the distinctly halakhic approach to the problem of conscience versus law that is an expression of the genius of classical, normative Judaism. The legal order provides a constitutional or higher law by which a man is commanded to disobey certain orders, even when they are made by the king or other high officers of the state. Halakhic normative Judaism thus speaks not of a right but of a duty, a legal duty of civil disobedience. Thus, while it recognizes conscience, or "the fear of God," or the laws written on the tablets of the heart, it converts morality into law by demanding that given proper circumstances, the higher law become the living law—a living law that contradicts, and even nullifies, the enacted law—or what wrongly pretends to be the law.[77]

This approach to the issue of civil disobedience serves as a caution to governmental officials to exercise their authority carefully and with appropriate deliberation and concern for implications in light of the higher law.

NOTES

1. Seymour Tobias Lachs, *Humanism in Talmud and Midrash*, p. 67.
2. *Avot* 2:5.
3. Lachs, *Humanism in Talmud and Midrash*, p. 68.
4. Rashi, *Perushei Rashi al haTorah* on Gen. 1:27.
5. *M. Sanhedrin* 4:5.
6. *Pesikta de-Rab Kahana*, Piska 12, p. 249.
7. Samuel Belkin, *Essays in Traditional Jewish Thought*, p. 93.
8. Simha Cohen, "Adam-Olam-Hevrah," in *El haMekorot*, vol. 3, p. 167.
9. *Baba Metzia* 62a.
10. *Berakhot*, 58a; *Sanhedrin* 72a. The principle is derived from exegesis of the biblical text, "If a thief be found breaking in, and be smitten so that he dieth, there shall be no bloodguiltiness for him" (Exod. 22:1). One may kill a thief who breaks

into his home, on the supposition that if the thief were exposed he would likely kill the proprietor in order to escape.

11. For an extensive discussion of the question of self-sacrifice to save others, and its treatment in rabbinic literature, see Shilo Rafel, "Mesirat haYahid leHatzalat haRabbim," and Nahum Rakover, "Yahid Mul Rabbim beHatzalat Nefashot," in *Torah Shebe'al Peh*, ed. Yitzhak Rafel.

12. David Novak, *Law and Theology in Judaism*, pp. 132–133.

13. Abraham Hen, *BeMalkhut haYahadut*, vol. 1, pp. 101–102.

14. Eugene Korn, "Tradition Meets Modernity: On the Conflict of Halakha and Political Liberty," *Tradition*, vol. 25, no. 4 (Summer 1991), p. 43.

15. Israel Mattuck, *Jewish Ethics*, p. 86.

16. It may be argued that this approach is contradicted by the biblical passage, "Send your bread forth upon the waters; for after many days you will find it. Distribute portions to seven or even to eight, for you cannot know what misfortune may occur on earth" (Eccles. 11:1). This has traditionally been understood as relating to the giving of charity and would therefore be seen as acknowledging self-interest, albeit not immediate, as an appropriate basis for philanthropy. However, this understanding of the text, although held by many traditional commentators, does not necessarily reflect its authentic meaning. Moreover, while this interpretation is cited by Rashi, he also provides alternative possible meanings. As Robert Gordis points out, "This reference to liberality is not in keeping with Koheleth's general outlook, nor is it relevant to the realistic tone of the section in which it occurs. Hence most modern commentators regard it as advice with regard to commerce: 'send your goods overseas,' where the profits are likely to be large, while the next verse urges diversifying one's undertakings to reduce the attendant risks. This is, by all odds, the most likely view of the passage" (*Koheleth: The Man and His World*, p. 320).

17. Emanuel Feldman, *On Judaism*, p. 244.

18. Ibid., p. 240.

19. *Baba Batra* 10a.

20. *Leviticus Rabbah* 34:8 (34:10 in some editions).

21. Milton R. Konvitz, "Man's Dignity in God's World," p. 27.

22. *Berakhot* 17a.

23. Joseph B. Soloveitchik, "The Lonely Man of Faith," *Tradition*, vol. 7, no. 2 (1965), pp. 13–14.

24. *Berakhot* 19b; *Menahot* 37b—38a. See also *Shabbat* 81b and 94b.

25. *Yevamot* 90b.

26. *Hagigah* 5a.

27. *Baba Batra* 9b.

28. *Mishnah Shekalim* 5:6.

29. Jacob Z. Lauterbach, *Rabbinic Essays*, p. 277.

30. *Baba Kamma* 79b; *Mekilta de-Rabbi Ishmael* (tractate *Nezikin* 12), vol. 3, p. 99. The Judaic penal code does not prescribe imprisonment for theft but the return of the article and payment of a fine equal to its value. In the case of sheep or cattle, the fine is multiplied, because both tend to graze far from home, making it easier to steal them. The increased penalties thus provide additional disincentives for the crime.

31. Maimonides, *Hilkhot Sanhedrin* 24:10.

32. Amnon Shapira, "Al 'Kavod haAdam' beMikra," *Beit Mikra*, no. 159, (January–March 1999), p. 129.

33. *Baba Metzia* 58b.

34. Ibid. 59a.

35. *Baba Kamma* 4b.

36. *M. Ketuvot* 3:4, 7; *M. Arakhin* 3:4.

37. Maimonides, *Hilkhot Hovel uMazik* 3.

38. *Kiddushin* 40b.

39. Maimonides, *Hilkhot Edut* 11:5.

40. *Pesahim* 113a.

41. Obadiah Sforno, *Biur al haTorah*, on Gen. 2:18.

42. Emanuel Rackman, *Modern Halakhah for Our Time*, p. 56.

43. *Berakhot* 58a. See also Maimonides, *The Guide of the Perplexed*, 1:72.

44. Sforno, *Biur al haTorah*, on Gen. 2:18.

45. Samson Raphael Hirsch, *The Pentateuch*, on Gen. 2:18.

46. *Leviticus Rabbah* 4:6.

47. *Sifra "Behukotai"* 7:5; *Shevuot* 39a.

48. *Kiddushin* 40b.

49. *Shevuot* 39a.

50. *Shabbat* 119b.

51. *Arakin* 16b.

52. Ibid.

53. Maimonides, *The Commandments, Positive Commandment* 205.

54. Aaron haLevi of Barcelona, *Sefer haHinukh* 218.

55. *Baba Kamma* 91b.

56. Lauterbach, *Rabbinic Essays*, pp. 274–275.

57. *Shabbat* 105b.

58. *Ketuvot* 50a.

59. *M. Baba Batra* 2:8–9.

60. Joseph Caro, however, would limit the ability to rescind such an agreement only if it were not formalized in an agreement whereby the neighbors received compensation for the anticipated environmental damage (*Shulhan Arukh: Hoshen Mishpat* 155:36).

61. Cited by Meir Tamari, *"With All Your Possessions,"* p. 291.

62. Ibid., p. 295.

63. *Tobit* 4:15.

64. *Shabbat* 31a.

65. Maimonides, *The Commandments*, part 2, 246. See also Aaron haLevi of Barcelona, *Sefer haHinukh* 525.

66. Maimonides, *Hilkhot Geneivah* 7:11. Translation used here is by Hyman Klein, *The Code of Maimonides: The Book of Torts*, p. 81. See also Joseph Caro, *Shulkhan Arukh: Hoshen Mishpat* 376.

67. *Shabbat* 85a.

68. See Tamari, *"With All Your Possessions,"* p. 108.

69. *Sifre on Deuteronomy*, Piska 188.

70. Jacob ben Asher, *Tur Hoshen Mishpat* 368.

71. *Tosefta Teruomot* 7:20.

72. Maimonides, *Hilkhot Melakhim* 3:8.

73. Basil F. Herring, *Jewish Ethics and Halakhah for Our Time*, p. 145.

74. *Sanhedrin* 74a.

75. *Kiddushin* 42b.

76. A minority view holds that the procurer of his services shares the culpability.

77. Konvitz, "Conscience and Civil Disobedience in the Jewish Tradition," pp. 175–176.

Chapter 6

Social Justice

The issue of justice was always a matter of prime concern to the prophets and sages of Israel, who considered it a critical factor in assuring the viability of the good society. "Justice, justice shalt thou follow, that thou mayest live, and inherit the land which the Lord thy God giveth thee" (Deut. 16:20). That is, the active pursuit of justice is a condition for Israel's continuing existence as a nation. However, it must be noted, as pointed out by Joseph H. Hertz, "that the idea of justice in Hebrew thought stands for something quite other than in Greek. In Plato's Republic, for example, it implies a harmonious arrangement of society . . . so that those who perform humble functions shall be content to perform them in due subservience to their superiors. It stresses the inequalities of human nature; whereas in the Hebrew conception of justice, the equality is stressed[.] . . . [W]hereas in Greek the idea of justice was akin to harmony, in Hebrew it is akin to holiness."[1]

The Judaic concept of justice as holiness is perhaps nowhere better articulated than in the assertion of the prophet, "But the Lord of hosts is exalted through justice [*mishpat*], and God the Holy One is sanctified through righteousness [*tzedakah*]" (Isa. 5:16). At the same time, the abiding Judaic concern for social justice in practice is reflected in the psalmist's aspirations for the just ruler: "That he may judge Thy people with righteousness [*tzedek*], and Thy poor with justice [*mishpat*]" (Ps. 72:2). It is noteworthy, as pointed out by Bible scholar Artur Weiser, that the righteousness demanded of the ruler "is ultimately not a relative human requirement of 'humanitarianism,' but a divine, and for that reason absolute, requirement of a religiously binding character. For behind the reign of the earthly king is God's rule as

King; the righteousness of the king is a function and the mirror-image of the righteousness of God which he has promised to his people in their need for protection."[2]

The key Hebrew terms *tzedek* and *mishpat* in these biblical texts, particularly in translation, are somewhat ambiguous and require further explication to decipher the authors' intent.[3] Samson R. Hirsch wrote in this regard, "'*Tzedek*,' 'right,' 'justice' is the firm, incorruptible right as proclaimed by God in His Law. '*Mishpat*' is the lawful order deriving therefrom. These two concepts constitute the prime indispensable basis for the state founded upon Divine Law."[4] In another place, Hirsch wrote, "*Mishpatim*, therefore, are God's pronouncements concerning those things which each man has a right—merely because God has created him a man—to demand of you, that is, to which he has a claim because he is a man. Hence every infringement of a *mishpat* is a sin not only against man but, for this very reason, also a sin against God; for you mock God by denying to a man that which God has allotted to him."[5]

Meir L. Malbim further defined these key terms. *Mishpat*, he wrote, is judgment rendered "in accordance with established norms." *Tzedek*, on the other hand, is judgment rendered "in accordance with the specific case, which may justify deviation from *mishpat*, going beyond the letter of the law in accordance with time, place, issue, and the person being judged." Accordingly, Malbim understands the psalmist as advocating that the proper ruler judge the people with *tzedek*, or righteousness, and, when circumstances dictate, that he place the needs of justice above the law. He offers as an example a situation in which a wealthy person has a legally effective case against a poor person but in which common sense indicates that an injustice will occur if the legal judgment is carried out. In such a case, the wealthy person should be compelled to act in accordance with the ethical principle that gives justice precedence over legality.[6] Thus, as Alexander Guttmann points out, "The quest for equity, the concept of resorting to general principles of fairness and justice when existing laws prove inadequate, has been present in Jewish law from biblical times to date."[7] Indeed, Malbim maintains that Judaism places a heavy moral burden on jurists not only to ensure the legality of judicial proceedings but also to ensure that substantive justice is rendered. "It is insufficient that one should adjudicate only according to the rules of law. He should see to it that his judgment be truly just, and if it appears to him that the law is deceptive [from the standpoint of justice,] he should not pronounce sentence based on it."[8]

As Hirsch put it, social justice requires that "everyone must know the limits of the legal claims which he may justly entertain against his fellow-man, and what claims of such nature his brother may properly hold against him. He must never exceed the former, and he must be willing to do justice to the latter at any time without first being reminded of his duty to do so. It shall be the prime concern of the king to spread recognition and respect for justice among the people."[9] In effect, justice rather than order takes precedence as the justification of the state; it becomes a primary obligation of government to ensure that justice prevails, not only in the operation of the judicial system but within the society itself. This notion is reflected most clearly in the prayer of King Solomon, "Give Thy servant therefore an understanding heart to judge Thy people, that I may discern between good and evil" (1 Kings 3:9).

It is, however, a notion alien to the political culture of much of the world. For example, to adherents of the Confucian theory of society, order takes precedence over justice. Recounting how this priority was reflected in the traditional political culture of Korea, one authority on the subject writes that Koreans of the Yi dynasty always considered the essence of a civilized life to be harmony and peace. Litigation and lawsuits meant that there was discord that required the intervention the state, something that signified political failure. Had the ruler been truly virtuous, social harmony would have prevailed and there would not have been a dispute in the first place. Accordingly, "When the ruler is truly virtuous and benevolent, he need not be a good judge. It is only if he fails in his virtue and is not able to permeate the entire society with harmony that a dispute arises, necessitating his judicial function. A reputation as a good judge therefore represents his failure as a truly effective and virtuous ruler. . . . The executive or the administrative function of government therefore was primary and the judicial was secondary." The writer then goes on to contrast this approach with that of Judaism.

If one remembers that the most virtuous and effective ruler in the eyes of the Jewish people was a king who possessed wisdom and the ability to judge his people and discern between good and bad (I Kings 3: 9), one cannot but be struck by the enormity of cleavage between the Jewish and Korean traditions. The Hebrew people even conceived of their God as a judge. They considered the judicial function to be a chief attribute of a political ruler. If we keep this fact in mind, it is not very difficult for us to see why a phrase such as "the supremacy of law" is easily accepted by Western people.[10]

It is also noteworthy that there is a school of thought in Judaism that attributes ultimate importance and value to the idea of social harmony; that school effectively defines justice as love. As Will Herberg put it, "The ultimate criterion of justice, as of everything else in human life, is the divine imperative—the law of love."[11] The sources for this perspective are the biblical imperatives, "And thou shalt love the Lord thy God with all thy heart, and with all thy soul, and with all thy might" (Deut. 6:5), and, "Thou shalt love thy neighbor as thyself" (Lev. 19:18). These imperatives were to form the basis for the ideal society envisioned by the Torah. Accordingly, Herberg writes, "The ethic of Judaism finds its source and power in the perfect love of God; therefore it is an ethic of total social responsibility." This is because man is ultimately responsible for his actions before God. "The law of love—as embodied, however, inadequately, in norms of justice—is ultimately the law of all social existence."[12] Justice, in effect, "is the institutionalization of love in society[;] . . . it is because love fails that justice is instituted among men. For without some structure of justice, the failure of love in social life would leave every man exposed to the unrestrained aggressions of every other and thus reduce society to chaos. In this sense, justice is indeed, as it is declared in tradition, the foundation of every social order, one of the pillars of the universe."[13]

Others, however, suggest that the biblical imperative to love one's neighbor, although vital to conditioning our sensitivity to the needs of our fellowman, is not an adequate basis for a just social policy, because its operative principle is the notion of self-sufficiency. In other words, if one has a low estimate of his own needs, he may assign the same estimate to the needs of others, an approach that does not necessarily lead to social justice. As the sage Ben Azzai put it, "You must not say, because I have been put to shame, let my neighbor also be put to shame."[14] This concern appears to be the issue behind the curious disagreement between Ben Azzai and R. Akiba that is recorded in the Talmud, and to which we referred in chapter 2.[15] "R. Akiba said: '"Love thy neighbor as thyself" is a great principle of the Torah.' Ben Azai said: 'An even greater principle is expressed in the verse "This is the book of the generations of Adam. In the day that God created man, in the likeness of God made He him" [Gen. 5:1].' "[16] The reason why Ben Azzai takes this position, according to Aaron Levine, is that "If man is created in the image of God, then only God's Torah, the source of moral truth, can determine for us what constitutes duty and virtue in interpersonal relations. Since we cannot rely on our own instincts to tell us what duty and virtue are in interpersonal relations, the 'love your neighbor as yourself' principle is not a self-sufficient social welfare philosophy."[17] Accordingly, a Judaic social welfare policy must be predicated on the specific halakhic guidelines and operative principles discussed below.

Byron Sherwin addresses this point from a different but instructive perspective, observing that the terms "charity" and "philanthropy," terms that are commonly employed to characterize aid to the indigent, really do not fit well with the Judaic concept of *tzedakah*. "Charity" derives from a Latin root that refers to love *(caritas)*, and "philanthropy" derives from a Greek word that refers to the love of other people. These terms suggest that we should help those in need because of our love for them. However, the harsh reality is that "the poor, the indigent, the insane, and the critically ill do not usually evoke our benevolence, our love, unless we are those rare saints that populate the world from time to time." As a result, aid to the needy based on love is too unreliable to help ensure their welfare. "The needs of the indigent are too constant and numerous, and their conditions often too precarious to rely upon the spontaneous altruism of the potential donor." For this reason,

Judaic ethics prefer to place aid to the indigent on the basis of social obligation. "For Jewish ethics, *zedakah* rather than 'charity' is required. *Zedakah* is etymologically related to the Hebrew word for 'righteousness,' *'zedek.'* In this view, one regularly helps the needy because it is right. *Zedakah* is a regular and continuous social obligation, and not the result of a passing passion."[18]

It should be clearly understood that the Judaic focus on *tzedakah* as a social and political obligation does not in any way denigrate charity or philanthropy, which are deemed to have even higher moral value as "acts of loving kindness" (*gemilut hasadim*). Indeed, the early sage Simeon ben Shetah declared *gemilut hasadim* to be one of the three pillars undergirding a truly human existence.[19] Such acts of benevolence, however, cannot be mandated and therefore cannot serve as the primary basis for assuring the well-being of the needy or otherwise disadvantaged in the properly ordered Judaic political society.

In Judaic tradition, Sodom, the city-state destroyed by God, typifies the irresponsible and therefore dysfunctional state. What was so wrong with Sodom that it merited annihilation by the hand of God? According to the prophet Ezekiel, God stated, "Behold, this was the iniquity of thy sister Sodom: pride, fullness of bread, and careless ease was in her and in her daughters; neither did she strengthen the hand of the poor and needy" (Ezek. 16:49). Sodom was dysfunctional because in addition to its immorality, it failed in its responsibility to deal with the essential needs of its people.

Reflecting an ethic of maximum social responsibility, the psalmist argues that the just ruler should demonstrate an overriding concern for the public welfare, with special attention to those at the bottom of the social ladder, who are least able to act effectively in their own interest. "May he judge the poor of the people, and save the children of the needy, and crush the oppressor. . . . For he will deliver the needy when he crieth; the poor also, and him that hath no helper. He will have pity on the poor and needy, and the souls of the needy he will save. He will redeem their soul from oppression and violence, and precious will be their blood in his sight" (Ps. 72:4, 12–14). Indeed, the ultimate disappearance of injustice and oppression is considered in rabbinic thought to be the goal of human history, and its realization as synonymous with the establishment of the divine kingdom on earth. This idea is clearly implicated in the prayer recited during the traditional New Year (Rosh Hashanah) service: "And therefore, the righteous shall see and be glad, the just exult, and the pious rejoice in song, while iniquity shall close its mouth and all wickedness shall vanish like smoke, when Thou removest the dominion of tyranny from the earth."[20]

In effect, it becomes the responsibility of the just ruler to prevent social and economic disparities among the people from disrupting the cohesiveness of the society. Israel Mattuck observed, "A society is just when it is informed by respect for the human rights of all its members. Therefore, the justice of a social order is tested and gauged by the provision it makes for its weakest members."[21] In other words, there is an implicit biblical concern with the consequences of wide social and economic inequality. This is clearly reflected in a series of biblically-imposed constraints on the behavior of the legitimate ruler, constraints that are designed in large part to ensure "that his heart be not lifted up above his brethren" (Deut. 17:20). This suggests further that the ruler and even the most downtrodden among the ruled are in some undefined sense equals and worthy of treatment as equals.

As discussed earlier, considered descriptively, men are held by Judaism to be universally equal, in the sense that they are all equally created in the image of God. This biblical concept clearly postulates a certain natural equality among all humans in this respect. However, this should not be construed as asserting that men are therefore intrinsically equal to one another in any other regard. Indeed, it is not entirely clear what the practical implications are of even the concept of an inherent natural equality among all human beings. Consider, for example, how the medieval commentator Solomon b. Isaac (Rashi) interprets the biblical verse, "And God said: Let us make man in our image, after our likeness" (Gen. 1:26). He understands the last clause of the citation to mean, "to comprehend and to discern."[22] This interpretation clearly does not reflect an egalitarian approach to expounding the intent of the passage. Suffice it to note that the attributes of comprehension and discernment are intellectual qualities, which most would admit are not distributed very equally among men.

The sages of the talmudic era were surely well aware of the inherent natural distinctions or inequalities that prevail among mankind. They taught, "If a man strikes many coins from one mold, they all resemble one another, but the supreme King of Kings, the Holy One, blessed be He, fashioned every man in the stamp of the first man, and yet not one of them resembles his fellow."[23] Given this perspective, it becomes rather unclear in what way men can be conceived as intrinsically equal to one another, if in fact they are not equal in fundamental human attributes. If such is the case, the presumed societal implications of the postulated intrinsic equality of men before God remain highly conjectural at best.

Moreover, as argued by Hirsch, the notion of the inherent equality of men is not at all applicable in the realm of economics. "The ideal of the equal distribution of wealth for all men is an unfortunate dream which is at variance with the natural state of the world's affairs and which, if it were to come true, would bring about the disintegration of human society.... For it would presuppose universal equality of intellectual ability, physical strength and potentialities, an equal number of members in every family, etc. Such a state of affairs would be contrary to the design of the Creator of Mankind."[24] This view is reaffirmed in contemporary times by a number of Judaic writers. Thus, Aaron Levine stresses that it is clear "that what Judaism calls for is responsibility to the poor, not income redistribution. It makes no judgment as to what constitutes equity in income distribution [, . . . although] many other factors work to enhance the economic well-being of the poor in the halakhic society."[25] In a similar vein, David Novak writes, "Society's distribution of the things necessary for the bodily needs of its members cannot be conducted on the basis of a strictly arithmetic equality and still be considered just by any rational criterion." Nonetheless, Novak argues, "The maldistribution of wealth—some getting too much and others too little—is considered to be an intolerable imbalance in the covenantal reality. It requires rectification."[26] The Judaic approach to achieving that rectification has some unique aspects.

Ideally, as asserted by Moses, "There shall be no needy among you . . . if only thou diligently hearken unto the voice of the Lord thy God, to observe to do all these commandment" (Deut. 15:4–5).[27] However, given man's inconstancy, it is more likely that "the needy shall never cease out of the land" (Deut. 15:11). The apparent contradiction between these almost adjacent passages may be resolved through a careful parsing of the earlier statement. As Israel H. Levinthal observed, the phrase "among you" may also be understood more literally as "in you." That is, there should not be "in you," or because of you, any reason for the poverty of others. "Even in the ideal state there will always be people who cannot work. But each man must see to it that no poverty should result because of his actions or his wrong or immoral economic way of life. When we are responsible for existing poverty, we are guilty of evil."[28] The Torah therefore sets forth a number of social laws designed to prevent the disparity between the "haves" and the "have nots" in society from reaching a point that will produce social instability—a problem that modern progressive societies have continued to deal with, and not very successfully.

One of the serious conceptual problems to be dealt with is the determination of what constitutes the desired characteristics of social justice. The latter, according to Daniel Nussbaum, "is conceived as that criterion which, when employed by a collectivity in its societal decision-making processes, propels the configuration of distribution in the direction of less inequality."[29] It seems quite evident that Judaism does not advocate a militant egalitarianism that would create virtual economic equality. As Sherwin puts it, "Jewish ethical teachings regarding social and economic welfare relate more to treating the dis-ease of the individual in need rather than trying to completely cure the economic or social afflictions of society as a whole."[30] Judaism's approach appears to comport better with a more moderate conception of social justice. Such a concept, Nussbaum writes, "when operative in social policy, translates all basic life-sustaining needs into human rights by providing all members of a community with resources sufficient to meet their needs. In this latter concept, distribution reduces inequalities only to the point of basic need satisfaction of all members of the community."[31] The question of just what constitutes a basic need begs a definitive answer, although, as will be seen, Judaic thinkers have always considered it to be at some point above mere subsistence.

Judaism has consistently refused to make a virtue of poverty, and for that reason among others it does not encourage asceticism. It does not accept the notion that voluntary poverty, ridding oneself of worldly goods, is the way to true piety. On the contrary, R. Eleazar b. Azariah taught that "if there is no meal there is no Torah."[32] Without the necessary material resources to satisfy his needs, man will not have the peace or presence of mind to devote himself to his spiritual well-being. Richard G. Hirsch wrote in this regard: "The common saying 'Poverty is no disgrace' may offer consolation—to those who are well off. As a statement of morality, an ethical imperative, it would have much to commend it—'Poverty should be no disgrace.' As a statement of fact, however, it is totally inaccurate. Poverty is a disgrace—for those who are poor. Poverty is destructive to the human personality."[33] Further, it should be borne in mind that the human personality being a reflection of the image of God, that which is destructive of it is an affront to God. Indeed, "Whoso mocketh the poor blasphemeth his Maker" (Prov. 17:5).

Poverty is considered to be an unmitigated disaster for a person. As the biblical sage put it, "The ruin of the poor is their poverty" (Prov. 10:15). The later sages taught, "Three things deprive a man of his senses and of a knowledge of his creator, and these are, idolaters, an evil spirit, and oppressive poverty."[34] Moreover, they pointed out, "Nothing is harder to bear than poverty; for he who is crushed by poverty is like one to whom all the troubles of the world cling and upon whom all the curses in Deuteronomy have descended. Our Teachers have said: If all the troubles were assembled on one side and poverty on the other, poverty would outweigh them all."[35] Poverty also causes a person to become insignificant in his own eyes, as well as an object of derision. Poverty leads to embarrassment and humiliation. "As soon as a man needs the support of his fellow creatures his face changes color."[36] Humiliation is the prelude to dehumanization, and Judaism, acknowledging the improbability of eliminating poverty entirely, demands that steps be taken to mitigate the severity of the problem. As Richard G. Hirsch put it, "To aid the poor is to 'rehumanize' children of God."[37]

With this purpose in mind, Judaism does not consider the right to private property absolute and inviolable, although it strongly affirms the principle. Indeed, no man is considered to have absolute control over what is conventionally considered to be his property. This view is a necessary corollary to the psalmist's assertion that "The earth is the Lord's and the fullness thereof" (Ps. 24:1). Herberg wrote in this regard, "The social attitude of Hebraic religion holds it to be the will of God that the resources of nature and the fruits of human creativity, which are a divine gift, should be used for the satisfaction of human needs and the enhancement of human welfare." Thus, while Judaism does not posit any preferred economic system, it does profess criteria for assessing the social adequacy and appropriateness of particular economic arrangements at a particular place and time. The ultimate criterion is the extent "to which humans are treated as ends in themselves, of equal worth and dignity as children of God and bearers of the divine image."[38]

In Judaism, human rights take precedence over property rights. The Mosaic Law thus imposes certain infringements on private property designed to reduce the gap between economic classes enough to make both extreme wealth and extreme poverty unlikely. One of these infringements is the law of the Sabbatical Year, which was introduced during the biblical period, perhaps primarily to attack the problem of gross economic inequalities within the context of the predominantly agricultural society of ancient Israel. Scripture specifies, "And six years thou shalt sow thy land, and gather the increase thereof; but in the seventh year thou shalt let it rest and lie fallow, that the poor of thy people may eat" (Exod. 23:10–11). This law quite clearly and explicitly impinges on one's rights to one's own property. Every seventh year, the produce of the land is denied to its owner and made available to the poor, who may help themselves to it without hindrance. In effect, the owner of the property temporarily loses some of his rights over the usufruct of the land.

The law of the Sabbatical Year was subsequently applied not only to agricultural products but also to matters of finance. In the agricultural society of ancient Israel, for which the biblical legislation was originally intended, every family had its own normally self-sufficient homestead; debts were contracted only in times of crop failure. Under such circumstances, loans to tide individuals over to the next season were considered acts of philanthropy rather than simple business transactions. Accordingly, "At the end of every seven years thou shalt make a release. And this is the manner of the release: every creditor shall release that which he hath lent unto his neighbor; he shall not exact it of his neighbor and his brother; because the Lord's release hath been proclaimed" (Deut. 15:1–2).

Abraham ibn Ezra suggested that the rationale behind the last clause of the biblical passage is that the required debt release is in deference to the honor of the Lord, who gave the creditor the money to lend in the first place.[39] Here again, the creditor effectively loses control of his assets through the mandatory cancellation of unpaid debts, an arrangement that gives the poor who needed to go into debt to survive an opportunity to start afresh every seventh year and thereby, ideally, work their way out of chronic poverty.

However, over time, there grew up in the economy of the society a commercial sector, in which loans were incurred as a normal part of business transactions; the biblical ordinance was increasingly seen as anachronistic in that sector. There was an understandable reluctance on the part of lenders to make loans the repayment of which would extend beyond the Sabbatical Year. To ease the burden on those who needed such loans for the viability of their enterprises, the sages adopted a legal fiction, the *prosbul*, designed for the purpose by Hillel at the beginning of the first century c.e. Because the requirement to cancel debts in the Sabbatical Year was addressed to the individual lender, the mechanism formally transferred the debt to the courts, which as collective bodies were not bound by the biblical injunction. They were therefore able to collect the debt on behalf of the lender, notwithstanding the biblical stricture. The *prosbul* stated, "I hand over [my notes] to you, So-and-so, the judges in such-and-such a place, so that I may be able to recover any money owing to me from So-and-so at any time I shall desire."[40] This effectively secured the loans and permitted normal financial transactions to take place, to the great benefit of those who needed to borrow funds for a period that extended beyond the Sabbatical Year. In this way, the rabbis employed rigorous textual analysis to interpret the biblical law in a manner that fulfilled its beneficent intent under circumstances not dealt with specifically in the biblical text.

There were also other approaches to rectifying the social balance, such as *tzedakah* and state welfare, which the Torah strongly encourages and which rabbinic thought and halakhah transformed into individual and communal obligations. It is noteworthy that, as Emanuel Rackman points out, "Judaism distinguishes between acts of charity and acts of benevolence and deems the latter far more significant. Charity involves parting with money; acts of benevolence require the commitment of one's person as well as one's purse."[41] The personal involvement of the individual in acts of benevolence gives it broader scope than charity. Charity can be given only to the poor, whereas benevolence can be extended even to the wealthy. Moreover, as the sages pointed out, charity can only be given to the living, whereas benevolence can be shown to the dead as well, by treating their wishes with respect and by according them burial with dignity. Rackman further suggests that the greatest contribution of Judaism to the concept of benevolence "is that it grafted the notion of justice on the concept of charity. In the Bible one invariably finds the two words 'charity and justice' as a compound phrase—both words almost always appear together."[42]

Philanthropy, in the Judaic perspective, is no longer merely an act of pure voluntarism; it is rather the fulfillment of a halakhic obligation to demonstrate empathy for the unfortunate. It is related in this regard that a Hasid once asked his master why God had to create both rich and poor people and then demand that the rich share their wealth with the poor—God surely could have distributed wealth in a manner that neither one would have to give nor the other to receive charity. The master's response was that if such had been the case, how would one have learned to care for his fellow and share in his sorrows? In effect, Judaism sets forth a moral basis for the authority of society to tax its members in order to provide for those who are unable to meet their own needs. As Meir Tamari puts it, "The Jewish concept that the market mechanism may, legally or morally, be distorted to assist the poor and weak at the expense of the property rights of the strong flows from this view of charity."[43]

Moreover, the impact of halakhic society's theocentricity may be clearly seen with regard to the problem faced in all societies where charity is entirely voluntary, namely, the inability to enforce promises. For example, under Anglo-American law it is extremely difficult to enforce payment of promises to charity, because of their unilateral nature. Because the promisee provides no consideration in return, the contractual character of the promise is moot. The situation is rather different under Jewish law. As pointed out by Rackman, "All such promises were deemed executed and not executory. They required no fulfillment because they were fulfilled as soon as they were uttered. Since God was the trustee of the poor, the promise was in effect to Him, and since His is the earth and all that is therein, He was in possession of the promisor's assets as soon as the promise was expressed." [44] The legal maxim upon which this rule is based is the dictum of the Mishnah, "Dedication to the Temple [i.e., to God] by word of mouth is equal to the act of delivery to a common person."[45] Indeed, if only it could be proved, the mere thought of a gift to the poor would also be enforceable, because God also knows the thoughts of man.[46]

The Judaic concept of *tzedakah* is perhaps unique in that it places the responsibility for taking the initiative in assisting those in need on the donor rather than the recipient. This notion is understood to be reflected in the biblical demand, "Thou shalt surely open thy hand unto thy poor and needy brother" (Deut. 15:11). As Immanuel Jakobovits noted, "In the imagery of the Torah it is not the poor man who stretches forth his hand begging for alms, but the donor who opens his hand so that the needy may help themselves."[47] This is made clear in the biblical adjuration, "And when ye reap the harvest of your land, thou shalt not wholly reap the corner of thy field, neither shall thou gather the gleaning of thy harvest. And thou shalt not glean thy vineyard, neither shalt thou gather the fallen fruit of thy vineyard; thou shalt leave them for the poor and for the stranger" (Lev. 19:9–10). Similarly, "When thou reapest thy harvest in thy field, and hast forgot a sheaf in the field, thou shalt not go back to fetch it; it shall be for the stranger, for the fatherless, and for the widow" (Deut. 24:19). In addition, a tithe, an obligatory tax of 10 percent, was imposed to provide support for the landless Levites, whose primary responsibilities lay in serving the needs of the Temple, and who were often destitute (Num. 18:21). Another provision in the Torah required the farmer to set aside a tenth of the produce of his fields every third year as a tithe to be consumed by "the stranger, the orphan, and the widow," in addition to the Levite (Deut. 14:28).

As suggested by Aaron haLevi of Barcelona, the biblical emphasis on the obligation of the donor rather than the recipient reflects the notion that the paramount objective of *tzedakah* is to instill in man the qualities of mercy and kindness. It wishes to ennoble the character of the donor, not simply alleviate the poverty of those in need.[48] Because striving toward this goal is required of all, rich and poor alike, the halakhah stipulates, as Joseph Caro states in his codification of the law, "Even a poor man who is supported by *tzedakah* is himself also obligated to give *tzedakah* out of what is given to him." Moreover, if he fails to donate the amount for which he has been assessed, the court may seize the unpaid balance from his assets to fulfill his communal responsibility.[49]

Isadore Twersky points out the interesting interplay between the responsibilities of the individual and the community in dealing with philanthropic needs.

A study of the laws of charity yields paradoxical conclusions. On the one hand, it seems that the central figure is the individual: to him are the [biblical] commandments addressed, he is enjoined to engage unstintingly in charity work, and assiduously to help his fellow man. . . . On the other hand, it is surprising to find that the Halakhah has assigned an indispensable, all-inclusive role to the community. The community acts not only as a supervisory, enforcing agency but occupies the center of the stage as an entity possessed of initiative and charged with responsibility. . . . Responsibility for the care of the needy—sick, poor, aged, disturbed—is communal. The individual makes his contribution to the community chest and with this he apparently discharges his obligations. He acts mechanically, almost anonymously, by responding to the peremptory demands of the collectors "who go about among the people every Friday soliciting from each whatever is assessed upon him."[50]

Tzedakah thus emerges as an individual obligation "which is fulfilled corporately. . . . The community does not step in and assume responsibility ex post facto, after individuals have shirked their duty or failed to manage matters properly. The community initially appears as a modified welfare city-state, with its special functionaries who collect the compulsory levy and act as trustees for the poor and needy."[51]

It is noteworthy that Judaism deals with the issues of public welfare both from an ideal as well as a reality-grounded perspective. The ideal is predicated on the biblical teaching, "If there be among you a needy man[,] . . . thou shalt not harden thy heart, nor shut thy hand from thy needy brother; but thou shalt surely lend him sufficient for his need in that which he wanteth" (Deut. 15:7–8). The critical question, which the sages attempted to answer in the most ideal fashion, is: how to define "sufficient for his need in that which he wanteth." The Talmud reports, "Our Rabbis taught: 'sufficient for his need' [implies that] you are commanded to maintain him, but you are not commanded to make him rich; 'in that which he wanteth' [might include] even a horse to ride upon and a slave to run before him."[52]

The presumption here is that "need" is subjective rather than objective and depends on the character of the deprivation one has experienced. The rich person who has fallen on hard times will have a different level of need than one who has long lived at the threshold of abject poverty, and each should ideally be treated accordingly. Thus, the sages taught that "if he had been accustomed to use vessels of gold, he is given vessels of silver; if of silver, he is given vessels of copper; if of copper, he is given vessels of glass."[53] That is, the community is not obligated to maintain a person's maximum prior lifestyle, but at the same time his personal level of need should not be ignored or denigrated. In his recapitulation of the halakhah, Maimonides affirms that if the person in need is used to riding on a horse (presumably this would translate into an automobile in contemporary times), the community is obligated to provide him with a comparable vehicle. As extreme as this halakhic approach may appear, the community should do this because it is biblically obligated to provide "sufficient for his need in that which he wanteth."[54] Thus far the ideal.

The rabbis, however, were also acutely aware of the prevailing human and economic realities, that welfare systems are subject to abuse, and that perhaps above all, the resources of the community are limited. They therefore sought, as a concession to practical reality, to establish guidelines with regard to what constituted basic necessities, who was to be eligible to receive them, and who was obligated to contribute to the community coffers. Maimonides defined the welfare system in all its aspects in his codification of the halakhah, in no less than 201 distinct provisions.

With regard to contributing to the welfare system, for example, the obligation fell on anyone who had resided in the community for thirty days, the obligation increasing in specific stages according to length of subsequent residence until it was equal to that of the regular members of the community. With regard to the recipients of welfare, the halakhah established specific, and rather stringent, criteria. For example, anyone who had sufficient food for two meals was precluded from receiving additional food from the *tamkhuy*, food set aside daily for those in extreme need. One who had sufficient food for fourteen meals was ineligible for funds from the community chest. Only a person with a net equity not exceeding a specified amount, not counting loans, could partake of the agricultural gifts discussed above. According to the Mishnah, the eligibility limit was two hundred *zuz* per person, which has been estimated to be approximately equivalent to 270 U.S. dollars (in 1996), the amount that presumably constituted the poverty line at the time.[55]

Maimonides went farther and drew a distinction between "idle" and "active" capital in determining the status of a welfare recipient. He ruled that fifty *zuz* actively invested in a business that produced income was roughly equivalent to the two hundred idle *zuz* that served to disqualify the holder from receiving welfare.[56] In other words, the halakhah established a comprehensive means test to determine eligibility for any of the various components of the welfare system.

It should be understood that in the traditional rabbinic view, the complex means tests are necessary to ensure societal equity. The individual and the community are obligated to provide basic necessities in goods and services to the needy, and the latter have the reciprocal obligation to demonstrate that they are entitled to them. It is worth emphasizing once again that from the Judaic perspective, the welfare system is not intended as a vehicle for the reallocation of wealth from the rich to the poor. Maimonides makes this clear in his assertion that it is not the obligation of the householder and the community to enrich the poor, only to give them the necessary support.[57] As Tamari observes, "It is owing to these guidelines and to the protection mechanisms that were put in place that living off charity and welfare never became a legitimate and acceptable way of living in Judaism, as has happened in many modern welfare systems—and which tends to expand such systems beyond the ability or willingness of the society to finance them."[58]

One additional aspect of the Judaic welfare system merits consideration here, namely, the responsibility for the redemption of captives, or *pidyon shevuyim*. The allocation of communal funds for the redemption of captives was held to take precedence over all other kinds of philanthropy, because the captive not only suffers all the hardships endured by the poor but also is under a continuing threat of bodily harm and even death. As Joseph Caro asserted in his law code, "Redemption of captives takes priority over support for the poor, and there is no greater precept than this. Accordingly, communal moneys raised for any other purpose may be diverted to the redemption of captives."[59] In the event that there are insufficient funds to pay all the demands for ransom, the halakhah stipulated detailed criteria, reflecting the value system of Judaism, according to which persons were to be redeemed in order of priority.[60]

Moreover, as a matter of practical policy, the halakhah set forth criteria for the amount of ransom to be paid. "Captives should not be ransomed for more than their value[,] as a precaution for the general good."[61] This restriction was held to apply to the community but not to individual families. Evidently reflecting a time when there was a vibrant international trade in slaves, the restriction recognized that excessive payments would only serve to encourage raiding and the taking of captives. It is noteworthy that the latter enterprise took on unprecedented dimensions throughout the world in the latter part of the twentieth century, leading to national policies of refusal to negotiate with terrorists and hijackers—policies that were often ignored in practice, effectively encouraging the continuation of such crime.

Maimonides extended application of this precept to the redemption of persons imprisoned because of indebtedness. Although deemed responsible for their situation, such persons were considered to be in danger and were therefore included in the category of *pidyon shevuyim*. However, certain constraints were imposed to prevent wanton abuse of the welfare system. The community was responsible for bailing such prisoners out twice, but no more, under normal circumstances. But, because of the importance attached to human life in Judaic thought, a prisoner whose life was believed to be in danger was to be redeemed as many times as necessary.[62]

Judaic teaching also emphasizes that because man, of necessity, lives within the framework of a society of his fellows, he must be concerned not only about the effects his actions may have on others; he must also be concerned with how he is affected by the acts of his fellows. Consequently, the idea of each individual's responsibility for his personal conduct is extended by the sages to the concept of the collective social and moral responsibility of each man for his fellow: "All of Israel are responsible for one another."[63] Thus, as Leo Jung pointed out, "Jewish Law demands as a minimum that we co-operate with our neighbor, that we help him in distress, that we prevent him from falling, that we work individually and collectively for the higher life: kindness, justice, and love. All this, however, Judaism demands not as an outcome of our generosity, but as the self-evident minimum of justice."[64]

It also seems clear that the biblical author believed strongly that the inequalities that would inevitably emerge among the people of Israel should do so from an equal economic-opportunity starting point, or at least as equal as possible given the natural differences and capabilities among people. Since ancient Israel was to be established on the basis of an agricultural economy, the Torah mandated that each of its citizens over the age of twenty should have an initial equal economic opportunity, through the equitable distribution of the land that was to become available. Thus after taking a census of the population over age twenty, according to the tribal structure of the nation (Num. 26:2), "the Lord spoke unto Moses, saying: Unto these the land shall be divided for an inheritance according to the number of names. To the more thou shalt give more inheritance, and to the fewer thou shalt give the less inheritance; to each one according to those that were numbered of it shall its inheritance be given" (Num. 26:52–54).[65] This would ensure that each mature member of the nation, to the extent practicable and consistent with the laws and customs of primogeniture, would have an equal initial opportunity for economic viability.

Recognizing that all parcels of land are not likely to be equally productive at all times, and that it might become necessary for some to sell land to meet the needs of their families, the Torah promulgated the unique institution of the "Jubilee": "And ye shall hallow the fiftieth year, and proclaim liberty throughout the land unto all the inhabitants thereof; it shall be a jubilee unto you; and ye shall return every man unto his possession, and ye shall return every man unto his family" (Lev. 25:10). This provided that any land sold had to be returned to the original owner in the fiftieth year of the national calendar, in effect to permit the equal opportunity process to begin anew. The institution was based on the biblical injunction, "And the land shall not be sold in perpetuity; for the land is Mine; for ye are strangers and settlers with Me" (Lev. 25:23–24). In other words, Scripture effectively distinguishes between ownership and possession of the land. That is, the people of Israel do not really own the land but merely enjoy divinely authorized possession of it. Such possession of the land does not entail the right to alienate it permanently; only God may do that. Accordingly, one who would purchase land from another must do so knowing that it will eventually have to be returned to the original possessor or his heir. In essence, what is being transferred temporarily through the sale is the usufruct of the land, not the land itself. Moreover, the Torah demands, "And in all the land of your possession ye shall grant a redemption for the land" (Lev. 25:24). That is, if the person who sold the land, presumably out of economic need, is subsequently able to redeem it before the onset of the Jubilee year, he is entitled to do so, and the current possessor is obligated to sell it back to him.

The institution of the Jubilee, if it was ever actually operational, has been defunct for millennia. This is primarily because the equal distribution of land upon which it was predicated required Israel's complete control of all the territory constituting the ancient land of Canaan, something that was realized only very briefly in the nation's troubled history. Nonetheless, the principle of equal economic opportunity that it sought to uphold remains valid to this day. It remains only to find appropriate ways of making the principle operative in a modern industrial or postindustrial environment.

PRESCRIPTIVE EQUALITY

The preceding discussion makes clear that there is an evident and significant disjunction in Judaic thought between the notions of "descriptive" and "prescriptive" equality. Considered from a descriptive standpoint, it is by no means self-evident that the concept of equality has deep roots in biblical and rabbinic literature. But, when we turn to the prescriptive conception of equality, we find a rather different situation. Judaism prescribes that all persons be treated as equals in certain respects regardless of whether they are equal in fact. As Sol Roth put it, "The imperative of equality . . . is rooted in a theoretical construction, a legal fiction, a declaration, independent of facts, that each person is to be regarded as if he were his equal. I must perceive and treat men as my equals whether they are equal to me or not." However, this Judaic concept of prescriptive equality is radically different in character from the descriptive equality that forms the basis of secular democratic political thought. Roth asserts, in effect, that Judaism is more concerned with quality than with equality.

Judaism affirms standards; it seeks excellence. It looks for the constant, uninterrupted spiritual growth of those who identify with it. It achieves this by recognizing differences and by the judgment that some are better than others, thereby motivating all to strive for the ideal. This approach differs radically from that adopted by advocates of equality in its American form who . . . push for the application of the principle of equality beyond the boundary even of its reasonable application. In America, this idea has come to mean that mankind must create the social conditions in which all men will achieve equality in fact, though this enterprise may well throttle the attainment of excellence.[66]

A rather different approach to the idea of equality is suggested by the Judaic notion of the "infinite worth" of the human personality, an idea introduced by Samuel Belkin as a critical element in the concept of democratic theocracy, discussed earlier. Roth, who notes that "Jewish tradition stresses not the equality of all human beings but rather the infinite value of the life of every human being, which is a more far-reaching concept," echoes this view.[67] This distinction between human equality and the infinite value of every human is highly significant in Judaic thought and requires closer examination.

Equality may be defined generally as a likeness in dimensions, values, attributes, qualities, or other characteristics. In a mathematical sense, equality may be understood as a one-to-one correspondence between two numbers or groups of numbers, each of which, in the aggregate, is identical or equivalent to the other. Applied within the context of a democratic political process, the vote of each eligible member of the society is equal in weight and value to every other comparable ballot. One consequence is that the votes of two people represent greater democratic value than the vote of a single person. Therefore, in a decision-making process governed by the democratic principle of majority rule, equal but conflicting votes cancel one another, effectively leaving the decision to be made in accordance with the number of the remaining uncontested ballots in favor of any particular choice.

The notion of infinite value, by contrast, implies a radically different conception of equality. The essence of this idea is perhaps best captured in the description of the mathematical concept of infinity offered by Bertrand Russell: "A collection of terms is infinite when it contains as parts other collections which have just as many terms as it has. If you can take away some of the terms of a collection, without diminishing the number of terms, then there are an infinite number of terms in the collection."[68] In other words, infinity is a unique condition of equality in which one part is equal not merely to another part but to the whole of which it itself is a part. Under this infinite-value conception of equality, the very notion of a majority vote would be quite devoid of meaning.

Roth argues that this unique conception of equality is inherent in the manner by which the halakhic system "defines the infinite value of every human being."[69] This principle of the infinite value attributed to each human life underlies and explains the following otherwise enigmatic rabbinic teaching: "For this reason was man created alone, to teach thee that whosoever destroys a single soul of Israel, Scripture imputes [guilt] to him as though he had destroyed a complete world; and whosoever preserves a single soul of Israel, Scripture ascribes [merit] to him as though he had preserved a complete world."[70] Abraham Hen insists that this is no mere rhetorical assertion but a precise statement of Judaism's values. He argues that when a person dies, all of existence perishes for him; it is all lost to him. All being becomes nothingness as far as he is concerned, and it makes no difference if the entire world should be transformed into a veritable Eden after his death.[71] That is, in terms of the value system of Judaism, where life itself is at stake, the part, the individual, is considered to be equal to the whole, the community.

This principle of infinite human value is given even more dramatic expression in another talmudic dictum: "If they say to you: Give us one of you that we may kill him, and if not we will kill all of you, they shall risk slaughter rather than hand over a single person."[72] When it comes to human life all men are considered intrinsically equal, and society, or the community, may not arrogate to itself priority of survival simply because it represents the collective interests of its members. The infinite value of the individual is considered equal to that of the whole of which he is part; the collectivity loses its corporate significance and is reckoned simply as an aggregation of individuals.

We can only speculate on how the moral dilemma implicit in this latter dictum might be resolved under the democratic principle of equality, but it seems reasonably certain that the resolution would be fundamentally different from that of the normative rabbinic teaching. An example of this may be seen in the argument made by the ethicist J. W. Hudson, who asserts the existence of a body of minimum rights in regard to which we all belong to one common and all-inclusive class. Nonetheless, he insists: "Yet even here equality is subject—if the means, such as food, are too limited to go around—to our ultimate criterion which assesses men according to their social value. If in an epidemic either the expert physician or the writer of this book must starve, the ideal answer, however tragic, is fairly clear."[73] The rabbis, however, categorically rejected this approach, insisting in effect that the democratic ideal of equality is unacceptable as the operative principle of society under the postulated circumstances. Instead, Judaism demands that the higher principle of infinite human value serve as the relevant norm.

In essence, we see here a fundamental difference of perspective. The position articulated by Hudson reflects the view that the significance of the individual is assessed in terms of his actual or potential value to society; that is, society takes precedence over the individual. In the Judaic perspective, the converse is held to be the case: every individual has the unqualified right to declare, "The world was created for me!"[74] Society is conceived as having been created solely for the purpose of enhancing the life of the individual, who alone has intrinsic value, as one created in the image of God.[75] Moreover, this applies equally to the gifted individual who is capable of rendering service to his fellow members of the society, and to the weak and incompetent whose existence brings no evident benefit whatever to the group. The inestimable value of the latter, just as of the former, is that they are human beings created in the image and likeness of God, and who for that reason have infinite worth.[76] In Judaic thought, the individual is conceived as a microcosm, a special and completely self-contained universe, that cannot be evaluated on the basis of its contribution to the well-being of others. The individual may not be sacrificed against his will for the good of the many.[77]

But, one may ask, given the centrality of the principle of infinite human value, how can the institution of slavery be condoned by the Torah, which sets forth a number of provisions regulating the practice? A rational answer to this question may reasonably be inferred from Maimonides' discussion of the institution of animal sacrifice, which is similarly regulated in great detail in the Torah but which, Maimonides argues, the Torah nonetheless actually opposes. He reasons that "a sudden transition from one opposite to another is impossible. And therefore man, according to his nature, is not capable of abandoning suddenly all to which he was accustomed." Thus, when the Torah tells us that "ye shall serve the Lord your God" (Exod. 23:25), it had to recognize that the common notion of what constituted appropriate worship of the divine at that time involved the offering of sacrifices. Accordingly, "His wisdom, may He be exalted, and His gracious ruse . . . did not require that He give us a Law prescribing the rejection, abandonment, and abolition of all these kinds of worship. For one could not then conceive the acceptance of [such a Law], considering the nature of man, which always likes that to which it is accustomed." Maimonides suggests that the problem that would have been encountered then is the same as that which we should encounter now if a prophet appeared and instructed us to cease all our current religious practices and to worship God through meditation alone. In effect, the regulations concerning the sacrificial rite were intentionally made exceedingly precise by the Torah and limited to the worship of God alone. Moreover, by limiting the actual performance of the rite to a designated priesthood, it progressively limited the involvement of the people, so that once the rite was brought to an end because of the destruction of the Temple, there was little interest in restoring it. "Through this divine ruse it came about that the memory of idolatry was effaced and that the grandest and true foundation of our belief—namely the existence and oneness of the deity—was firmly established, while at the same time the souls had no feeling of repugnance and were not repelled because of the abolition of modes of worship to which they were accustomed."[78]

The same reasoning would apply to the institution of slavery, which was pervasive in world of antiquity and, indeed, continues to exist to this very day in some societies.[79] One need but recall that slavery was abolished in the United States only 136 years ago. In principle, Judaism strongly disapproves of slavery in any form, first of all because it is viewed as an affront to the sovereignty of God—"For unto Me the children of Israel are servants; they are My servants whom I brought forth out of the land of Egypt" (Lev. 25:55). Second, it is an affront to the dignity of man and as such should not be countenanced, unless absolutely necessary, and then only under a regulatory regime that discourages it. Jakobovits argued that the Judaic attitude toward slavery is perhaps best expressed in the nomenclature it uses to describe the practice.

The Jewish bondman is, throughout the Bible and Talmud, always referred to as *eved ivri*, meaning "Hebrew servant." Nowhere in the legal portions of the Torah and rabbinic literature is a Jew ever called "Hebrew"; he is invariably "Israel." The difference between the two terms is that the former connotes merely the racial origin and attachment of the Jew, whereas the latter is the name of honor given to the people that accepted the Divine Law. A Jew sold into slavery to another cannot be a true "Israelite"; he is simply a "Hebrew."[80]

The biblical regulations concerning slavery, while catering to conventional thinking about its legitimacy, imposed heavy burdens on the slave owner that made it increasingly less attractive. Indeed, it may be argued that the Torah effectively nullified the idea of chattel slavery with the following demand: "And if thy brother be waxen poor with thee, and sell himself unto thee, thou shalt not make him to serve as a bondservant [slave]. As a hired servant, and as a settler, he shall be with thee" (Lev. 25:39–40). In other words, biblical law does not allow an Israelite to become a slave in the conventional connotation of the term. The sages went so far as to suggest, "Perhaps he should not be called 'slave' at all, it being a term of opprobrium?"[81] In addition, Hebrew slaves could only serve for six years and had to be released in the seventh, even earlier if a Jubilee year occurred during his indenture. "And when thou lettest him go free from thee, thou shalt not let him go empty; thou shalt furnish him liberally out of thy flock, and out of thy threshing floor, and out of thy wine-press; of that wherewith the Lord thy God hath blessed thee" (Deut. 15:13–14).

The Torah also took into account the possibility that such a slave might be reluctant to leave his servitude "because he loveth thee and thy house, because he fareth well with thee" (Deut. 15:16). The sages taught with regard to this last clause, "He must be with [i.e., equal to] thee in food and drink, that thou shouldst not eat white bread and he black bread, thou drink old wine and he new wine, thou sleep on a feather bed and he on straw. Hence it was said, 'Whoever buys a Hebrew slave is like buying a master for himself.' "[82] Jacob Lauterbach suggested that "the principle which underlies these regulations is, that only the product of the servant's labor belongs to the master. This alone the master pays for and has a right to demand. The personal honor and human dignity of the servant are his own sacred rights, which the master dare not infringe upon. The servant is to be treated as a fellow-man in all respects."[83] Indeed, the author of the Book of Job makes clear that the inherent dignity of one's servant is in every way equal to that of his master. "If I did despise the cause of my man-servant, or of my maid-servant, when they contended with me—What then shall I do when God riseth up? And when He remembereth, what shall I answer Him? Did not He that made me in the womb make him? And did not One fashion us in the womb?" (Job 31:13–15.)

At the same time, the pervasiveness of slavery in the ancient world made it necessary for the Torah to draw certain distinctions between a Hebrew and an alien slave. That is, Israel's legislation could demonstrate greater liberality toward slaves from among its own people, in the context of domestic policy. This situation was quite different, however, in terms of interstate relations that demanded reciprocity. It was politically infeasible to have a policy toward enslaved captives that was radically different from that of other nations toward enslaved Israelite captives. There were no Geneva Conventions in antiquity, setting standards for international behavior. Nonetheless, Israel's laws concerning alien slaves were markedly more liberal than those of its neighbors. As Maimonides, writing in reference to his codification of the halakhah, put it, "All the commandments that we have enumerated in Laws concerning Slaves are all of them imbued with pity and benevolence for the weak. Thus great pity is manifested in the prescription according to which a Canaanite slave is set free if he has been deprived of a limb. . . . This applies even if he has only been made to lose a tooth, and all the more in the case of other parts of the body."[84]

The issue of international reciprocity may be seen to underlie the rule established in the Mishnah: "If the ox of an Israelite gored the ox of a gentile [Canaanite], the owner is not culpable. But if the ox of a gentile gored the ox of an Israelite, whether it was accounted harmless or an attested danger, the owner must pay full damages."[85] The seemingly evident inequity in this rule was discussed in the Talmud. R. Abbahu explained, "God beheld the seven commandments [the Noahide Laws] which were accepted by all the descendants of Noah, but since they did not observe them, He rose up and declared them to be outside the protection of the civil law of Israel [with reference to damage done to cattle by cattle]."[86] That is, as one modern commentator on the Talmud, E. W. Kirzner, put it, "As the Canaanites did not recognize the laws of social justice, they did not impose any liability for damage done by cattle. They could consequently not claim to be protected by a law they neither recognized nor respected."[87] By analogy, the same principle of reciprocity appears to be applied by the Torah with regard to the regulation of slavery: "In ancient Israel as in the modern state the legislation regulating the protection of life and property of the stranger was on the basis of reciprocity. Where such reciprocity was not recognized, the stranger could not claim to enjoy the same protection of the law as the citizen."[88]

Perhaps the clearest example of the Torah's disdain for slavery may be seen with regard to its approach to the issue of an escaped slave, compared to that of the Code of Hammurabi, which reflected the culture of the ancient Middle East. The latter stipulates, "If a seignior has harbored in his house either a male slave or a female slave belonging to the state or to a private citizen and has not brought forth [the slave] at the summons of the police, that householder shall be put to death."[89] By contrast, the Torah stipulates, "Thou shalt not deliver unto his master a bondman that is escaped from his master unto thee; he shall dwell with thee, in the midst of thee, in the place which he shall choose within one of thy gates, where it liketh him best; thou shalt not wrong him" (Deut. 23:16). Moreover, it seems quite evident that this biblical law is intended to encourage the escape of slaves who are maltreated, and indirectly to encourage slaveholders to behave more humanely toward them. In this regard, Ben Sira writes, "If you have but one slave, deal with him as a brother; your life's blood went into his purchase. If you mistreat him and he runs away, in what direction will you look for him?"[90]

As in the case of sacrifices, the practice of slavery was regulated in a manner that deviated dramatically from that which prevailed in other societies, while retaining the familiar façade of the institution. Before God, as emphasized by Job, there was no distinction between slave and slaveholder. "Did not He that made me in the womb make him? And did not One fashion us in the womb?" (Job 31:15). It seems clear that the biblical authors considered slavery as a societal aberration. The sages of the Talmud effectively eliminated the legal basis for slavery in Israel, with the assertion the "the law of the Hebrew slave applies only as long as the Jubilee applies, as it is said: He shall serve with thee unto the year of Jubilee" (Lev. 25:40). However the law of Jubilee was no longer in effect in postbiblical times.[91]

The rabbis went so far as to assert that the principle of infinite human value generally outweighed even God's commandments as set forth in the Torah, arguing that its supreme importance was implicit in the biblical text. The divine imperative is, "Ye shall therefore keep My statutes, and Mine ordinances, which if a man do, he shall live by them" (Lev. 18:5). But the sage, Samuel, interpreted the final clause of the injunction as stating, "He shall live by them, but he shall not die because of them."[92] This would suggest that because human life is held to be of infinite value, all the laws of the Torah might be abrogated if necessary to preserve it. The sages evidently felt that this would take the matter too far, that there were in fact some biblical injunctions that should not be violated even to preserve one's life. Accordingly, after deliberating the issue, they stipulated some specific exceptions to the rule. "By a majority vote, it was resolved ... that with regard to every [other] law of the Torah, if a man is commanded: 'Transgress and suffer not death' he may transgress and not suffer death, except for idolatry, incest [which includes adultery], and murder."[93] These three injunctions were not to be violated under any circumstances, even under pain of death. It is noteworthy that each of these three exceptions concerns acts that, in the rabbinical view, clearly devalue the infinite worth of human life.

EQUALITY BEFORE THE LAW

The idea of prescriptive equality is also reflected in the Judaic conception of the equality of all men before the law. Scripture declares, "Ye shall have one manner of law, as well for the stranger, as for the home-born; for I am the Lord your God" (Lev. 24:22). That is, because the Lord is the God of both the Jew and the non-Jew, His law must apply equally to both. As Samson R. Hirsch put it, "Just as all the rights and all the high value of human beings are rooted in the Personality of God, so does this form the basis for complete equality in law and justice."[94] Similarly, the sages declared, "All are equal before the law. The duty of observance is for all."[95] The implication of all this, as Emanuel Rackman has argued, is that "since God created all men equal, their natural inequality can only be justified with reference to His service, which means the fulfillment of the very equality God had willed."[96]

The Judaic concept of equality before the law may perhaps best be understood as a synthesis of the professed natural equality of men with respect to their Creator and the acknowledged natural inequality of men with respect to one another. The idea of the natural equality of men before God is given expression in the classical literature in the form of a homily. "R. Judah b. Shalom said: If a poor man comes and pleads before another, that other does not listen to him; if a rich man comes, he receives and listens to him at once. God does not act in this manner; all are equal before Him—women, slaves, rich and poor."[97]

The problem of the natural inequality of men with respect to one another is addressed in the literature as well—perhaps with a poignant touch of irony—in the midrashic recounting of a purported dialogue between King David and the Lord: "David said, 'Lord of the Universe, make equality in Thy world.' God replied, 'If I made all equal, who would practice faithfulness and loving kindness?' "[98] This latter teaching, of course, is principally concerned with man's moral posture rather than with the more obvious distinctions between persons that may be drawn with regard to their intellectual and physical attributes and capacities. Nevertheless, the general point it makes is unmistakable: there are in fact significant differences among men, differences that can be equalized only in certain limited respects. This presents a major challenge for government in the Judaic political society.

While the Judaic concept of social justice is predicated on the ideal of intrinsic equality, it also takes into account that the tangible differences among men may be very great, not only in terms of innate capacities but also with regard to their social and economic circumstances. Consequently, if persons characterized by significant intrinsic and extrinsic inequalities were treated as equals before the law—without special consideration being accorded to those differences—the fundamental principle of justice might be seriously compromised in the process of arriving at a judicial determination. The interests of true justice therefore require that the significant differences between persons be taken fully into account, so that unequals may be effectively equalized before the law.

It becomes a basic responsibility of government to order society so as to bring about the equivalent of equality. At the same time it must preserve those essential qualities manifested in the differences among people that derive from the gift of the Creator, or from the practical consequences of the operation of His law in the social and economic spheres. The scales of justice must be balanced in such a manner as to produce the greatest possible social cohesion and harmony. The necessary guidelines for the successful fulfillment of this momentous task are considered to have been provided in the precepts of the Torah.

NOTES

1. Joseph H. Hertz, *The Pentateuch and Haftorahs*, p. 821.

2. Artur Weiser, *The Psalms: A Commentary*, p. 503.

3. For a detailed, in-depth, and extensive analysis of the biblical use and meanings of these terms see Eliezer Berkovits, *Man and God: Studies in Biblical Theology*, chaps. 5 and 7.

4. Samson Raphael Hirsch, *The Psalms*, vol. 1, p. 497.

5. Samson Raphael Hirsch, *Horeb: A Philosophy of Jewish Laws and Observances*, vol. 1, p. 222.

6. Meir L. Malbim, *Mikraei Kodesh* on Psalm 72:2.

7. Alexander Guttmann, "The Role of Equity in the History of the Halakhah," p. 71.

8. Malbim, *HaTorah vehaMitzvah* on Deut. 16:18.

9. S. R. Hirsch, *The Psalms*, vol. 1, p. 497.

10. Hahm Pyong-Choon, *The Korean Political Tradition and Law: Essays in Korean Law and Legal History*, pp. 29–30.

11. Will Herberg, *Judaism and Modern Man*, p. 148.

12. Ibid., p. 134.

13. Ibid., pp. 148–149. Herberg's reference is to the teaching of R. Simeon ben Gamliel, "The world stands on three things, on truth, on judgment, and on peace" (*Avot* 1:18).

14. *Genesis Rabbah* 24:7.

15. For an extensive analysis of this difference of views see, Hayyim Z. Reines, *Torah uMusar*, pp. 180–183.

16. *J. Nedarim* 9:4.

17. Aaron Levine, *Economics and Jewish Law*, p. 108.

18. Byron L. Sherwin, *Jewish Ethics for the Twenty-first Century*, pp. 132–133.

19. *Avot* 1:2.

20. *High Holiday Prayer Book*, p. 74.

21. Israel Mattuck, *Jewish Ethics*, p. 86

22. Solomon b. Isaac, *Perushei Rashi al haTorah* on Gen. 1:26.

23. *Sanhedrin* 37a.

24. S. R. Hirsch, *The Psalms*, vol. 1, p. 497.

25. Levine, *Economics and Jewish Law*, p. 135.

26. David Novak, *Jewish Social Ethics*, pp. 206, 210.

27. There is a distinction in Hebrew between *ani*, meaning "poor" or "low income," and *evyon*, meaning "needy," the latter term being used in this biblical verse. One who is *evyon* is considered to be seriously impoverished, a degree worse off than "poor."

28. Israel H. Levinthal, *Judaism Speaks to the Modern World*, p. 108.

29. Daniel Nussbaum, "Social Justice and Social Welfare in Jewish Tradition," p. 230.

30. Sherwin, *Jewish Ethics for the Twenty-first Century*, p. 131.

31. Nussbaum, "Social Justice and Social Welfare in Jewish Tradition," p. 230.

32. *Avot* 3:21.

33. Richard G. Hirsch, "There Shall Be No Poor," p. 237.

34. *Eruvin* 41b.

35. *Exodus Rabbah* 31:14.

36. *Berakhot* 6b.

37. R. G. Hirsch, "There Shall Be No Poor," p. 238.

38. Herberg, *Judaism and Modern Man*, pp. 151–152.

39. Abraham ibn Ezra, *Perushei haTorah leRabbenu Avraham ibn Ezra*, ad loc.

40. *M. Sheviyit* 10:4; *Gittin* 36a.

41. Rackman, *Modern Halakhah for Our Time*, p. 57.

42. Ibid., p. 58.

43. Meir Tamari, "With All Your Possessions," p. 52.

44. Rackman, *Modern Halakhah for Our Time*, pp. 28–29.

45. *Mishnah Kiddushin* 1:6.

46. Rackman, *Modern Halakhah for Our Time*, p. 29.

47. Immanuel Jakobovits, *Journal of a Rabbi*, p. 114.

48. Aaron haLevi of Barcelona, *Sefer haHinukh* 66.

49. Joseph Caro, *Shulhan Arukh: Yoreh Deah* 248:1.

50. Maimonides, *Hilkhot Mattanot Aniyyim* 9:1.

51. Isadore Twersky, "Some Aspects of the Jewish Attitude toward the Welfare State," p. 229. The Talmud considered the existence of a communal charitable fund as absolutely essential and asserted that a person who served as a role model for others might not live in a town that did not have, among other things, a community chest for the needy (*Sanhedrin* 17b).

52. *Ketuvot* 67b.

53. *J. Peah* 8:7.

54. Maimonides, *Hilkhot Mattanot Aniyyim* 7:3.

55. A *zuz*, in talmudic times, was equivalent to a dinar, or one-twenty-fifth of a golden dinar. It would be very difficult to compare a *zuz* to contemporary currencies, especially in terms of buying power. Nonetheless, it would seem fair to assert that possession of two hundred *zuz* would put one above the established poverty

line. For an extensive discussion of the poverty line according to the halakhah, see Shlomo Goren, *Torat haMedinah*, pp. 358–384.

56. Maimonides, *Hilkhot Mattanot Aniyyim* 9:13.

57. Ibid. 7:3.

58. Tamari, *"With All Your Possessions,"* p. 258.

59. Caro, *Shulhan Arukh: Yoreh Deah* 252:1.

60. *Horayot* 13a.

61. *M. Gittin* 4:5.

62. Maimonides, *Hilkhot Mattanot Aniyyim* 8:13.

63. *Sanhedrin* 27b. This idea also finds expression in the Midrash in a number of formulations, such as "Why is Israel compared to a nut? Just as with a nut, if you remove one from the heap the rest tumble down and roll one after another, so it is with Israel. When one is affected, all feel it" (*Canticles Rabbah* 6:17). In a variation on this theme, another homily asks: "Why is Israel compared to a sheep? Just as with a sheep, if it receives a blow on the head or on one of its limbs all of its limbs feel it, so it is with Israel. When one sins, all feel it" (*Leviticus Rabbah* 4:6).

64. Leo Jung, *Living Judaism*, p. 266.

65. There is a major disagreement, based on complex exegesis of the biblical text, among the classic commentators, Rashi and Nahmanides, regarding the character of the initial land allocation. I have adopted the view of Rashi, who argued that the allocations to the tribes were not equal but rather in accordance with the relative sizes of their populations. The opposing view of Nahmanides—that each of the tribes received an equal share of the land, shares that were subsequently to be allocated equally to its members—would have created structural inequality among the people as a whole from the outset; it does not seem plausible.

66. Sol Roth, *Halakhah and Politics*, pp. 60–61.

67. Roth, "Judaism and Democracy," in *The Torah U-Madda Journal*, vol. 2 (1990), p. 67.

68. Bertrand Russell, *Mysticism and Logic*, p. 81.

69. Roth, "Judaism and Democracy," p. 68.

70. *Sanhedrin* 37a; *The Fathers According to Rabbi Nathan*, chap. 31.

71. Abraham Hen, *BeMalkhut haYahadut*, vol. 1, p. 112.

72. *J. Terumot* 8:4. Maimonides, *Hilkhot Yesodei haTorah* 5:5. Note that this principle is not held to apply if the individual demanded is specifically identified and is in fact guilty of a capital crime.

73. Jay William Hudson, *Why Democracy: A Study in the Philosophy of the State*, p. 187.

74. *M. Sanhedrin* 4:5.

75. Moshe Avigdor Amiel, "HaTzedek haSotziali vehaTzedek haMishpati vehaMusari Shelanu," p. 33.

76. Ibid., p. 35.

77. The situation discussed here is radically different from that discussed earlier with regard to the priority criteria established by the halakhah when insufficient resources are available for the redemption of captives. In the latter case, value to society is not the principal relevant criterion. "Our Rabbis taught: If a man and his father and his teacher were in captivity he takes precedence over his teacher and his teacher takes precedence over his father, while his mother takes precedence over all of them" (*Horayot* 13a).

78. Maimonides, *Guide of the Perplexed*, 3:32, pp. 526–527.

79. For a discussion of this point, see Simon Federbusch, *Mishpat haMelukhah beYisrael*, pp. 159–160.

80. Jakobovits, *Journal of a Rabbi*, p. 88.

81. *Mekilta de-Rabbi Ishmael* (tractate *Nezikin* 1), vol. 3, p. 4.

82. *Kiddushin* 20a.

83. Jacob Z. Lauterbach, *Rabbinic Essays*, p. 278.

84. Maimonides, *Guide of the Perplexed*, 3:39, pp. 553–554.

85. *M. Baba Kamma* 4:3.

86. *Baba Kamma* 38a.

87. Ibid. (Soncino, ed.), 37b, n. 6., p. 211.

88. M. Guttmann, "The Term 'Foreigner' Historically Considered," *Hebrew Union College Annual*, vol. 3 (1926), pp. 1–20.

89. James B. Pritchard, ed., *The Ancient Near East*, p. 141, para. 16.

90. The Wisdom of Ben Sira [Ecclesiasticus] 33, p. 403.

91. *Arakin* 29a.

92. *Yoma* 85b.

93. *Sanhedrin* 74a.

94. S. R. Hirsch, *The Pentateuch*, on Lev. 24:22.

95. *Sifre Deuteronomy*, "Ekev" 11:22.

96. Rackman, *One Man's Judaism*, p. 145.

97. *Exodus Rabbah* 21:4.

98. Ibid. 31:5.

Chapter 7

National Security

It was evident to the biblical authors as well as to the sages of the Talmud that even an ideal Judaic society could not exist in a political vacuum, that it was necessary to provide guidelines that would govern its relations with other nations and states, and their citizens. Reflecting the realities of the political environment in antiquity, which has not changed very much in the Middle East over the millennia, the principal concerns of prophet and sage in the field of foreign affairs related to issues of national security. Primary attention was given to the subject of war—when and under what circumstances it might be undertaken as a legitimate means of achieving national objectives, by whose authority might a war be initiated, and what the fundamental rules of engagement were for combatant forces.

This focus on war seems to be inconsistent with one of Judaism's principal values—peace. "R. Simeon b. Gamliel used to say: By three things does the world endure: justice, truth and peace."[1] Indeed, there is a minor tractate of the Talmud, *Perek Hashalom*, that is devoted exclusively to extolling the blessings of peace. It opens with the following teaching: "R. Joshua b. Levi said: Great is peace, for peace is to the world as leaven is to dough. Had not the Holy One, blessed be He, given peace to the earth, the sword and the beast would have robbed the world of its children."[2] Judaism's primary interest, however, is more with life in the real world than with an ideal world to come. "Judaism, therefore," as Emanuel Rackman observed, "is more concerned with regulating the circumstances that would permit the exercise of violence—by individuals, by groups, and by states—than it is with the elimination of violence at all costs. Violence is at one and the same time

an important way both to destroy and to conserve one of the most important values in the system of Judaism—human life." Accordingly, if one is to
engage in war and violence, it must be justified on the basis of halakhah and
conducted in behalf of the value ascribed to life or to an even higher value.
War for war's sake is considered the essence of evil and must be prevented.[3]

The sages of the talmudic period sought to formulate the applicable
halakhah in this field within the framework of the guidance of the Torah.
They therefore bore in mind that one of the principal objectives they had set
for themselves was to project the establishment of a society that could serve
as a model of social justice and morality. They recognized that to achieve
this goal it would be necessary to constrain the ability of the government,
whether a monarchy or some other regime, to use war as a vehicle for expanding the power of the state. Accordingly, they set out to define carefully
the terms and conditions under which the public might be mobilized for
war, and thereby bring about governmental compliance with halakhic
norms and requirements.

The essential nature of the concern of the sages was well articulated by
the prophet Samuel, in his response to the demands placed on him by the
elders of the society. The latter wanted to transform the structure and character of the existing political society, by establishing a state with a central
government, in lieu of the loosely organized confederacy of tribal governments. Samuel reacted strongly to their expressed desire to have a monarchy comparable to those that existed among their neighbors. He warned
the people that the monarch they were requesting would have power and
authority unprecedented in the nation's history. The monarch would mobilize their youth in his service, as well as levy taxes on all the sources of
wealth in the country in order to defray the costs of his regime and to finance the wars in which he might engage. The prophet declared:

This will be the manner of the king that shall reign over you: he will take your sons,
and appoint them unto him, for his chariots, and to be his horsemen; and they shall
run before his chariots. And he will appoint them unto him . . . to plow his ground,
and to reap his harvest, and to make his instruments of war, and the instruments of
his chariots. . . . And he will take the tenth of your seed, and of your vineyards, and
give to his officers, and to his servants. (I Sam. 8:11–15)

It should be noted that while the biblical text and the halakhic writings
discuss these issues in terms of a monarch, the principles apply to political
leadership generally. Thus, Abraham Isaac Kook wrote, "It would seem
that at a time when there is no king, given that the laws of the kingdom
touch upon the welfare of the people, the rights contained within those
laws revert to the people as a whole." Thus, when someone is subsequently
appointed a leader with the consent of the public and the court, "he certainly stands in place of the king with regard to those laws of the kingdom
that touch upon the leadership of the collectivity."[4]

While this power to tax and mobilize the resources of the society might be necessary and proper, both prophet and sage were concerned about the abuses of legitimate authority that might ensue from such seemingly arbitrary power. Accordingly, the rabbis sought to mitigate the concerns evinced by the prophet by making the legitimate authority of the government subject to halakhic norms. As these halakhic constraints were codified by Maimonides, the king "may take whatever he requires from the craftsman, put them to work for him and pay them their wages; he may take all the livestock, menservants and maidservants for his work, and pay for their use or value."[5]

This halakhic formulation significantly modifies the legitimate authority of the government, clearly limiting its confiscatory powers. The people may indeed be mobilized for military or other forms of national service, and their property may be commandeered to serve the public need, but appropriate compensation must be paid. Legitimate rulers, moreover, may not trample on the residual rights of the people.

THE AUTHORITY TO MAKE WAR

The sages were also concerned that a monarch or other ruler not be given unrestricted latitude to enhance the authority of the regime or pursue arbitrary policies at the expense of the public, in terms of either human or material resources. Their concern was especially acute with respect to the question of war, which entailed high risks of death and dismemberment for its participants, the ultimate sacrifice that a government might demand of the governed. The sages therefore sought to delimit governmental authority in this field, by defining different fundamental categories or classes of war and specifying the criteria by which the legitimacy of a government determination to engage in a conflict could be assessed.

They asserted that from the standpoint of halakhah there are two principal types of war: mandated war (*milhemet mitzvah*), and discretionary war (*milhemet reshut*). The legitimate involvement of the state in either class of conflict required strict compliance with a distinct set of legitimating criteria. The halakhah stipulated the circumstances or conditions under which the government might legitimately declare war unilaterally, and those under which it was obligated to seek the prior concurrence of the independent supreme judicial body—the Great Sanhedrin, or high court. In principle, it was held that a mandatory war might be initiated at the discretion of the government, whereas a discretionary war required legitimation by the high court. This principle is reflected in the mishnaic dictum: "A discretionary war may be waged only by the authority of a court of seventy-one."[6]

What is the basis for this rule? In the opinion of the sage R. Abbahu, it is derived from a traditional interpretation of the biblical passage that discusses the succession of Joshua to the leadership position held by Moses:

"And he shall stand before Eleazar the priest, who shall inquire for him by the judgment of the Urim before the Lord; at his word shall they go out, and at his word they shall come in, both he, and all the children of Israel with him, even all the congregation" (Num. 27:21).[7] According to the sage, this passage is to be understood as stipulating that a voluntary decision to go to war must first receive religious sanction from the high priest, at whose word "they shall go out" to war. This is considered to apply to the king or ruling authority as well as the people. The reference to "all the congregation" is held to refer to the Sanhedrin, or high court, which must consent to the decision. In other words, the decision for a discretionary war requires both religious and political sanction from the appropriate communal authorities.

According to Nahmanides, however, the referenced biblical text does not clearly distinguish between a mandatory and a discretionary war. He therefore suggests that the requirement to request prior sacerdotal and political consent applies equally to both types of war.[8] If Nahmanides is correct, this requirement could have been carried out in practice only during the First Temple period, when, according to tradition, it was customary to ask the high priest to inquire of the Urim and Thummim, the stones that adorned his breastplate; in them he was to perceive an oracular response. For reasons that are not entirely clear, this practice was discontinued during the Second Temple period.[9] Maimonides asserts that the elimination of the requirement to inquire of the high priest was the direct result of the serious decline in the spiritual quality of the priesthood. "Why was not inquiry made of them? Because the divine spirit was absent, and one does not inquire of a priest who does not speak with divine spirit, or upon whom the *shekhinah* does not rest."[10] In his critical notes on Maimonides' work, Abraham ben David (Rabad) suggests that the probable reason the practice was discontinued is simply that the Urim and Thummim were no longer in existence after the destruction of the First Temple.[11]

In any case, it is clear that in accordance with rabbinic tradition, the authority to authorize a discretionary war during the Second Temple period and afterward rested exclusively with the high court. However, the classical rabbinic literature is silent with regard to why it was considered necessary that there be judicial authorization of a discretionary war. It is only recently that Reuven Margaliot offered a cogent explanation of this halakhic requirement. He suggested that the reason for requiring judicial sanction for a discretionary war is the analogy that can be drawn between the mortality implications of such a war and the halakhic requirement that decisions concerning the capital punishment of groups of people be made only by the high court. Margaliot argued that a decision for war places large numbers of people in mortal danger, which makes it analogous to a mass death sentence—which can properly be rendered only by the high court.[12]

In Margaliot's view, it becomes the responsibility of the high court to determine whether the risk of casualties is acceptable in terms of the public interest, or whether the war is being initiated for reasons that will not stand such a test. Applying this concept to contemporary times, when there exists no high court in the talmudic sense, Simon Federbusch suggests that such legitimating authority may be assumed by whatever high tribunal does in fact exist. In his view, "every high court has the authority to determine [whether a proposed war] is a moral war, and after having received its concurrence it is incumbent upon the government to declare war in order to save the people and for justice to prevail."[13]

In the same vein, Yehuda Gershuni suggests that if a discretionary war is approved by a popular consensus, such public sanction should be considered equivalent to approval by a high court. He argues that if the people have the right to appoint elders, to sanctify the new moon, and to make certain necessary calendar adjustments, all of which actions are halakhically considered to be the traditional prerogatives of the high court, they can also authorize a discretionary war. Such authorization would presumably come through a referendum or some equivalent device. Accordingly, he insists, "The public in the Land of Israel is equivalent to the high court[,] . . . and therefore, if all Israel decides on a discretionary war, they have the same power as the high court."[14]

CLASSIFICATION OF WARS

The principal criterion for distinguishing between a mandatory and a discretionary war is whether the war is biblically ordained or merely condoned. A mandatory war would be one that Scripture indicated was explicitly commanded by God, whereas a discretionary war would be one that was not specifically commanded but that served the interests of the nation or state. The distinctions between the two categories relate primarily to the process by which a decision for war is taken and the extent of mobilization authorized in each case.

Because the Torah ordains a mandatory war, no additional approval is required from any other institution. By contrast, because the Torah does not explicitly command a discretionary war, it cannot be initiated at the sole discretion of the government. Pointing out clear examples of each type, the talmudic sage Raba observed, "The wars waged by Joshua to conquer [Canaan] were obligatory in the opinion of all; the wars waged by the House of David for territorial expansion were voluntary in the opinion of all."[15] Raba thus drew a distinction between wars undertaken for the purpose of securing the territory and frontiers of the land promised to the Israelites and that were specifically authorized by Scripture, such as those that were fought by Joshua, and wars that were undertaken for expansionist purposes.

The determination that a war is to be classified as mandatory is highly significant, because it affects the manner in which the requirement that citizens perform national military service is treated when it conflicts with other halakhic obligations. As stated in the Talmud, "One who is engaged in the performance of a commandment [*mitzvah*] is exempt from the performance of another commandment."[16] Moreover, the halakhah provides for a series of exemptions and deferments from national military service that, in the opinion of the majority of the sages, apply "to voluntary wars [*reshut*]." However, "in the wars commanded by the Torah [*mitzvah,*] all go forth, even a bridegroom from his chamber and a bride from her canopy."[17] While this ruling would facilitate total mobilization of the nation's resources in the case of a mandatory war, it also effectively limits the capacity of the government to undertake an aggressive foreign policy on its own initiative. Since a discretionary war does not automatically cancel the halakhic exemptions and deferments from mobilization, the ability of the government to mobilize the necessary resources to enable it to prosecute such a war are constrained.

In his codification of these principles, Maimonides subdivided the class of mandatory wars into three categories.[18] These included the biblically ordained wars against the seven nations that occupied the land of Canaan at the time of the exodus from Egypt, and the biblically mandated war to be prosecuted against Amalek. Finally, although it was only implied and not specifically mandated in the Torah, Maimonides accepted the minority view of the sage R. Judah and considered a war to defend Israel from attack as biblically obligatory. However, as will be discussed below, there is some disagreement over the parameters of a defensive war, as well as over whether such a conflict is to be considered obligatory in the same sense as the other two categories of mandatory war. Although reason itself would obligate the nation to undertake a defensive war, what is at issue in the matter of classification is whether such a war may be undertaken by the unilateral decision of the government, as is the case with the other types of mandatory wars.

The biblical commandment to wage total war against the seven nations appears quite explicit and unequivocal:

When the Lord thy God shall bring thee into the land whither thou goest to possess it, and shall cast out many nations before thee, the Hittite, and the Girgashite, and the Amorite, and the Canaanite, and the Perizzite, and the Hivite, and the Jebusite, seven nations greater and mightier than thou; and when the Lord thy God shall deliver them up before thee, and thou shalt smite them; then thou shalt utterly destroy them; thou shalt make no covenant with them, nor show mercy unto them; neither shalt thou make marriages with them. . . . But thus shall ye deal with them: ye shall break down their altars, and dash in pieces their pillars, and hew down their Asherim, and burn their graven images with fire. (Deut. 7:1–5)

The rationale for this extremely harsh policy, as given in another biblical text, is to ensure that they "teach you not to do after all their abominations, which they have done unto their gods, and so ye sin against the Lord your

God" (Deut. 20:18). The modern view of war is that it is but one instrument of politics; the biblical view as expressed in these passages reflects a rather different conception of war, at least of that which has been designated as a mandatory war. There is no interest here in compelling the surrender of the enemy; what is desired is its destruction as a national and cultural entity.

The biblical mandate seems clearly intended to enable Israel to occupy and settle the land promised to it in a manner that will leave the land completely free of any of the morally and spiritually corrupting influences that these seven pagan nations may have been capable of exerting. The text implicitly suggests that the very existence of any tangible manifestation of the Canaanite religion within its territory will constitute a mortal and therefore intolerable threat to the internal security of the nation.

There is a separate and distinct biblical mandate to destroy Amalek, because of the unwarranted animosity it displayed toward Israel during its trek through the desert, following the exodus from Egypt:

Remember what Amalek did unto thee by the way as ye came forth out of Egypt; how he met thee by the way, and smote the hindmost of thee, all that were enfeebled in thy rear, when thou wast faint and weary; and he feared not God. Therefore it shall be, when the Lord thy God hath given thee rest from all thine enemies round about, in the land which the Lord thy God giveth thee for an inheritance to possess it, that thou shalt blot out the remembrance of Amalek from under heaven; thou shalt not forget. (Deut. 25:17–19)

Implicit in this is the consideration that Israel had posed no threat to the interests of Amalek; its attacks on Israel had been completely unwarranted aggressions, effectively challenging the right of the nation of Israel to exist. An enemy of this kind, in the biblical view, must be rendered totally incapable of future aggression, and the only certain way to achieve this is by nullifying its existence as a threat. It has been suggested that the biblical mandate to war against Amalek may also be understood to extend to other nations who behave in comparable fashion to Amalek. This opinion is based on the biblical assertion "that the Lord will have war with Amalek from generation to generation" (Exod. 17:16). The implicit presumption of this statement is that the war with Amalek, or with others that are Amalek-like, may persist throughout history—a constant struggle by Israel to ensure its survival. Accordingly, Yehuda Gershuni suggests, war against those who would seek to destroy Israel, today as yesterday, is halakhically mandated.[19]

The third category of mandatory war, according to Maimonides, is a defensive war, one undertaken in order to guarantee the security of the nation in a time of international crisis—or as he put it, "to deliver Israel from the enemy attacking him."[20] Menahem Meiri concurs with Maimonides' halakhic position concerning the kinds of conflicts that may be included under the rubric of obligatory wars. He too would include a defensive war as one in which the approval of the high court is not required to order the compulsory mobilization of the people.[21] It is noteworthy that contemporary halakhists define the "enemy attacking him" to include an enemy that sends missiles across the nation's borders without physically crossing them with its troops.[22]

The biblical mandate for defensive warfare may be found in the passage, "And when ye go to war in your land against the adversary that oppresseth you, then ye shall sound an alarm with the trumpets; and ye shall be remembered before the Lord your God, and ye shall be saved from your enemies" (Num. 10:9). However, even without explicit scriptural sanction, it would seem that a defensive war might be justified as a mandated war on the basis that it constitutes a reasonable collective extension of the natural obligation of self-preservation. As Maurice Lamm put it, "It is a defense of one's land, one's family. Such a war is a moral reflex, calling forth a unanimous and instinctive response. It requires no convening of judges, leaves no options to the people. There are no draft exemptions whatever for all males between ages 20 to 60, including students, cowards and the physically defective."[23]

Nonetheless, Rashi takes a much narrower view of the biblical mandate and places a historical restriction on the classification of any war as mandatory. In his view, the mandatory categorization applies exclusively to the wars actually fought by Joshua to conquer the land of Israel.[24] All other wars, presumably including those to complete the conquest of the land, are therefore discretionary by definition. It has been suggested that Rashi omits any reference to the wars against Amalek because these are mandated unequivocally and are to be prosecuted relentlessly. However, the mandatory wars against the seven nations may be considered to be in a somewhat different category, because the timing of the fulfillment of the biblical mandate is clearly a matter of judgment, as may be gleaned from a close reading of the biblical text: "I will not drive them out from before thee in one year, lest the land become desolate. . . . By little and little I will drive them out before thee, until thou be increased, and inherit the land" (Exod. 23:29–30). Accordingly, Rashi may be understood as considering it appropriate that the consent of the high court be obtained before prosecuting such a war.[25]

Although not as restrictive as Rashi in his approach, Obadiah of Bertinoro similarly asserts that all wars other than those biblically commanded against the seven nations and Amalek are to be considered discretionary.[26] In their view, contrary to the opinion of Maimonides, a defensive war must be considered a discretionary war and thus is not to be prosecuted without prior authorization from the high court. Jonathan of Lunel would go even farther in making it difficult for a Judaic government to proclaim a defensive war. In his opinion, not only must the king receive the prior authorization of the high court, but he must have the agreement of all lower courts as well. He would require that the judicial system as a whole vote and decide whether it is permissible to undertake any discretionary war, including one that is clearly defensive in nature.[27] Although this perspective on the discretionary nature of a defensive war appears to be a minority view, there is generally a strong tendency among Judaic thinkers to emphasize limitations on the prosecution of discretionary wars. David S. Shapiro writes in this regard,

Its purpose may not be conquest, plunder, or destruction. It may be waged only for the protection of Israel and for the sanctification of the name of God, that is, the imposition of the Seven [Noahide] Commandments. When the prophets, singers, and sages of Israel speak of the extension of Israel's boundaries through war or of the dominion of Israel over other nations, they do not have in mind physical domination, but rather the sway of Israel's principles, the sovereignty of Israel's spiritual ideals. No war may be waged against a nation that has not attacked Israel, or that lives up to the fundamentals of the Universal Religion.[28]

PREVENTIVE AND PREEMPTIVE WAR

There is a fundamental difference of opinion among the rabbis as to whether the category of defensive war includes preventive or preemptive wars. The central issue is whether the concept of defense, as it relates to the halakhic definition of a mandatory war, is limited to what might be termed in contemporary jargon a "second strike" defense doctrine or also encompasses the idea of a "first strike" defense. That is, is a defensive war obligatory only in reference to military action taken when the nation is under actual attack? Or should its definition be extended to include a preemptive attack against an enemy who is planning and mobilizing resources for war in the foreseeable future? The self-evident purposes of such a preemptive war would be either to prevent the enemy from attaining the level of military readiness that would enable him to initiate hostilities, or to ensure that the coming conflict is fought on the enemy's territory rather than on one's own.

The moral, as well as the halakhic, basis for preemption may be derived from an extrapolation of the principle announced in the Talmud with regard to the safety of an individual: "If he come to slay you, forestall it by slaying him." The sage Raba applied this principle even to the case of a thief who breaks into one's house. His rationale was that people are expected to take action to protect their property. The thief, knowing this, must be assumed to have reasoned that in the event of resistance from the householder he (the thief) might have to do him severe harm, perhaps even kill him.[29] From this and related discussions in the sources, Shlomo Goren concluded that a person who finds himself in a position of probable, let alone certain, peril has the right to forestall such peril at all costs. If he can prevent it by wounding the assailant, he should do so; if not, he is permitted to kill him. Moreover, a third party who is in a position to prevent injury to the one subject to attack by acting against his assailant is obligated to do so as well, again preferably by merely wounding the offender. However, if the only way to stop the assault is to kill the assailant, there is a moral obligation to save the attacked even at the cost of the life of the attacker.[30] It would seem clear that what applies to the individual in peril surely also applies to the nation anticipating an attack.

The rabbis disagreed, however, over whether a preventive or preemptive war should be considered a biblically mandated war. On the one hand, it could be argued that since such a war is intended to forestall a future attack, defense against which would surely be obligatory, it should be treated as obligatory. On the other hand, it could be argued that since the danger to which such a war is a response is not imminent, and there is time to obtain the considered judgment of the high court, it should be classified as a discretionary war. It appears that in the opinion of the majority of the sages, a war "against heathens so that these should not march against them,"[31]— that is, a preventive war—should be categorized as a discretionary war, requiring the prior consent of the high court. R. Judah, representing a minority view, maintained that although such a conflict did not fall into the mandated category of *milhemet mitzvah*, it should nonetheless be considered obligatory; he introduced a third category of war, *milhemet hovah*, or obligatory war, to characterize preventive war as not biblically mandated but obligatory war.[32] In his view, the national executive (the monarch) was invested with discretionary authority to enter into such a war on its own initiative. It is noteworthy that, as noted above, in his codification of the halakhah Maimonides adopts this minority opinion as normative.

The discussion of preventive war in the halakhic literature, touched upon above, is primarily concerned with the implications of such a war for domestic policy—conscription and mobilization of resources—implications that will vary in accordance with the category to which preemptive wars are assigned. However, it is clear that preventive or preemptive wars are held to be legitimate means of assuring national security. As J. David Bleich put it:

There is no halakhic requirement that defensive war be limited to elimination of the immediate danger. The crucial issue, then, is whether such actions are entirely preventive in nature or whether a given action is undertaken in response to prior attack. Intermittent cessation of hostilities by the enemy does not signify termination of aggression. On the other hand, the purpose of such a war is not punishment of the enemy, but "to deliver Israel," i.e., to prevent Jewish casualties. Hence, prudence would dictate that such action be undertaken only if casualties as a result of a military response are likely to be lower than anticipated losses in the absence of such a response.[33]

Maurice Lamm adopts a similar position with regard to the legitimacy of preventive war:

"Permitted War," today, refers to only one type—the preventive war which reaches out to a known enemy who is judged to be preparing for a future attack, who has the men and weapons and motivation to invade. This war is initiated to enable a first strike, in the enemy's cities and amidst his civilian population. Such a war is "permitted" because it is not a clearly-defined, morally-instinctive response, and, therefore, requires (even according to R. Judah who quarrels with the more conservative Sages) not only the declaration of the Chief Executive, but the authorization of the Sanhedrin. The decision involves choosing among a hierarchy of values, the assessment of the possibilities of defeat, a strategic evaluation of military and political alternatives and a determination of the immediacy of the enemy's threat. There undoubtedly was included a judgment of the moral criteria involved in the just war—determining the possibility of victory and the proportionality of the means.[34]

Although it may be possible to subject a decision for a preventive war to such a comprehensive consultative and deliberative process, this approach may prove impracticable with regard to preemption. Given the lethality of modern weapons and the rapidity with which payloads can be delivered in the missile age, a preemptive strike at an enemy may be vital to national survival. Presumably, if consultation with judicial and legislative authorities is to be undertaken prior to taking action in this type of discretionary war, the necessary procedures would have to take into account the possible need for a decision in a matter of minutes—hardly enough time for a thorough and deliberate examination and assessment of the threat.

RULES OF MOBILIZATION

As already indicated, the classification of a conflict has a direct impact on the government's mobilization authority. The basic rules governing conscription for, and deferments from, military service are derived directly from Scripture.

When thou goest forth to battle against thine enemies[,] . . . the officers shall speak unto the people, saying: "What man is there that hath built a new house, and hath not dedicated it? Let him go and return to his house, lest he die in the battle, and another man dedicate it. And what man is there that hath planted a vineyard, and hath not used the fruit thereof? Let him go and return unto his house, lest he die in the battle and another man use the fruit thereof. And what man is there that hath betrothed a wife, and hath not taken her? Let him go and return unto his house, lest he die in the battle, and another man take her." And the officers shall speak further unto the people, and they shall say: "What man is there that is fearful and fainthearted? Let him go and return to his house, lest his brethren's heart melt as his heart." (Deut. 20:1–8)

The sages concluded on the basis of the majority opinion that these exemptions from national military service applied only "to discretionary wars [reshut]." However, in the case of mandated wars (mitzvah), "all go forth, even a bridegroom from his chamber and a bride from her canopy."[35] In other words, there are no exemptions from mobilization in the case of a mandatory war of persons otherwise capable of national service; according to Avraham Horowitz, a contemporary halakhic authority, this precludes any religious deferments. "In such a war, there are no rabbis or Torah scholars. Everyone is obligated to go out to the battlefield to destroy the enemy."[36] Moreover, even in the case of a discretionary war, those exempted from combatant service "return home and provide water and food and repair the roads."[37] In other words, even those deferred from active military duty may be mobilized for support services behind the lines.

THE ROLE OF WOMEN IN WAR

The assertion of the sages that in a mandatory war, "all go forth, even a bridegroom from his chamber and a bride from her canopy," cited by Maimonides verbatim in his codification of the halakhah,[38] raises the intriguing question of the role of women in war. Were women, in Maimonides' view, to serve in combatant roles alongside the men in a mandatory war? David ibn Abi Zimra indicated his perplexity at Maimonides' apparently positive assertion in this regard. "Is it the way of women to make war?" he asked. He therefore suggested that the dictum of the sages be understood as intending that "since the bridegroom leaves his chamber the bride leaves her canopy, they do not have a honeymoon. However, it is possible that during a mandated war the women were responsible for supplying food and drink to their husbands."[39]

Similarly, Samuel Strashun wrote, "'A bride from her canopy,' would suggest that women also go out to war, and this is a novellae. Perhaps it means that that they go out [to the field of combat] only to cook and to bake and such—i.e., preparation of food and arms, and the administration of the economy of the state—to meet the needs of the male soldiers."[40] However, the more conservative scholar Israel Lipschutz was adamant that "a woman is not a soldier, but she does go out to provide food and to maintain the roads."[41]

In this regard, Horowitz points out that even in the course of a defensive war there are many things and services needed both by soldiers at the front and by the population, under stress at home, that cannot be ignored or stopped but must be maintained. "And for this reason the Torah placed the responsibility for the administration and ordering of affairs and these necessities on the women," in order not to draw men away from the soldiering at the front.[42] However, Horowitz emphasizes that although, according to halakhah, women are not to serve in combat at the front, "in order to defend her life and home, a woman is obligated, weapon in hand[,] . . . to serve behind the lines."[43] At the same time, he would eliminate any war-related role whatever of women during a discretionary war, in accordance with the assertion of Aaron haLevi of Barcelona that everything pertaining to a discretionary war is reserved exclusively to the male population.[44]

RULES OF MILITARY CONDUCT

In setting up the parameters and regulations governing the initiation and prosecution of war, the Torah also seeks to place constraints on the behavior of the army in the field, constraints that are designed to limit wanton destruction and abuse of the defeated. First and perhaps foremost, the sages and their disciples undertook to interpret the guidance of Scripture so as to reduce the number of unnecessary casualties, especially those of the civilian population of a city under attack. Thus R. Nathan understood the biblical text "And they warred against Midian, as the Lord commanded Moses" (Num. 31:7), as meaning that Moses was instructed to attack from no more than three directions, leaving a forth open for the people to flee to safety.[45]

Maimonides subsequently codified this evidently minor opinion as halakhah. "When siege is laid to a city for the purpose of capture, it may not be surrounded on all four sides but only on three in order to present an opportunity for escape to those who would flee to save their lives. . . . It has been learned by tradition that that was the instruction given to Moses."[46] Yehudah Gershuni suggests that Maimonides took this approach because it represented a sound tactical approach to warfare. If an enemy finds itself with no way out of a trap it can choose to fight to the last man. If it does, that might result in unnecessary casualties to the attacking army, which would not gain any strategic advantage.[47] By contrast, Nahmanides takes the position that the purpose of the halakhah is to teach the virtue of mercy, even to one's enemies during warfare. Accordingly, Nahmanides elevates this rule to one of the 613 fundamental precepts of Judaism.[48]

The sages further interpreted the biblical statement "When thou drawest nigh unto a city to fight against it" (Deut. 20:10) as meaning "not to reduce it through lack of food or water nor to slay its inhabitants through disease."[49] The evident implication of this teaching, as suggested by Simon Federbusch, is the proscription of blockades designed to starve a city into surrender, and the prohibition of the use of biological or chemical agents against an enemy population.[50]

A specific case in point is the remarkable biblical rule concerning the treatment of trees during a siege.

When thou shalt besiege a city a long time, in making war against it to take it, thou shalt not destroy the trees thereof by wielding an axe against them; for thou mayest eat of them, but thou shalt not cut them down; for is the tree of the field man, that it should be besieged of thee? Only the trees of which thou knowest that they are not trees for food, them thou mayest destroy and cut down, that thou mayest build bulwarks against the city that maketh war with thee, until it fall. (Deut. 20:19–20)

The sages went so far as to prohibit the damage to trees that might result from the diversion of a water conduit.[51] Commenting on the biblical rule, Gerhard von Rad wrote, "The fact that Deuteronomy contains in the contexts of its laws concerning war a rule to protect fruit-growing is probably unique in the history of the growth of a humane outlook in ancient times. Deuteronomy is really concerned to restrain the vandalism of war and not with considerations of utility."[52] Maimonides explains, "By this prohibition we are forbidden to destroy fruit trees during a siege in order to cause distress and suffering to the inhabitants of the besieged city." Moreover, he continues, "all [needless] destruction is included in this prohibition: for instance, whoever burns a garment, or breaks a vessel needlessly, contravenes the prohibition."[53] Federbusch would extend this prohibition to include anything built to support agriculture, and by further inference any factory or industry that serves the civilian needs of the population.[54] This elaboration on the biblical statement was already in acceptance a millennium before Maimonides, as may be seen from the writings of Flavius Josephus. Speaking of those matters ordained by "our legislator," Josephus asserts, "He also would have us treat those that are esteemed our enemies with moderation; for he doth not allow us to set their country on fire, nor permit us to cut down those trees that bear fruit: nay, farther, he forbids us to spoil those who have been slain in war. He hath also provided for such as are taken captive that they may not be injured, and especially that the women may not be abused."[55]

With regard to the latter, the Torah also sets forth a unique and probably unprecedented demand about the treatment of female captives:

When thou goest forth to battle against thine enemies, and the Lord thy God delivereth them into thy hands, and thou carriest them away captive, and seest among the captives a woman of goodly form, and thou hast a desire unto her, and wouldest take her to thee to wife; then thou shalt bring her home to thy house; and she shall shave her head, and pare her nails; and she shall put the raiment of her captivity from off her, and she shall remain in thy house, and bewail her father and her mother a full month; and after that thou mayest go in unto her, and be her husband, and she shall be thy wife. And it shall be, if thou have no delight in her, then thou shalt let her go whither she will; but thou shalt not sell her at all for money, thou shalt not deal with her as a slave, because thou hast humbled her. (Deut: 21:10–14)

In his codification of the halakhah, Maimonides amplifies the biblical ordinance by asserting that a soldier in the invading army may, if overpowered by passion, cohabit with a captive woman. But Maimonides makes clear, echoing the Talmud, that this is merely a pragmatic concession to man's evil impulse.[56] However, even so, he may not behave savagely.

"How do we know that he must not force her to yield to him in the open field of battle? Because it is said: Then thou shalt bring her home to thy house, that is, he shall take her to a private place and cohabit with her." He may not, however, simply disavow her after having cohabited with her. Moreover, "he is forbidden to cohabit with her a second time before he marries her."[57] In other words, the Torah recognizes that men are wont to behave savagely during and immediately following battle. It therefore seeks to constrain such behavior, most notably with regard to female captives, normally considered prizes of war, by insisting on building in delays during which the passions of the moment may abate.

MILITARY ASSISTANCE

It seems self-evident that a political society has an obligation to see to its own self-defense. Is there a similar obligation to come to the defense of another that is suffering from unprovoked aggression?

The prophet Obadiah appears to be indicating that such an obligation exists when he roundly condemns Edom for failing to come to the aid of Jerusalem in its hour of need. "In the day that thou didst stand aloof, in the day that strangers carried away his substance, and foreigners entered into his gates, and cast lots upon Jerusalem, even thou wast as one of them" (Obad. 11). The clear implication of this passage is that Edom bears guilt because it stood by and allowed a neighbor to be attacked and despoiled. In other words, the prophetic message seems to be that adoption of a stance of neutrality in the presence of an obvious aggression is morally equivalent to passive complicity with the aggressor.

Support for this position may also be inferred from the mishnaic dictum that "he who pursues after his neighbor to slay him" must be saved from committing such a transgression, even at the cost of his life.[58] Moreover, the sages taught that "if a man sees his fellow drowning, mauled by beasts, or attacked by robbers, he is bound to save him."[59] Based on these sources, Federbusch argues that in a case where a weak nation or people is the target of unprovoked aggression, it is incumbent upon all others to come to the aid of the victim, even if it means waging war against the aggressor to force him to desist. Indeed, Federbusch argues that notwithstanding a general halakhic prohibition about endangering one's life unnecessarily by serving in a foreign army, in the case of unwarranted aggression it is both permitted and encouraged in order to render assistance to the victim.[60]

There is some question, however, about whether it is legitimate to extrapolate, as does Federbusch, from the case of an individual to a people, particularly an alien people. Given that unjustified wars have been endemic throughout history, acceptance of an obligation to intervene in all such conflicts seems quite unrealistic as a practical matter. Moreover, even if it were feasible, it would surely be undesirable, because of the onerous

burden it would place on the people. However, this does not make a case
for isolationism; it merely suggests that there will be many instances when
neutrality will be the only viable policy.

A related issue is whether it is permissible to supply weapons to others
as a means of military assistance short of direct intervention. Once again,
although the classic literature does not deal with this question directly, it
does provide a basis for drawing some inferences and conclusions. Thus,
there is a mishnaic rule that one may not sell anything to a gentile "which
may injure the public."[61] More specifically, the sages taught that "one
should not sell them either weapons or accessories of weapons, nor should
one grind any weapon for them." Furthermore, the prohibition holds
whether one sells directly or through a reseller.[62] One sage went farther and
insisted that "one should not sell them bars of iron. Why?—Because they
may hammer weapons out of them."[63] The clear implication of all this,
translated into contemporary terms, seems to be that it is halakhically im-
permissible to sell offensive weapons that may be used for aggression.
However, this rule would not appear to apply in a case where such sales are
to be made within the context of a mutual security pact.[64]

On a related question, there is a significant difference of opinion over
whether it is permissible to sell defensive weapons. "Our Rabbis taught: It
is forbidden to sell them shields; some say, however, that shields may be
sold to them."[65] The dispute is over the difficult question of whether a
shield, intended to serve as a defensive device, can be used for offensive
and aggressive purposes. Notwithstanding the opposition of the early
sages, the halakhah was ultimately determined to be in accord with the
views of those who would permit the sale of defensive armaments.[66] As
stated by Maimonides, "It is forbidden to sell any weapons of war to gen-
tiles, nor may one sharpen their weapons or sell them knives, chains, leg
irons, weapons grade iron, bears, lions, or anything that could be used to
cause widespread injury. However, one may sell them shields that are
purely for defense."[67] In another place, Maimonides adds that making such
sales to someone who intends to resell them to the proscribed recipients is
also prohibited.[68] It has been observed "that the nature of the weapons
themselves, and not the purported intentions of their users, determines the
prohibitions."[69]

NATIONAL SECURITY POLICY

The sage and president of the ancient Sanhedrin, R. Simeon b. Gamliel,
taught that the world is sustained by three things: truth, law, and peace.[70]
The idea of peace is thus one of the principal value concepts of Judaism; it is
lauded, preached, and encouraged throughout the traditional literature.
Indeed, there is a minor tractate of the Talmud on the subject of peace, and it
concludes with the words, "As for him who loves peace, pursues peace,

and gives the greeting of peace and responds with peace, the Holy One, blessed be He, will cause him to inherit life in this world and life in the world to come."[71] Consistent with the general importance attributed to the search for peace, a similar concern for peace becomes a major aim in the conduct of foreign relations, even when belligerency has become necessary. As the sages put it, "Great is peace, for even in their war Israel requires peace."[72]

As a general proposition, peace with one's neighbors is clearly to be preferred over war. However, this assertion should not be misconstrued. It does not suggest that capitulation, compromise, or accommodation is always preferable to war. Both from the biblical and rabbinic perspectives, this clearly is not the case. There are times when war is necessary, indeed obligatory. However, even at such times, it is desirable to avoid bloodshed if at all possible. Thus, the Torah instructs us, "When thou drawest nigh unto a city to fight against it, then proclaim peace unto it" (Deut. 20:10).

The only biblical qualification to this rule is that it pertains to "all the cities which are very far off from thee, which are not of the cities of these nations" (Deut. 20:15). The biblical author appears to have drawn a sharp distinction between foreign and domestic policy, between the laws of war that applied generally to conflicts with foreign nations and the laws of war that applied exclusively to the seven nations that were to be completely uprooted from the Land of Israel itself.[73] The rabbis were thus confronted by the difficult problem of reconciling the desire and inclination for peace with the explicit and rather unequivocal language of the Bible with regard to the treatment to be accorded to the seven nations: "Howbeit of the cities of these peoples, that the Lord thy God giveth thee for an inheritance, thou shalt save alive nothing that breatheth, but thou shalt utterly destroy them" (Deut. 20:16–17).

On the one hand, there is a tradition recorded in the rabbinic literature that during the conquest of the Land of Israel, Joshua published an edict in every place he planned to conquer that stated: Whoever wishes to leave, let him go; whoever desires peace, let him make peace; whoever prefers to make war, let him do so.[74] This clearly implies that it was proper to make an offer of peace even to the seven nations. Joseph H. Hertz, a strong modern advocate of this position asserted, with some exaggeration, "All traditional commentaries agree that these offers of peace had to be made to all enemy cities, to those of the Canaanites as well."[75] A further implication, for proponents of this view, is that the biblical mandate does not unequivocally call for the annihilation of the civil population of the proscribed nations within the country. This would also seem to be suggested by the warning against intermarrying with them. Thus, it would appear that the goal of the divine mandate is to obliterate the threat and not necessarily and unequivocally everything of Canaanite provenance that breathed. Accordingly, the extreme anathema would probably apply only in instances where the

Canaanites chose to fight to the last man rather than accept the terms they were offered. A major commentator of the nineteenth century, Meir L. Malbim, suggested that the biblical mandate could be fulfilled by relocating the dispossessed peoples to a contained region where they might settle, completely segregated from the people of Israel.[76]

The importance attached by the sages to peaceful accommodation with one's neighbors is exemplified further in a midrash that has Moses disobeying a divine command in an attempt to avoid the necessity for war with the Amorites, one of the seven condemned nations. Thus it is noted that during the trek from Sinai to the eastern bank of the Jordan, prior to the invasion of Canaan, Moses is instructed to challenge "Sihon, the Amorite king of Heshbon, and contend with him in battle" (Deut. 2:24). Instead, Moses first sends messengers to Sihon with words of peace (Deut. 2:26).[77]

On the other hand, there are those who argue strenuously in favor of retaining the sharp distinction between foreign and domestic military policy. In this regard, it is important to recall that the biblical reason given for the need to utterly destroy and uproot the seven nations is that "they teach you not to do after all their abominations, which they have done unto their gods, and so ye sin against the Lord your God" (Deut. 20:18). In other words, what is at issue here are the religious and cultural practices of the Canaanite nations that are considered too abominable to be permitted to coexist alongside the higher teachings of the Torah. Accordingly, R. Simeon maintained, the harsh terms demanded by the Torah applied only to the members of the seven nations who actually lived within the territory of the Land of Israel. In his view, they did not apply to members of the seven nations who resided outside its boundaries. Accordingly, the latter could be permitted to survive if they gave up their idolatrous practices, whereas such an option was not open to those within the country.[78] Moreover, because the extreme penalty did not apply to them, it was not necessary to offer them peace before the opening of hostilities.[79] R. Judah adopted an even harder position on this question, denying the acceptability of making peace with members of the seven nations even outside the country. It was his opinion that they could not be trusted, because their moral corruption was total; they were therefore considered to be beyond redemption.[80]

It would seem that some of the sages sought to dispose of the problem by arguing that the biblical requirement to offer peace before beginning an attack only applies in the case of a discretionary war.[81] Rashi later unequivocally reaffirmed this position.[82] Given that the wars against the seven nations were biblically mandated, the entire question becomes moot. Nahmanides, however, rejected this interpretation, which he insisted simply referred to the fact that the two categories of war, mandatory and discretionary, were alluded to in the biblical passage. "But the [requirement] to offer peace applied even in a mandated war, obligating an offer of peace even to the seven nations."[83] A similar position was taken by Maimonides, who also insisted that the biblical requirement applied to all wars, without any distinction between discretionary and mandatory wars in regard to a prior offer of peace.[84]

In the view of Maimonides, the biblical command to eliminate the seven nations is strictly religious, not political, in intent. "Do not think that this is hard-heartedness or desire for vengeance. It is rather an act required by human opinion, which considers that everyone who deviates from the ways of truth should be put an end to and that all the obstacles impeding the achievement of the perfection that is the apprehension of Him, may He be exalted, should be interdicted."[85] In other words, as the biblical passage explains, the seven nations are condemned because of their beliefs and practices and not because of their physical presence in the land. But if this is the case, it is reasonable to conclude that should these nations be brought to repudiate their beliefs and practices, they need not be destroyed. From this standpoint, the wars against the seven nations may be seen as wars of religious conquest rather than as struggles to displace the nations who occupied the land. This comports with Maimonides' halakhic ruling concerning a city that accepts the offer of peace. He insists that one does not conclude a treaty with them until they reject idolatry, destroy all related pagan sanctuaries, and accept the seven Noahide laws that provide the basis for a morally acceptable society—rejection of the Noahide laws to be considered a capital offense.[86] Accordingly, it would seem, viewed from this perspective, that if the members of the seven nations put aside their beliefs and practices and adopted the Noahide laws, the biblical command to destroy them could be fulfilled without bloodshed and even without forcing them out of the country.

Nahmanides, however, took issue with Maimonides over the true character of the conquest of the Land of Israel. In his view, the conquest was primarily political in nature, its principal purpose being to take control of the territory and to settle it. Accordingly, Nahmanides scored Maimonides for his failure to include the conquest of the land in his tabulation of the principal precepts of Judaism, despite the fact that the Torah states quite clearly, "And ye shall drive out the inhabitants of the land, and dwell therein; for unto you have I given the land to possess it" (Num. 33:53). Nahmanides therefore concluded that Israel was commanded to conquer the land and to exercise dominion over it. Because of this, it was not necessary in his view literally to destroy the members of the seven nations; it was sufficient to bring them to accept that the land had changed hands permanently and was no longer theirs, and that they had forfeited any residual rights to it.[87] From his perspective, it was perfectly legitimate to offer peace to the seven nations as long as there could be no doubt that the land in its entirety had become the exclusive patrimony of Israel.

It is noteworthy, notwithstanding the differences between Maimonides and Nahmanides over the question of the intrinsic purpose of the biblical demand for obligatory war against the seven nations, that both halakhists imputed a far-from-self-evident meaning to the biblical language. Although it seems to call explicitly for the obliteration of these peoples, they effectively transformed the harsh biblical doctrine into one more in accord with the claims of reason. This approach may be seen already in the earlier rabbinic tradition about the manner in which Joshua pursued the conquest of these very peoples. This tendency to moderate the seemingly unequivocal obligations imposed by Scripture through interpretation is taken a step farther in the case of the Ammonites and the Moabites.

The biblical text states with respect to these two peoples: "Thou shalt not seek their peace nor their prosperity all thy days for ever" (Deut. 23:7). In the event of a war with Ammon or Moab, and in light of this provision, is there any obligation to offer peace before opening hostilities? The general response of the sages to this question is negative. Indeed, the argument is made that the very fact that this verse concerning the two nations follows the one requiring the offer of peace suggests that it is intended to limit the application of the latter. Accordingly, while one might assume that the obligation to offer peace terms applies to the Ammonites and Moabites as well as to all others, the second biblical verse specifically excludes them from the scope of that obligation.[88]

Nonetheless, there is a significant disagreement among the sages over another biblical dictum relating to the treatment of Ammonites and Moabites that is of great relevance to the issue under consideration here. It is stated, "An Ammonite or a Moabite shall not enter into the assembly of the Lord, even to the tenth generation" (Deut. 23:4). R. Gamliel took this statement at its face value and ruled that no member of either nation can become part of the community of Israel. However, R. Joshua, who was also willing to accept the text at face value, argued that historical events had eroded the force of the biblical injunction. He suggested that the national identities of the peoples of the region had been effectively obliterated during the Assyrian invasion and occupation of the region more than eight hundred years earlier.[89] As a consequence, it was no longer possible, as a practical matter, to know who was truly an Ammonite or a Moabite. Adopting the position of R. Joshua, Maimonides asserted that it was by then halakhically permissible to accept people who identified themselves as Ammonites or Moabites into the community of Israel.[90]

Consequently, if one accepts that there is no way of knowing who really is a true Ammonite or Moabite, it does not seem reasonable to exclude them from the scope of the requirement to offer peace terms. Seeking a middle ground on this issue, and deferring to the explicit biblical injunction concerning them, Maimonides stated that it was not necessary to offer either the Ammonites or Moabites peace terms. But he asserted that if they took the initiative and sought peace, it was permissible to respond favorably to them.[91]

NEGOTIATING PEACE

Because Judaism places such a high value on peace, it seeks to limit the circumstances and conditions under which war is an acceptable, let alone obligatory, policy. To emphasize this further, it insists that the purpose and objectives of war be truly in the public interest. Consequently, the halakhah seeks to place certain constraints on the negotiation of peace terms in order to ensure that the public interest in pursuing a war policy is not negated at the peace table. In other words, if it becomes necessary to go to war, for whatever reason, and if prior to the actual initiation of hostilities the enemy is invited to capitulate, to avoid unnecessary bloodshed and destruction, and agrees to do so, the peace negotiations need not result in an agreement that essentially restores the situation that prevailed before the decision for war was taken in the first place. Once a decision for war is taken, the peace agreement that is subsequently negotiated must reflect the essence of what would have been achieved had the conflict been permitted to run its course. Anything less would indicate that the purposes for which the war was originally justified had been overstated, thereby raising questions about the integrity and legitimacy of the initial policy decision.

This perspective may be seen as implicit in the guidance provided by the biblical author regarding the negotiation of peace with an enemy, appropriate allowances being made for the specific conditions, circumstances, and practices that prevailed in antiquity: "When thou drawest nigh unto a city to fight against it, then proclaim peace unto it. And it shall be, if it make thee answer of peace, and open unto thee, then it shall be, that all the people that are found therein shall become tributary unto thee, and shall serve thee" (Deut. 20:10–11). This suggests that one does not undertake a military initiative against a foreign city or state unless there is a clear intent, at a minimum, to establish one's suzerainty and political control over it. Accordingly, any peace negotiated with such a city must contain terms that will achieve this original intent. The sages took this a step farther, emphasizing that these basic terms had to be fulfilled in their entirety and were not negotiable or subject to partial fulfillment. Thus, in reference to the minimum biblical terms requiring tribute and servitude, the sages insisted that both conditions had to be accepted and fulfilled completely if war was to be avoided.[92]

In codifying the halakhah in this regard, Maimonides gave greater specification to the substantive content of these conditions, particularly the requirement of servitude. He required that they accept permanent inferior status, which would preclude them from ever being in a position to exercise any authority over an Israelite. Moreover, they must be prepared to respond to any levies that were imposed upon them for either money or labor for the purpose of public works.[93] In effect, they must be prepared to live as second-class citizens, under foreign domination. Nahmanides, however, prefers a more compassionate approach that avoids treating such people as servants. In his opinion, their status should be that of "hired" persons, who must receive compensation for their labors. In this approach, the nature of their servitude would be limited to the requirement that they carry out the work demanded of them regardless of how demeaning they may find it. But they must be paid a fair wage for their labors.[94] It is noteworthy that at least one contemporary commentator suggests on the basis of an extensive analysis of Maimonides' writings on the subject that Maimonides, in effect, drew a distinction between peace with contiguous states and with states far off. If this is correct, the preceding discussion would apply only to the former category. With regard to distant states, a peace treaty on equitable terms would be acceptable.[95]

Once having achieved the upper hand in a conflict, Israel remains under an unequivocal obligation to abide by the terms of the peace agreement, an obligation that has become a fundamental principle of international law—namely that agreements entered into freely must be honored. As Maimonides declared, "It is forbidden to be false to the treaty made with them, and to deceive them after they have made peace and accepted the Noahide laws."[96]

The only incentive for the city under threat to meet these mandatory peace terms was the knowledge that the price that might have to be paid should it reject them would be very high. "And if it will make no peace with thee[,] . . . thou shalt smite every male thereof with the edge of the sword; but the women, and the little ones, and the cattle, and all that is in the city, even all the spoil thereof, shalt thou take for a prey unto thyself" (Deut. 20:12–14). For the reason given above, it seems plausible that it was the hope of the biblical author that such harsh punitive measures would never have to be carried out against an enemy with whom it was possible to make peace. Such a hope, however, could be realized only if the force arrayed against the city was clearly overwhelming. This suggests further that the offer of peace would be disingenuous unless it was accompanied by a display of the military capability necessary to make credible the threat of annihilation. That is, from a biblical perspective, a satisfactory peace can only be negotiated from a position of overpowering strength. Indeed, the psalmist has been interpreted as alluding to this notion in his meditation, "The Lord will give strength unto his people; the Lord will bless His people with peace" (Ps. 29:11). As understood by one contemporary writer, with regard to the current nonbelligerency treaty between Israel and Egypt, the implication of this statement is that "first, God gave strength to His people, and because of that blessed them now with peace. This obligates us to remain strong always."[97]

This is a very different concept from one that supposes a real peace can be reached only by a willingness of each of the antagonists to make substantial concessions to the other, as takes place in commercial contract negotiations. Although this latter approach to peacemaking has become very popular in contemporary times, there is no evidence whatsoever that it is a viable approach in the world of international politics, where the stakes are usually much higher and far more complex than in the world of business. Indeed, viewed from a realistic rather than an idealistic political perspective, the biblical approach to peacemaking reflects a profound insight into the true nature of international relations.

NOTES

This chapter is based in part on an unpublished essay on war and peace in rabbinic thought prepared by my spouse, Ahouva Sicker, and submitted to Baltimore Hebrew University in 1992 in partial fulfillment of the requirements for the degree of Master of Arts. I am grateful to her for allowing me to elaborate on her original work.

1. *Avot* 1:18.
2. *Perek Hashalom* 1.
3. Emanuel Rackman, *Modern Halakhah for Our Time*, pp. 75–76.
4. Abraham Isaac Kook, *Mishpat Kohen* 142.
5. Maimonides, *Hilkhot Melakhim* 4:3.
6. *M. Sanhedrin* 1:5, 2:4.
7. *Sanhedrin* 16a.
8. Nahmanides, *Hassagot Rabbeinu Moshe bar Nahman*, near the end of the section on the negative commandments. This interpretation is problematic, in that if the decision on an obligatory war is subjected to such an approval process, it cannot be truly obligatory. See discussion of this issue in Yehuda Gershuni, "Milhamot Yisrael, Giyus leTzavah, veT'nai'ei Milhamah," *Or HaMizrach*, vol. 33 (1985), no. 1, pp. 27–29.
9. *Yoma* 21b.
10. Maimonides, *Hilkhot Klei haMikdash* 10:10.
11. Rabad, ad loc. Maimonides' assertion that the Urim and Thummim existed during the Second Temple period is apparently based on a veiled hint in *Kiddushin* 31a.
12. Reuven Margaliot, *Margaliot haYam: Sanhedrin*, vol. 1, no. 29, p. 8.
13. Simon Federbusch, *Mishpat haMelukhah beYisrael*, p. 203.
14. Yehuda Gershuni, "Milhemet Reshut uMilhemet Mitzvah," in *Torah Shebe'al Peh*, vol. 13, p. 149.
15. *Sotah* 44b.
16. Ibid.
17. *M. Sotah* 8:7.
18. Maimonides, *Hilkhot Melakhim* 5:1. It should be noted that in his earlier commentaries on *M. Sanhedrin* 2:4 and *M. Sotah* 8:7 Maimonides limits his definition of mandatory wars to the first two categories only.
19. Yehuda Gershuni, "Milhemet Reshut uMilhemet Mitzvah," p. 151.
20. Maimonides, *Hilkhot Melakhim* 5:1.
21. Menahem Meiri, *Bet haBehirah al Massekhet Sanhedrin*, 15b, p. 50.
22. Yeshayahu A. Steinberger, "Mivtzah 'shalom haGalil' miBehinat haHalakhah," *Or HaMizrach*, vol. 31, nos. 3–4 (1983), p. 200.

23. Maurice Lamm, "After the War—Another Look at Pacifism and Selective Conscientious Objection (SCO)," in *Contemporary Jewish Ethics*, ed. Menachem M. Kellner, pp. 235–236.

24. Perush Rashi on *Sanhedrin* 2a.

25. See discussion of issue in Jacob Ettlinger, *Arukh leNer: Sanhedrin*, p. 2.

26. Perush R. Obadiah miBertinoro on *M. Sanhedrin* 1:5.

27. Perush Rabbenu, *Yehonatan haKohen miLunel* 1:10. Elsewhere in his commentary, he writes, "Any war that is not for the purpose of conquering the Land of Israel is classified as a discretionary war" (ibid. 2:6).

28. David S. Shapiro, "The Jewish Attitude towards Peace and War," in *Israel of Tomorrow*, ed. Leo Jung, p. 216.

29. *Sanhedrin* 72a; *Berakhot* 58a and 62b.

30. Shlomo Goren, *Mishnat haMedinah*, p. 68.

31. *Sotah* 44b.

32. *M. Sotah* 8:7.

33. J. David Bleich, "Preemptive War in Jewish Law," *Tradition*, vol. 21, no. 1 (1983), pp. 29–30.

34. Lamm, "After the War," p. 236.

35. *M. Sotah* 8:7.

36. Avraham Horowitz, "Tehukat haTzavah haIvri leOr haHalakhah," p. 108.

37. *M. Sotah* 8:2.

38. Maimonides, *Hilkhot Melakhim* 7:4.

39. David ibn Abi Zimra (Radbaz), commentary on Maimonides, *Hilkhot Melakhim* 7:4.

40. Samuel Strashun, commentary on *Sotah* 44b.

41. Israel Lipschutz, *Tiferet Yisrael* on *Mishnah Sotah* 8:7.

42. Horowitz, "Tehukat haTzavah haIvri leOr haHalakhah," p. 107.

43. Ibid., p. 108.

44. Aaron haLevi of Barcelona, *Sefer haHinukh* 526.

45. *Sifre al Sefer Bamidbar* (Horowitz ed.), *Piska* 157, p. 210.

46. Maimonides, *Hilkhot Melakhim* 6:7.

47. Yehuda Gershuni, "Milhamot Yisrael, Giyus leTzava, veTenai'ei Milhamah," *Or HaMizrach*, vol. 23, no. 1 (1984), pp. 29–30. It is of interest that this discussion echoes that to be found in the work of the ancient Chinese general and strategist Sun Tzu and that of his commentators. Thus, Sun Tzu asserted, "To surround an enemy you must leave a way of escape," to which Tu Mu commented: "Show him there is a road to safety, and so create in his mind the idea that there is an alternative to death. Then strike." Further elaborating the point, another commentator noted that "wild beasts, when at bay, fight desperately. How much more is this true of men! If they know there is no alternative they will fight to the death" (Sun Tzu, *The Art of War*, pp. 109–110).

48. Nahmanides, *Hasagot Rabbeinu Moshe bar Nahman, Positive Commandment 5*. For further analysis of the different approaches of Maimonides and Nahmanides, see Meir Simhah haKohen, *Meshekh Hokhmah* on Num. 31:7.

49. *Sifre on Deuteronomy* (Hammer ed.), *Piska* 199, p. 217.

50. Simon Federbusch, *Mishpat haMelukhah beYisrael*, p. 209.

51. *Sifre on Deuteronomy* (Hammer ed.), *Piska* 203, p. 219.

52. Gerhard von Rad, *Deuteronomy: A Commentary*, p. 133.

53. Maimonides, *The Commandments, Negative Commandment 57*, pp. 54–55.

54. Federbusch, *Mishpat haMelukhah beYisrael*, p. 209.

55. Flavius Josephus, *Against Apion* 2:30, in *Josephus: Complete Works*, p. 632.

56. *Kiddushin* 21b.

57. Maimonides, *Hilkhot Melakhim* 8: 2–4.

58. *M. Sanhedrin* 8:7.

59. *Sanhedrin* 73a.

60. Federbusch, *Mishpat haMelukhah beYisrael*, p. 225.

61. *M. Avodah Zarah* 1:7.

62. *Avodah Zarah* 15b.

63. *Avodah Zarah* 16a.

64. R. Ashi justified the sale of iron used for making weapons to the Persians on the grounds that the latter protected the Jewish community (*Avodah Zarah* 16a). See Maimonides, *Hilkhot Avodat Kokhavim* 9:9, where he legitimates such sale of weapons as a means of communal self-defense.

65. *Avodah Zarah* 15b.

66. "There are some who say that the reason for not permitting [the sale of] shields is this: When they have no weapons left, they might use these for killing. But there are others who say that shields may be sold to them, for when they have no more weapons they run away. Said R. Nahman in the name of Rabbah b. Abbuha: The halakhah is with the 'others'" (*Avodah Zarah* 16a).

67. Maimonides, *Hilkhot Rotzeah* 12:12.

68. Maimonides, *Hilkhot Avodat Kokhavim* 9:8.

69. Everett E. Gendler, "War and the Jewish Tradition," in *Contemporary Jewish Ethics*, ed. Menachem M. Kellner, p. 202.

70. *Avot* 1:18.

71. Perek haShalom, in *The Minor Tractates of the Talmud*, vol. 2, p. 602.

72. *Sifre Devarim*, *Piska* 199.

73. Ibid. 201.

74. *T. J. Sheviyit* 6:1; *Deuteronomy Rabbah* 5:14.

75. Joseph H. Hertz, *The Pentateuch and Haftorahs*, p. 832, n. 10. In fact, the great medieval commentator, Rashi, as will be pointed out shortly, maintained the opposite opinion.

76. Meir L. Malbim, *HaTorah vehaMitzvah* on Deut. 7:2.

77. The Midrash then concludes: "God said to him: I have commanded you to make war with him, but instead you began with peace; by your life, I will confirm your decision; every war upon which Israel enter, they shall begin with [a declaration of] peace" (*Deuteronomy Rabbah* 5:13).

78. *Sotah* 35b. R. Simeon's position is also adopted in *Sifre Devarim*, *Piska* 200.

79. See Rashi's commentary on *Sotah* 35b.

80. *Sotah* 35b.

81. *Sifre on Deuteronomy*, *Piska* 199.

82. Solomon b. Isaac [Rashi], *Perushei Rashi al haTorah*, commentary on Deut. 20:10.

83. Nahmanides, *Perushei haTorah*, commentary on Deut. 20:10.

84. Maimonides, *Hilkhot Melakhim* 6:1.

85. Maimonides, *Guide of the Perplexed* 1:54, p. 127.

86. Maimonides, *Hilkhot Melakhim* 8:9.

87. Nahmanides, *Hasagot al Sefer Mitzvot,* Positive Commandnent no. 4 (omitted by Maimonides).

88. *Sifre Devarim, Piska* 251.

89. *M. Yadayim* 4:4.

90. Maimonides, *Hilkhot Issurei Biah* 12:25.

91. Maimonides, *Hilkhot Melakhim* 6:6.

92. *Sifre Devarim, Piska* 200.

93. Maimonides, *Hilkhot Melakhim* 6:1.

94. Nahmanides, *Perushei haTorah* on Deut. 20:11.

95. Shmuel B. Werner, "Kritat Brit veAsiyat Shalom Bain Yisrael leAmim—leOr haHalakhah," p. 55.

96. Maimonides, *Hilkhot Melakhim* 6:3.

97. Hayyim David Halevi, "HaShalom veHashlakhotav," p. 48.

Selected Bibliography

Because the subject matter of this book, the political culture of Judaism, is touched upon in several different fields of Jewish studies but does not as yet constitute a distinct subject area, it is not possible to construct a focused bibliography. The following selected works are those cited and consulted in the preparation of this book.

CLASSICAL RABBINIC TEXTS

The Babylonian Talmud. 18 vols. Translated under the editorship of I. Epstein. London: Soncino Press, 1978.

The Fathers According to Rabbi Nathan. Translated by Judah Goldin. New Haven, Conn.: Yale University Press, 1955.

Mekilta de-Rabbi Ishmael. 3. Vols. Edited and translated by Jacob Z. Lauterbach. Philadelphia: Jewish Publication Society, 1949.

Midrash Mishlei. Edited by Solomon Buber. Vilna: Romm Brothers, 1893; facsimile edition: Jerusalem, 1965.

Midrash Rabbah. 10 vols. Translated under the editorship of H. Freedman and Maurice Simon. London: Soncino Press, 1983.

The Minor Tractates of the Talmud. 2 vols. Translated under the editorship of A. Cohen. London: Soncino Press, 1971.

The Mishnah. Translated by Herbert Danby. Oxford: Oxford University Press, 1933.

Pesikta de-Rab Kahana: R. Kahana's Compilation of Discourses for Sabbaths and Festal Days. Translated by William G. Braude and Israel J. Kapstein. Philadelphia: Jewish Publication Society, 1975.

Shishah Sidrei Mishnah. 13 vols. Jerusalem: Meorot, 1976.

Sifra [*Torat Kohanim*]. With Commentary by Israel Meir Kagan (Hafetz Hayyim). Jerusalem: Sachs Family, n.d.

Sifre: A Tannaitic Commentary on the Book of Deuteronomy. Translated by Reuven Hammer. New Haven, Conn.: Yale University Press, 1986.

Sifre al Bamidbar ve'al Devarim. (Printed in Malbim, *HaTorah vehaMitzvah.*)

Sifre al Sefer Bamidbar veSifre Zuta. Edited by H. S. Horovitz. Jerusalem: Shalem Books, 1992.

Sifre on Deuteronomy (Hebrew). Edited by Louis Finkelstein. New York: Jewish Theological Seminary, 1969.

Talmud Bavli veYerushalmi. 20 vols. New York: Otzar Hasefarim, 1959.

Talmud Yerushalmi. 3 vols. Zhitomer, 1866; facsimile edition: Jerusalem, 1968.

Torat Kohanim. 2 vols. Husyatin: Dovevei Siftei Yeshainim, 1908; facsimile edition: Israel, 1968.

Tosefta. Edited by M. S. Zuckermandel. Jerusalem: Wahrman, 1970.

MISCELLANEOUS WORKS

Aaron haLevi of Barcelona (c 1300). *Sefer haHinukh.* Edited by Charles B. Chavel. Jerusalem: Mossad Harav Kook, 1966.

Abi Zimra (Radbaz), David ibn (1479–1573). Commentary on Maimonides' *Mishnah Torah.* (Printed in Maimonides, *Mishnah Torah.*)

Albo, Joseph (c. 1420). *Sefer Ha-'Ikkarim.* 4 vols. Edited and translated by Isaac Husik. Philadelphia: Jewish Publication Society, 1946.

Amiel, Moshe Avigdor. *HaTzedek haSotziali vehaTzedek haMishpati vehaMusari Shelanu.* Published in volume entitled *Bein Adam leHavero: Massekhet Yahasei Enosh beYahadut.* Jerusalem: Mossad Harav Kook, 1975.

Anatoli, Jacob ben Abba Mari (13th cent.). *Malmad haTalmidim.* Lyck, Poland: Mekitze Nirdamim, 1866; reprinted Israel: n.p., 1968.

Arama, Isaac (c. 1420–1494). *Sefer Mishlei im Perush Yad Avshalom.* Leipzig edition; reprinted Israel: n.p., 1968.

Asher ben Jehiel [Rosh] (c. 1250–1327). *Sefer Rabbenu Asher.* (Printed in *Talmud Bavli veYerushalmi.*)

Belkin, Samuel (1911–1976). *Essays in Traditional Jewish Thought.* New York: Philosophical Library, 1956.

———. *In His Image: The Jewish Philosophy of Man as Expressed in Rabbinic Tradition.* New York: Abelard-Schuman, 1960.

Ben-Artzi, Haggai. "HaYahid mul haMemsad beHevrah Halakhatit." *Sinai,* vol. 94 (1984).

Berav, Jacob (c. 1474–1546). *Sefer Sheilot uTeshuvot.* Jerusalem: n.p., 1958.

Berkovits, Eliezer (b. 1900). *Man and God: Studies in Biblical Theology.* Detroit: Wayne State University Press, 1969.

———. *Not in Heaven: The Nature and Function of Halakha.* New York: Ktav Publishing House, 1983.

Bin-Nun, Yoel. Interview. In *Medinat Yisrael: Bain Yahadut leDemokratia,* edited by Yossi David. Jerusalem: HaMakhon haYisraeli leDemokratia, 2000.

Bleich, J. David. "Preemptive War in Jewish Law." *Tradition,* vol. 21, no. 1 (1983).

Blidstein, Gerald J. "Halakha and Democracy." *Tradition,* vol. 32, no. 1 (1997).

Buber, Martin (1878–1965). *Israel and the World.* New York: Schocken Books, 1948.

Caro, Joseph (1488–1575). *Shulhan Arukh.* 10 vols. New York: Otzar haHalakhah, 1959.

Chernik, Michael. "HaHevdel bain Mitzvah veHalakhah beTorato shel haRambam." *CCAR Journal: A Reform Jewish Quarterly* (Spring 1997).

Chouraqui, André. *A History of Judaism.* New York: Walker, 1962.

Clark. Eli D. " 'After the Majority Shall You Incline': Democtaric Theory and Voting Rights in Jewish Law." *The Torah U-Madda Journal,* vol. 8 (1998–1999).

Cohen, Shaar Yashuv. "Kriyah leShalom beMilhemet Yisrael." In *Torah Shebe'al Peh: Hartzaot beKinus haArtzi haEsrim veEhad leTorah Shebe'al Peh,* edited by Yitzhak Rafel. Vol. 21. Jerusalem: Mossad Harav Kook, 1989.

Cohen, Simha. "Adam-Olam-Hevrah." In *El haMekorot: Otzar Mamarim beHashkafat haYahadut.* Vol. 3. Israel: Tenuat Moreshet Avot, 1982–84.

David, Yossi ed., *Medinat Yisrael: Bain Yahadut leDemokratia.* Jerusalem: HaMakhon haYisraeli leDemokratia, 2000.

Eidelberg, Paul. *Jerusalem vs. Athens: In Quest of a General Theory of Existence.* Lanham, Md.: University Press of America, 1983.

———. *Judaic Man: Toward a Reconstruction of Western Civilization.* Middletown, N.J.: Caslon, 1996.

Eidels, Samuel (1555–1631). *Hiddushei Agadot.* (Printed in *Talmud Bavli veYerushalmi.*)

Elazar, Daniel J., ed. *Kinship and Consent: The Jewish Political Tradition and Its Contemporary Uses.* Washington, D.C.: University Press of America, 1983.

Elon, Menahem. *HaMishpat haIvri: Toldotav, Mekorotav, Ikronotav.* Jerusalem: Magnes Press, 1992.

Entziklopedia Talmudit. Vol. 9. Jerusalem: Talmudic Encyclopedia Publishing, 1971.

Ettlinger, Jacob (1798–1871). *Arukh leNer: Sanhedrin.* Warsaw: Isaac Goldman, 1874.

Federbusch, Simon (1892–1969). *Mishpat haMelukhah beYisrael.* Jerusalem: Mossad Harav Kook, 1973.

Feldman, Emanuel. *On Judaism.* New York: Shaar Press, 1994.

Finkelstein, Louis (b. 1895). "Hebrew Sources: Scripture and Talmud." In *Foundations of Democracy,* edited by F. Ernest Johnson. New York: Cooper Square Publishers, 1964.

———. "Human Equality in the Jewish Tradition." In *Aspects of Human Equality; Fifteenth Symposium of the Conference on Science, Philosophy and Religion,* edited by Lyman Bryson et al. New York: Harper and Brothers, 1956.

Fishbane, Michael A. *Judaism: Revelation and Traditions.* San Francisco: HarperCollins, 1987.

Frank, Daniel H., ed. *Commandment and Community: New Essays in Jewish Legal and Political Philosophy.* Albany: State University of New York Press, 1995.

Frishtik, Gidi. "Dina deMalkhuta vehaMinhag haBeinleumi: LeKeviat Hogenet Din haMalkhut." *Sinai,* no. 110 (1992).

Gershuni, Yehuda. "Milhamot Yisrael, Giyus leTzavah, veT'nai'ei Milhamah." *Or HaMizrach,* vol. 33, no. 1 (1985).

———. "Milhemet Reshut uMilhemet Mitzvah." In *Torah Shebe'al Peh: Hartzaot beKinus haArtzi haSheloshah Assar leTorah Shebe'al Peh,* edited by Yitzhak Rafel. Vol. 13. Jerusalem: Mossad Harav Kook, 1971.

———. *Mishpat haMelukhah.* 2nd ed. Jerusalem: Moznaim Publishing, 1984.

Goodenough, Erwin R. *The Politics of Philo Judaeus: Practice and Theory*. New Haven, Conn.: Yale University Press, 1938.

Gordis, Robert (b. 1908). "Democratic Origins in Ancient Israel: The Biblical Edah," in *Alexander Marx Jubilee Volume*. New York: Jewish Theological Seminary, 1950.

———. *Judaic Ethics for a Lawless World*. New York: Jewish Theological Seminary, 1986.

———. *Koheleth: The Man and His World*. New York: Bloch Publishing, 1955.

———. *Torat haMedinah: Mehkar Halakhati Histori beNosim haOmdim beRomah shel Medinat Yisrael me'az Tekumatah*. Jerusalem: Idrah Rabbah, 1996.

Goren, Shlomo. *Mishnat haMedinah: Mehkar Halakhati Histori beNosim haOmdim beRomah shel Medinat Yisrael me'az Tekumatah*. Jerusalem: Idrah Rabbah, 1999.

Greenberg, Simon. *Foundations of a Faith*. New York: Burning Bush Press, 1967.

Guttmann, Alexander. "The Role of Equity in the History of the Halakhah," in *Justice, Justice Shalt Thou Pursue: Papers Assembled on the Occasion of the 75th Birthday of the Reverand Dr. Julius Mark*, edited by Ronald B. Sobel and Sidney Wallach. New York: Ktav Publishing House, 1975.

Guttmann, M. "The Term 'Foreigner' Historically Considered." *Hebrew Union College Annual*, vol. 3 (1926).

Halevi, Hayyim David. "HaShalom veHashlakhotav." In *Torah Shebe'al Peh: Hartzaot beKinus haArtzi haEsrim veEhad leTorah Shebe'al Peh*, edited by Yitzhak Rafel. Vol. 21. Jerusalem: Mossad Harav Kook, 1989.

Hen, Abraham (1878–1958). *BeMalkhut haYahadut: Pirkei Hagut uMahshavah*. 3 vols. Jerusalem: Mossad Harav Kook, 1959–70.

Herberg, Will. *Judaism and Modern Man: An Interpretation of Jewish Religion*. Philadelphia: Jewish Publication Society, 1951.

Herring, Basil F. *Jewish Ethics and Halakhah for Our Time: Sources and Commentary*. New York: Ktav Publishing House/Yeshiva University Press, 1984.

Hertz, Joseph H. (1872–1946), ed. *The Pentateuch and Haftorahs*. 2nd ed. London: Soncino Press, 1966.

High Holiday Prayer Book. Compiled and arranged by Morris Silverman. Hartford, Conn.: Prayer Book Press, 1951.

Hirsch, Richard G. "There Shall Be No Poor." In *Judaism and Human Rights*, edited by Milton R. Konvitz. New York: W. W. Norton, 1972.

Hirsch, Samson Raphael (1808–1888). *Horeb: A Philosophy of Jewish Laws and Observances*. 2 vols. Translated by Isidor Grunfeld. London: Soncino Press, 1962.

———. *The Pentateuch*. 5 vols. Translated by Isaac Levy. New York: Judaica Press, 1972.

———. *The Psalms*. 2 vols. Translated by Gertrude Hirschler. Jerusalem—New York: Feldheim Publishers, 1976.

Hoffman, Lawrence A. *The Art of Public Prayer: Not for Clergy Only*. Washington, D.C.: Pastoral Press, 1988.

Horowitz, Avraham. "Tehukat haTzavah haIvri leOr haHalakhah." In *Torah Shebe'al Peh: Hartzaot beKinus haArtzi haSheloshim leTorah Shebe'al Peh*, edited by Yitzhak Rafel. Vol. 30. Jerusalem: Mossad Harav Kook, 1989.

Hudson, Jay William. *Why Democracy: A Study in the Philosophy of the State.* New York: Appleton-Century, 1936.

Ibn Ezra, Abraham (1092–1167). *Perushei haTorah leRabbenu Avraham ibn Ezra.* 3 vols. Edited by Asher Weiser. Jerusalem: Mossad Harav Kook, 1976.

Jacob ben Asher [Baal haTurim] (c. 1270–c. 1343). *Arbah Turim.* 7 vols. New York: Otzar Hasefarim, 1959.

———. *Kitzur Piskei haRosh.* (Printed in *Talmud Bavli veYerushalmi.*)

Jakobovits, Immanuel. *Journal of a Rabbi.* New York: Living Books, 1966.

Jonathan of Lunel (c. 1135–after 1210). *Perush Rabbenu Yehonatan haKohen miLunel al haMishnah vehaRif leMassekhet Sanhedrin.* Edited by Judah Kuperberg. In *Sanhedrei Gedolah*, vol. 2. Jerusalem: Makhon Harry Fischel, 1969.

Josephus, Flavius (c. 38–c. 100). *Complete Works of Josephus.* Grand Rapids, Mich.: Kregel Publications, 1977.

Jung, Leo (1892–1987). *Living Judaism.* 2nd ed. New York: Night and Day Press, 1927.

Jung, Leo, ed. *Israel of Tomorrow.* New York: Herald Square Press, 1949.

Kahana, Kalman. *The Case for Jewish Civil Law in the Jewish State.* London: Soncino Press, 1960.

Kaniel, Michael. "Judaism: 'Godocracy,' rather than Democracy." *Jerusalem Post International*, week ending April 20, 1991.

Kaplan, Mordecai M. (1881–1983). *Judaism as a Civilization.* New York: Thomas Yoseloff, 1957.

Kellner, Menachem M., ed. *Contemporary Jewish Ethics.* New York: Sanhedrin Press, 1978.

Klausner, Joseph (1874–1958). *Yahadut veEnoshiut.* 2 vols. Jerusalem: Madda, 1955.

Konvits, Milton R. "Conscience and Civil Disobedience in the Jewish Tradition." In *Judaism and Human Rights,* edited by Milton R. Konvitz. New York: W. W. Norton, 1972.

———. "Man's Dignity in God's World." In *Judaism and Human Rights*, edited by Milton R. Konvitz. New York: W. W. Norton, 1972.

Kook, Abraham Isaac (1865–1935). *Mishpat Kohen.* Jerusalem: Mossad Harav Kook, 1966.

Korn, Eugene. "Tradition Meets Modernity: On the Conflict of Halakha and Political Liberty." *Tradition*, Vol. 25, no. 4, Summer 1991.

Lachs, Samuel Tobias. *Humanism in Talmud and Midrash.* Rutherford, N.J.: Fairleigh Dickinson University Press, 1993.

Lauterbach, Jacob Z. (1873–1942). *Rabbinic Essays.* Cincinnati, Ohio: Hebrew Union College Press, 1951.

Levenson, Jon D. *Sinai and Zion.* New York: Harper and Row, 1988.

Levine, Aaron. *Economics and Jewish Law.* New York: Yeshiva University Press, 1987.

Levinthal, Israel H. *Judaism Speaks to the Modern World.* New York: Abelard-Schuman, 1963.

Lew, Myer S. *The Humanity of Jewish Law.* London: Soncino Press, 1985.

Lichtenstein, Aaron. *The Seven Laws of Noah.* New York: Rabbi Jacob Joseph School Press, 1981.

Lipschutz, Israel (1782–1860). *Tiferet Yisrael.* (Printed in *Shishah Sidrei Mishnah*)

Maimon, Judah L (1875–1962). *Hiddush haSanhedrin beMedinatenu haMehudeshet.* Jerusalem: Mossad Harav Kook, 1967.

Maimonides, Moses [Rambam] (1135–1204). *The Code of Maimonides: The Book of Judges*. Translated by A. M. Hershman. New Haven: Yale University Press, 1949.

———. *The Code of Maimonides: The Book of Torts*. Translated by Hyman Klein. New Haven: Yale University Press, 1954.

———. *The Commandments*. Translated by Charles B. Chavel. New York: Soncino Press, 1967.

———. *The Guide of the Perplexed*. Translated by Shlomo Pines. Chicago: University of Chicago Press, 1963.

———. *Mishnah Torah*. 6 vols. New York: Rambam Publishers, 1956.

———. *Perush haMishnayot*. (Printed in *Talmud Bavli veYerushalmi*.)

———. *Sefer haMitzvot lehaRambam*. New York: Jacob Shurkin, 1955.

———. *Treatise on Logic*. Edited and translated by Israel Efros. New York: American Academy for Jewish Research, 1938.

Malbim, Meir Leibush (1809–1879). *HaTorah vehaMitzvah*. 2 vols. Jerusalem: Pardes, 1956.

———. *Mikraei Kodesh*. 2 vols. Jerusalem: Pardes, 1956.

Manasseh ben Israel (1604–1657). *The Conciliator*. Vol. 1. New York: Hermon Press, 1972.

Margoliot, Moses (d. 1781). *Pnei Moshe*. (Printed in *Talmud Yerushalmi*.)

Mattuck, Israel (1883–1954). *Jewish Ethics*. London: Hutchinson House, 1953.

Meiri, Menahem (c. 1249–c. 1310). *Perush haMeiri al Sefer Mishlei*. Jerusalem: Otzar HaPoskim, 1969.

Meir Simhah haKohen (1853–1926). *Meshekh Hokhmah*. Jerusalem: Eshkol, n.d.

Mendelssohn, Moses (1729–1786). *Biur Millot haHigayon*. Berlin: B. Kohn, 1925.

———. *Jerusalem: Or on Religious Power and Judaism*. Translated by Allan Arkush. Hanover, N.H.: University Press of New England, 1983.

Morell, Samuel. "The Constitutional Limits of Communal Government in Rabbinic Law." *Jewish Social Studies* (April—July 1971).

Munk, Elie (1900–1981). *La Justice Sociale en Israel*. Neuchatel, Switz.: A La Baconniere, 1948.

Nahmani, Hayim S. *Human Rights in the Old Testament*. Tel Aviv: Joshua Chachik Publishing House, 1964.

Nahmanides (1194–1270). *Hasagot Rabbeinu Moshe bar Nahman*. (Printed in Maimonides, *Sefer haMitzvot lehaRambam*.)

———. *Perushei haTorah*. 2 vols. Edited by Charles B. Chavel. Jerusalem: Mossad Harav Kook, 1969.

Nathan of Rome (1035–c. 1110). *Sefer haArukh*. Tel Aviv: Sifrei Kodesh, n.d.

Novak, David. *Jewish Social Ethics*. New York: Oxford University Press, 1992.

———. *Law and Theology in Judaism*. New York: KTAV Publishing House, 1974.

———. *Natural Law in Judaism*. Cambridge: Cambridge University Press, 1998.

Noveck, Simon, ed. *Great Jewish Thinkers of the Twentieth Century*. Washington, D.C.: B'nai B'rith, 1963.

Nussbaum, Daniel. "Social Justice and Social Welfare in Jewish Tradition: A Case Study in Religious Values and Social Policy." In *Jewish Civilization: Essays and Studies*, edited by Ronald A. Brauner. Vol. 3. Philadelphia: Reconstructionist Rabbinical College, 1985.

Pardes, Hayyim. "Milhemet Mitzvah uMilhemet Reshut." In *Torah Shebe'al Peh: Hartzaot beKinus haArtzi haSheloshim leTorah Shebe'al Peh*, edited by Yitzhak Rafel. Vol. 30. Jerusalem: Mossad Harav Kook, 1989.

Philo (c. 20 b.c.e.—50 c.e.). Vol. 8. Translated by F. H. Colson. Cambridge, Mass.: Harvard University Press, 1968.

Pontremoli, Raphael Chiyya (c. 1825–1885). *Yalkut MeAm Lo'ez: The Book of Esther*. Translated by Aryeh Kaplan. New York: Maznaim Publishing, 1978.

Priest, James E. *Governmental and Judicial Ethics in the Bible and Rabbinic Literature*. New York: KTAV Publishing House, and Malibu, Calif.: Pepperdine University Press, 1980.

Pritchard, James B. *The Ancient Near East: An Anthology of Texts and Pictures*. Princeton, N.J.: Princeton University Press, 1958.

Rabinowitz, Abraham H. *The Jewish Mind: In Its Halachic Talmudic Expression*. Jerusalem: Hillel Press, 1978.

Rackman, Emanuel. *Modern Halakhah for Our Time*. Hoboken, N.J.: KTAV Publishing House, 1995.

———. *One Man's Judaism*. New York: Philosophical Library, 1970.

Rad, Gerhard von (1901–1971). *Deuteronomy: A Commentary*. Translated by Dorothea Barton. Philadelphia: Westminster Press, 1966.

Rafel, Shilo. "Mesirat haYahid leHatzalat haRabbim." In *Torah Shebe'al Peh: Hartzaot beKinus haArtzi haSheloshim veShishah leTorah Shebe'al Peh*, edited by Yitzhak Rafel. Vol. 36. Jerusalem: Mossad Harav Kook, 1995.

Rakover, Nahum. "Yahid Mul Rabbim beHatzalat Nefashot." In *Torah Shebe'al Peh: Hartzaot beKinus haArtzi haSheloshim veShishah leTorah Shebe'al Peh*, edited by Yitzhak Rafel. Vol. 36. Jerusalem: Mossad Harav Kook, 1995.

Rawls, John. *A Theory of Justice*. Cambridge, Mass.: Harvard University Press, 1971.

Reines, Hayyim Z. *Torah uMusar*. Jerusalem: Mossad Harav Kook, 1954.

Rosenberg, Shalom. "Demokratia veHalakhah: Perspectivah Filosofit." In *Medinat Yisrael: Bain Yahadut leDemokratia*, edited by Yossi David. Jerusalem: HaMakhon haYisraeli leDemokratia, 2000.

Roth, Sol. *Halakhah and Politics: The Jewish Idea of the State*. New York: Ktav Publishing House, 1988.

———. *The Jewish Idea of Community*. New York: Yeshiva University Press, 1977.

———. "Judaism and Democracy." *The Torah U-Madda Journal*, vol. 2 (1990).

Russell, Bertrand. *Mysticism and Logic*. Garden City, N.Y.: Doubleday, 1957.

Saadia Gaon (882–942). *The Book of Beliefs and Opinions*. Translated from the Arabic by Samuel Rosenblatt. New Haven, Conn.: Yale University Press, 1948.

Samuel ben Meir [Rashbam] (c. 1080–c. 1158). *Commentary on the Talmud*. (Printed in *Talmud Bavli veYerushalmi*.)

Samuel haNagid (993–1055). *Mavo haTalmud*. (Printed in *Talmud Bavli veYerushalmi*, vol. 1.)

Sforno, Obadiah (1475–1550). *Biur al haTorah*. Edited by Zeev Gottlieb. Jerusalem: Mossad Harav Kook, 1980.

Shapira, Amnon. "Al 'Kavod haAdam' beMikra." *Beit Mikra*, no. 159 (January—March 1999).

Sherwin, Byron L. *Jewish Ethics for the Twenty-first Century: Living in the Image of God*. Syracuse, N.Y.: Syracuse University Press, 2000.

Shilo, Shmuel. *Dina deMalkhuta Dina*. Jerusalem: Defus Akademi deYerushalayim, 1975.

Sibley, Milford Q. *Political Ideas and Ideologies*. New York: Harper and Row, 1970.

Sicker, Martin. *The Judaic State: A Study in Rabbinic Political Thought*. New York: Praeger, 1988.

———. "Reading the Pentateuch Politically." *The Jewish Bible Quarterly*, vol. 27, no. 4 (October—December 1999).

———. *What Judaism Says about Politics: The Political Theology of the Torah*. Northvale, N.J.: Jason Aronson, 1994.

Slotki, Judah J. *Commentary on Judges*. London: Soncino Press, 1950.

Solomon ben Isaac [Rashi] (1040–1105). *Perushei Rashi al haTorah*. Edited by Charles B. Chavel. Jerusalem: Mossad Harav Kook, 1983.

Soloveitchik, Joseph B. (1903–1995). "The Lonely Man of Faith." *Tradition*, vol. 7, no. 2 (Summer 1965).

Steinberger, Yeshayahu A. "Mivtzah 'shalom haGalil' miBehinat haHalakhah." *Or haMizrakh*, vol. 31, nos. 3–4 (1983).

Stevens, Elliot L., ed. *Rabbinic Authority*. New York: Central Conference of American Rabbis, 1982.

Strashun, Samuel (1794–1872). *Commentary on Sotah*. (Printed in *Talmud Bavli veYerushalmi*.)

Tamari, Meir. *"With All Your Possessions": Jewish Ethics and Economic Life*. New York: Free Press, 1987.

Teshuvot haGeonim: Shaarei Teshuvah. Notes and index by Z. W. Leiter. New York: Philipp Feldheim, 1946.

Tomaschoff, Avner, ed., *Contemporary Thinking in Israel*. Vol. 1, *Halacha*. Jerusalem: World Zionist Organization, 1976.

Sun Tzu. *The Art of War*. Translated by Samuel B. Griffith. New York: Oxford University Press, 1963.

Twersky, Isadore (1930–1999). "Some Aspects of the Jewish Attitude toward the Welfare State." In *A Treasury of "Tradition,"* edited by Norman Lamm and Walter S. Wurzburger. New York: Hebrew Publishing, 1967.

Urbach, Ephraim E. *The Halakhah: Its Sources and Development*. Translated by Raphael Posner. Tel Aviv: Massada, 1986.

Walzer, Michael, Menachem Lorberbaum, and Noam J. Zohar, eds. *The Jewish Political Tradition*. Vol. 1, *Authority*. New Haven, Conn.: Yale University Press, 2000.

Weiler, Gershon. *Teocratiya Yehudit*. Tel Aviv: Am Oved, 1976.

Weinryb, Elazar. *Dat uMedinah: Hebetim Filosofiyim*. Tel Aviv: Hakibbutz Hameukhad, 2000.

Weiser, Artur. *The Psalms: A Commentary*. Philadelphia: Westminster Press, 1962.

Werblowsky, R. J. Zwi, and Geoffrey Wigoder. *The Encyclopedia of the Jewish Religion*. New York: Holt, Rinehart and Winston, 1966.

Werner, Shmuel B. "Kritat Brit veAsiyat Shalom Bain Yisrael leAmim: leOr haHalakhah." In *Torah Shebe'al Peh: Hartzaot beKinus haArtzi haEsrim veEhad leTorah Shebe'al Peh*, edited by Yitzhak Rafel. Vol. 21. Jerusalem: Mossad Harav Kook, 1989.

Whitehead, Alfred North. *The Principle of Relativity*. London: Cambridge University Press, 1922.

The Wisdom of Ben Sira. Translation and notes by Patrick W. Skehan. Introduction
and commentary by Alexander A. Di Lella. New York: Doubleday, 1987.

Wolfson, Harry A. (1887–1974). *Philo: Foundations of Religious Philosophy in Judaism,
Christianity and Islam*. 2 vols. Cambridge, Mass.: Harvard University Press,
1948.

Index

About the Author

MARTIN SICKER is a private consultant and lecturer who has served as a senior executive in the U.S. government and has taught at the American University and George Washington University. Dr. Sicker has written extensively in the field of political science and international affairs. He is the author of seventeen earlier books, including *The Judaic State: A Study in Rabbinic Political Theory* (Praeger, 1988). His most recent book is *Between Man and God: Issues in Judaic Thought* (Greenwood, 2001).